COWBOYS, CREATURES, AND CLASSICS

THE STORY OF REPUBLIC PICTURES

CHRIS ENSS AND HOWARD KAZANJIAN

Guilford, Connecticut

An imprint of The Rowman & Littlefield Publishing Group, Inc.
4501 Forbes Blvd., Ste. 200
Lanham, MD 20706
www.rowman.com

Distributed by NATIONAL BOOK NETWORK

British Library Cataloguing in Publication Information available
Library of Congress Cataloging-in-Publication Data

Names: Enss, Chris, 1961- author. | Kazanjian, Howard., author.
Title: Cowboys, creatures, and classics : the story of Republic Pictures /
    Chris Enss and Howard Kazanjian.
Description: Guilford, Connecticut : Lyons Press, 2018. | Includes
    bibliographical references and index.
Identifiers: LCCN 2018017577 (print) | LCCN 2018020422 (ebook) | ISBN
    9781493031306 (ebook) | ISBN 9781493031283 (hardcover)
Subjects: LCSH: Republic Pictures Corporation.
Classification: LCC PN1999.R4 (ebook) | LCC PN1999.R4 E58 2018 (print) | DDC
    384/.80979494--dc23
LC record available at https://lccn.loc.gov/2018017577

Printed in the United States of America

CONTENTS

ACKNOWLEDGMENTS

In the beginning motion pictures seemed a magic thing, born yesterday and full of growth today. There was plenty of opportunity to be a part of that magic if you wanted. What an experience it must have been to contribute to the start of an industry that would change the world. It's that simple idea that needs to be acknowledged because it led to the desire to write about a studio that broke new ground and delighted hundreds of thousands of children that flocked to see Saturday matinees.

Among the kind individuals who helped make this book a possibility are Linda Harris Mehr, director at the Margaret Herrick Library, and Kristine Krueger, NFIS director at the Academy of Motion Picture Arts and Sciences;

Cindy Brightenburg, head of the Special Collection Department at Brigham Young University and her hard-working staff who graciously made available the Republic Pictures' archives on file at the facility;

The men and women at the Library of Congress who supplied numerous documents and images of Hollywood's glory days;

And finally, to Executive Editor Rick Rinehart for agreeing to produce Republic Pictures' story.

FOREWORD

Republic Pictures was one of the busiest, and most profitable, studios in Hollywood's Golden Era. While it often lacked the critical prestige of other studios such as Paramount, MGM, and Warner Bros., it made up for it in box office receipts.

The studio understood what appealed to its audience and gave it to them in bulk: westerns, crime dramas, and serials. Lots of action, maybe some romance and a few singing cowboys thrown into the mix. Herbert Yates, who founded and ran the studio, kept the budgets lean, but he knew how to make a dollar stretch in his productions. For actors at the studio, work was plentiful and quick. An actor could film his role in a crime drama on Monday and Tuesday, jump over to work in a serial on Wednesday, and then finish the week on a western. Republic's back lot of standing sets (city and residential streets, jungle, lake, and western streets), not to mention the soundstages, were in constant use. Just as soon as one production finished filming, another would step in.

Republic Studios, like the major studios, had certain stars under contract such as Gene Autry, Roy Rogers, and John Wayne, and numerous character actors and actresses found steady employment in a variety of roles. The crews were kept busy year-round. One veteran makeup artist, who spent six years working at Republic, said the only days off he had were Sundays, Thanksgiving, and Christmas. Despite the lack of days off, employees enjoyed working at Republic. Many considered the studio a second home, and fellow cast and crew members were their extended families.

Howard Kazanjian and Chris Enss give Republic Pictures its proper spotlight in the annals of film history. Just like a Republic picture, this book is fast paced and riveting, with a unique cast of characters. Herbert Yates would be proud.

—Michael F. Blake

Emmy Award–winning makeup artist and best-selling author

INTRODUCTION

Not so many generations ago, boys and girls of all ages flocked to movie houses across the country to watch gallant heroes in white hats outwit sinister bankers or corrupt government officials. They shrieked as lovely damsels in distress dangled precariously on a branch high above a yawning chasm. They cheered when the good guy rescued the frightened female and applauded when the villain in the black hat was hauled off to the hoosegow. Only a handful of Hollywood movie companies in the post-Depression era produced such films, and among those only one dominated the business: Republic Pictures.

Some of Hollywood's most notable stars and best known characters of the 1930s, 1940s, and 1950s rose to prominence at Republic Pictures. For nearly twenty-five years, the studio produced Saturday afternoon serials starring such characters as Rocket Man, Dick Tracy, The Lone Ranger, Zorro, Captain Marvel, and countless "cowboy operas" or singing cowboy pictures starring such well-known figures as Roy Rogers and Gene Autry. The studio helped launch the career of the legendary John Wayne, who made thirty-three films for the company including such notable efforts as *Sands of Iwo Jima*, *The Quiet Man*, and *The Fighting Seabees*.

Under Republic Pictures' majestic banner of an eagle perched high atop a mountain peak, low-budget action films such as *Spy Smasher* and the *Perils of Nyoka* were made. Big-budget motion pictures such as *Macbeth* and *Man of Conquest* were also produced by the company, recognized as one of history's most prolific studios. More than eleven hundred movies were made by Republic Pictures during the twenty-four years the studio was in existence.

Republic was the brainchild of Herbert J. Yates, who founded the studio in 1935 when he convinced several smaller studios such as Chesterfield, Monogram, and Mascot to consolidate under one banner. The company wasted no time in establishing itself as one of the most productive and efficient in Hollywood.

Yates assembled a talented group of directors, technicians, and performers who merged into a hard-working, dedicated team. Republic's special effects duo of Howard and Theodore Lydecker was hailed as the best in the business. Its music department was equally effective. Such notables as future Broadway producer Cy Feuer and eventual Academy Award–winner Victor Young scored films for the studio.

At Republic, stunt work became an art. Yakima Canutt, David Sharpe, and Tom Steele were among the stuntmen who worked there, and all three became legends within the movie world.

Republic's filming techniques were just as fast-paced as its final products. Whereas major studios might shoot only three or four scenes in a day, Republic would shoot dozens. The directors of the high-energy, thrill-a-minute chapter plays were driven, talented men such as Joseph Kane, John English, and William Witney. Kane, English, and Witney directed the majority of the westerns and cliffhanger serials produced by the studio. Between 1939 and 1942, Republic turned out sixty-six multipart, cliffhanger serials.

Yates depended on the speed and flexibility of his stable of actors, writers, directors, and behind-the-scenes talent to bring to life the topical projects he believed audiences wanted to see. For example, within a week after the Japanese bombed Pearl Harbor, Republic writers were at work on a script built around the incident. In less than six months, *Remember Pearl Harbor* was playing in the nation's theaters.

Yates not only built plots around current events but on popular songs, too. When the tune "Pistol Packin' Mama" became a hit, Yates quickly put out a film with the title.

Republic produced a number of low-budget or "B" horror and mystery films, but it was the cowboy westerns and serials that remained the company's bread-and-butter throughout its history. Extremely popular with moviegoers, those B pictures usually ended with the bad guy being arrested or killed.

When television exploded on the scene in the 1950s, it signaled the beginning of the end of Republic Pictures. People no longer needed to go to the theater to see their heroes save the day. The little pictures for which the studio was noted became less and less profitable due to rising costs and the allure of television. The studio closed in 1959.

Cowboys, Creatures, and Classics: The Story of Republic Pictures tells the story of the ambitious film company that made a big impact on Hollywood and influenced some of today's most gifted filmmakers and industry leaders. It's a tribute to cheap thrills and guilty pleasures.

Included in the book is information about the actors who helped to make Republic Pictures popular and one in particular many believe responsible for the studio's decline. The careers of the special effects artists, stuntmen, and the films that brought them fame and fortune are examined in the book, too.

So, grab a bag of popcorn and a bottle of soda pop and relive the excitement and thrills of those wonderful, bygone days before television when Republic Studios was king and B pictures ruled the box office.

The Republic Pictures name proudly displayed on a building in the studio lot AUTHOR'S COLLECTION

CHAPTER 1

Herbert Yates' Republic

Herbert Yates, a tall, compact man in his mid-fifties, stood staring out the window of his magnificent office at Republic Pictures in Studio City, California, surveying the domain spread before him. A scene from a western film was being rehearsed in the middle distance. The usual, turbulent activity surrounded it: extras, makeup women, cameramen, grips, assistants, set designers, etc. Yates lit a cigar the size of a baby's leg and held it tightly in his teeth. He took a long puff and blew the smoke out the corner of his mouth and checked the pockets of his charcoal gray Brooks Brothers suit for the additional cigars he had tucked away. He patted them reassuringly, then rolled the fat stogie from one side of his mouth to the other.

Yates had acquired his taste for cigars while working as a salesman at the American Tobacco Company. Paired with a stiff bow tie, a receding hairline, and a dour expression, the cigar added a layer of seriousness to his persona. As head of a burgeoning motion picture studio, he felt the look was necessary. He wanted to appear menacing. More often than not, his business approach was "never underestimate the power of good, old-fashioned intimidation."[1]

Herbert Yates founded Republic Pictures in 1935, but his history working in the movie industry began twenty years prior to the creation of the studio. Yates' introduction to cinema came by way of a film-processing business called Hedwig Laboratories. He learned all about developing celluloid and relationships with some of the most profitable filmmaking executives in the field. He parlayed his knowledge into his own processing venture called Consolidated Film Industries. In a short time, Consolidated Film Industries became the leading laboratory in Southern California.

President of Republic Pictures, Herbert Yates AUTHOR'S COLLECTION

They processed negatives and made prints for the majority of movies produced by studios such as First National Pictures, Warner Bros., and Fox Film Corporation. Consolidated Film Industries proved to be extremely profitable for Yates, and he sought other areas of the industry of which to be a part. He acquired record companies and financed ventures for director Mack Sennett and comedic actor Fatty Arbuckle.

Within eight weeks of advancing funds to Sennett and Arbuckle, Yates received a 100 percent return on his investment. The speed in which his funds were replenished intrigued him. Yates saw the profit to be made in producing motion pictures, and it whetted his appetite for further opportunities.[2]

Among the studios Consolidated Film Industries developed films for was Mascot Pictures. Mascot was run by filmmaker Nat Levine. Levine was the pioneer of serial films,* most notably *King of the Kongo*. Made in 1929, it was the first serial to have sound. In 1931, Mascot Pictures introduced the first all-talkie western entitled *The Phantom of the West*. Yates kept a close eye on the studio's interworking and the money earned from the release of Levine's pictures. Because he saw massive earning potential in film, he never hesitated to advance funds to Levine for his projects. By the mid-1930s, Yates was bankrolling the majority of Mascot Pictures' projects.

The serial work Levine was doing was extremely popular. Audiences flocked to theaters each week to find out how cowboy heroes like Johnny Mack Brown, Ken Maynard, and Tom Mix fared against the bad guys and to learn if equine stars like Rex, the King of Wild Horses, and canine actor Rin Tin Tin managed to save their pal Smiley Burnette from the villainous Harry Woods. Levine wanted to expand his moviemaking and looked to acquire the Mack Sennett production lot and facilities in order to make it happen. He approached Monogram Pictures' executives Trem Carr and

---

* A motion picture form popular during the first half of the twentieth century, consisting of a series of short subjects exhibited in consecutive order.

W. Ray Johnston about a merger. Neither was interested in combining his resources to purchase Mack Sennett. Both men felt the cost to run such a business would be too much to sustain. Yates heard about Levine's proposal and offered to finance the deal. With Yates' considerable wealth behind the enterprise and the promise that the two could share the responsibility of studio chief, Carr and Johnston decided to participate. The owners of Liberty and Majestic Studios also agreed to merge with Mascot and Monogram. The talent and resources of

Republic Studio boss Herbert Yates in a meeting with two of his executives, c. 1945 AUTHOR'S COLLECTION

each small motion picture company were pooled and a distribution arm was also added to the corporation.[3]

Republic Pictures was born in June 1935. As the money behind the venture, Yates wasted no time in asserting his authority. Although Johnston and Carr were installed as managers, Yates made it clear that he would make all major decisions regarding the company. The two executives were outraged by the mogul's behavior but were compelled to stay with the new studio because they now lacked the means to start their own business. Nat Levine clashed with Yates, too, but chose to keep quiet in favor of making movies. He churned out a number of modest yet successful films during the first four years Republic was in operation.[4]

Undeterred by the conflicts with his managing staff, Yates announced in a press conference with his top personnel that Republic Pictures would produce fifty-two films a year. Edward A. Golden, general sales manager for the studio, added that the company would strive to make exceptional pictures and cited problems with finances in the industry as a whole for the reason some companies delivered inferior products. Johnston shared his belief that not only financing played a part but that the lack of quality material was a contributing factor to bad movies being made. Johnston outlined Republic Pictures' program to produce classics and the works of famous authors and urged American authors to "write better stories for screen production."[5]

Throughout the summer of 1935, Republic Pictures and its qualified staff made news. Stories about the ambitious independent studio's line of pictures and the controversial comments about the industry appeared on the front pages of the newspapers. Johnston, an actor in his early days in Hollywood and a member of Franklin Roosevelt's motion picture code authority, had definite thoughts about the salary lead actors at Republic should expect to earn. "Stars of today are paid according to their drawing power," he told the *Associated Press*. "What they get is all right if they bring it back through the box office. Many of them don't do that, however. We at Republic Pictures will pay according to the draw."[6]

Scarcity of name players and general casting difficulties (established actors cited Republic's insistence that they ensure the films they were to star at least made what the studio invested in them as a problem) persuaded the studio to develop its own stock company. In pursuance of this policy, the company signed several promising, young players and gave them a chance at feature parts as soon as they qualified. The first player to be signed was Barbara Pepper. Barbara was a former Goldwyn Girl and a leading performer in several movies at the time. Her first role for Republic was entitled *Waterfront Lady*.[*,7]

---

* Goldwyn Girls were a musical stock company of female dancers employed by Samuel Goldwyn.

In early August 1935, Republic hired a director that had proved himself sufficiently talented not only at making motion pictures but also at acting in and producing quality work with a limited budget. Lew Ayres taught himself to use a camera, direct, and edit the films he shot. With only $160.00, he made an impressive featurette starring his wife Ginger Rogers and family friend Sterling Holloway entitled *The Disinherited*. The picture received the attention of Herbert Yates, who asked Ayres to join the Republic Pictures family as a director.[8]

A number of other gifted performers signed with Republic in their infancy. Lester "Smiley" Burnette, William Ching, Dale Evans, Roy Rogers, and John Wayne were just a few Republic hoped would make money for the studio and force competitors to take the company seriously. Of the fifty-two pictures Yates announced would be produced in the first year the studio was formed, twenty-two were mystery/adventure films, ten were dramas, four were serials, and sixteen were westerns starring either John Wayne or Gene Autry.

Republic Pictures had approximately forty-five writers on staff who worked on creating original material and adapting stories from magazines and popular news items. The studio developed many scripts from articles written by Allan Vaughan Elston. A story he penned entitled "Corpus Delicti" appeared in *Cosmopolitan*, and the popular thriller was acquired by Yates to be made into a film.[9] The former rancher and railroad employee signed on with Republic to write a number of mysteries and westerns. Elston eventually moved on to work for Alfred Hitchcock. Barry Shipman was another accomplished author hired by Yates. Shipman wrote several cliffhangers for Republic including those for the *Dick Tracy* and *Zorro* serials. He later graduated to writing full-length features for the studio.[10]

In addition to the talented actors and writers on staff with Republic Pictures were several stuntmen, cinematographers, and special effects experts. Cameraman Joseph Ruttenberg, one-time newsboy and runner for William Randolph Hearst, was a brilliant innovator with cranes and dolly devices. Ruttenberg would be nominated for an Academy Award ten times for best cinematographer. Yakima Canutt, world champion rodeo rider, perfected numerous horse falls and wagon wreck tricks that when filmed looked amazing; brothers Howard and Theodore Lydecker used low-tech artistry to elevate Republic's serials to new heights.

Herbert Yates held producers to a modest budget of eighteen thousand to thirty-seven thousand dollars to make serial pictures. The average US feature cost $375,000 to make. Republic Pictures did two westerns a month, and the actors and crew worked a seven-day schedule. Those westerns were referred to by the studio as Jubilee Pictures. Bigger westerns, action adventure films, and musicals were called Anniversary Pictures. The average budget for those films was $120,000 with a work schedule of two weeks. Deluxe Pictures were filmed over a twenty-two day schedule and cost three hundred thousand to five hundred thousand dollars to make. Premiere Pictures, which featured name actors and directors, were shot over a month-long schedule and had a one million dollar budget.

Given the minuscule funds to work with, the behind-the-scenes talent at the studio was challenged to be as inventive as it could. Republic's creative team did wonders, and the films were profitable, sometimes grossing more than $250,000. Yates was thrilled with the outcome. Turning out a low-cost, high-yield product was everything for which the shrewd businessman hoped. It did not inspire him to invest more funds in the pictures, however. He was convinced that his moviemaking principle was sound and that it inspired his creative departments to develop mechanisms that would revolutionize the medium.

Among the top money-making films for Republic in 1935 was the John Wayne western *Westward Ho*. The movie was about the onward movement of the new frontier from Dodge City, Kansas, to Grass Valley, California. The story covered a period of fifteen years and narrated the exploits of a band of roving vigilantes, headed by Wayne, who bring law and order to the covered wagon trails. *Westward Ho* was Wayne's twenty-fifth western production in a three-year span. During that period, he rose from an unknown property man to the top ranks of western players and one of the best-liked cowboy actors on the screen.[11]

Movie columnist Louella Parsons kept the public informed with news about the projects Republic was developing and the books the studio hoped to procure to make into motion pictures. She reported on the up and coming stars at the company, the hiring of key personnel such as talent scout Jules Schermer, and on the problems between Yates and fellow executives at the studio.[12] Citing difficulties working with Yates, Republic Pictures' president Trem Carr left the company on December 17, 1935.[13]

Independent film producer Walter W. Vincent joined the Republic Pictures team when W. Ray Johnston was announced as the person who would share the role of president of the company with Nat Levine.[14] By August 1936, Johnston had vacated the position, and Levine wasn't far behind. Johnston and Carr made it known to stockholders at Republic that they feared Yates' personality was too abrasive to attract quality executives who would stay for any length of time. Yates let the bottom line speak for his ability to efficiently run the studio. Republic Pictures grossed over $2.5 million in the first year of its existence.[15] Frustrated that no one at the studio would listen to them, Johnston and Carr decided to compete with Republic by reviving the Monogram organization.

By late 1936, the confidence stockholders had in Yates was in question. In the fall of that year, the Securities and Exchange Commission launched an investigation into Consolidated Film Industries. According to the October 23, 1936, edition of the *Detroit Free Press*, Consolidated Film

Industries had withheld certain information from stockholders. The commission made public the findings Yates failed to disclose.[*,16]

By early 1937, Yates and Consolidated Film Industries had bounced back from the negative press brought on by problems with the Securities and Exchange Commission. All major studio executives considered Consolidated Film Industries to be the best sound laboratory in Hollywood, and the high praise overshadowed any difficulties that had arisen. In terms of respect and acceptance by its peers, Republic Pictures was being recognized as a studio with massive possibility of one day becoming an industry leader.[17] Yates reveled in the acceptance the company received. He wanted Republic to grow into a studio that made more premiere pictures than Jubilee and reap the financial reward for such investments as MGM, Paramount, and Warner Bros. enjoyed.

In May 1937, all Republic Pictures' franchise owners in the United States and Canada, studio executives in New York and Los Angeles, and sale supervisors met at the Roosevelt Hotel in Hollywood to hear Chief Executive Officer Herbert Yates announce the slate of pictures scheduled for 1937 to 1938. The May 28, 1937, edition of the *Harrisburg Telegraph* reported that Republic Pictures would produce thirty features, twenty-four westerns, and four serials. Yates proudly informed the studio personnel that the new lineup also called for "four anniversary special pictures" on which the company was centering all its production resources. Those four pictures would be suitable to play in any class A theater. Ten Jubilee and sixteen action adventure money makers would be made.[18]

"Gene Autry again heads a series of twenty-four westerns with eight pictures," the *Harrisburg Telegraph* article noted:

---

* Gladys Baker, Marilyn Monroe's mother, worked for Consolidated Film Industries as a negative film cutter. Her father, Charles Stanley Gifford, was also employed by the company.

There will be eight *Three Mesquiteers* westerns from Bob Steele and four serials.

Phil Regan, singing star, is down for four productions. The comedy team of Alison Skipworth and Polly Moran is set for a pair, as are Ole Olsen and Chic Johnson. Republic plans to use Max Terhune, ventriloquist hit of the *Hit Parade*, in more important roles for the coming season.

Barry Perowne, creator of the famous character, Raffles; Mildred Cram, Everett Freeman, William Colt MacDonald, William Chester, Lucian Cary, Armstrong Sperry, Malcolm Wheeler-Nicholson and Ann Lawrence are a few of the nationally prominent authors whose stories will be brought to the screen by Republic.[19]

Yates left the corporate meeting at Roosevelt Hotel determined to realize his vision for Republic Pictures. His focus was seriously derailed on two occasions during the summer of 1937. In June, the studio was hit with a twenty-five thousand dollar lawsuit by actor, stuntman, and horse trainer Tracy Layne and his horse, Zane. Tracy had appeared in several serials directed by Nat Levine as did his trick horse Zane. Tracy was suing Republic because Zane didn't receive screen credit for his work.[20]

According to Tracy, Zane's feelings were hurt, and compensations for his pain had to be satisfied. In exchange for the job the horse did in the serial production, *Rex, King of the Wild Horses*, Zane was to be paid two hundred dollars and his name was to appear in the opening film credits. "The screen credit was not forthcoming," Tracy explained to a United Press journalist. The case was eventually settled out of court.[21]

Although the suit involving recognition for a movie horse was done more for publicity reasons by the trainer, it was a time-consuming issue for Yates and that annoyed him. The film executive wanted to concentrate

Rex, King of the Wild Horses

on making Republic one of the most profitable companies in the industry. On July 9, 1937, his goal met with a major setback when director Nat Levine announced he was leaving Republic to work for Louis B. Mayer at MGM. Levine was known for being one of the busiest executives in Hollywood. He helped make Republic an important action studio. He perfected the use of two directors and two separate filming units, with one shooting the main players and dialogue while a second unit filmed stunts, action sequences, location, and establishing shots. Levine's serials generated mass interest in short, cliffhanger movies that kept audiences returning to the theaters again and again to see how the hero and heroine survived certain danger.[22]

Levine didn't stay long at MGM, just a short two years. Mayer put him to work in the second unit department of the studio, and Levine had hoped for more of a role as a director of major films. By 1939, he had departed MGM and succumbed to a gambling habit. He lost his entire fortune betting on horses. He eventually took a job managing a movie theater in Redondo Beach.[23]

Herbert Yates managed to find suitable replacements for Levine. Directors Joseph Kane, Harry Fraser, and Norman Hall had all worked as production assistants under Levine and became key players for the studio.

In the fall of 1937, Republic launched a promotional campaign for the studio that ran in newspapers, magazines, and on the radio. It extolled the virtues of the company, its talented directors, actors, and writers, and touted the countless hours of "genuine entertainment" offered to the moviegoing audience. The storied advertisement read:

> Republic Pictures creates Happy Hours! Republic Pictures is tai-
> lored to fit the exacting requirements of Mr. and Mrs. America
> and their entire family. That's the program of Republic Pictures.
> That's the policy which in three years has made the name of

Republic Pictures on theater screens from coast to coast mean satisfied audiences and which now permits Republic to present an even stronger series of sure-fire hits filled with stars of the screen, the stage, and radio. Such favorites as Phil Regan, Ramon Navarro, Alison Skipworth, Polly Moran, Gene Autry, Jimmie Gleason, and Max Terhune. Here they are in stories by such outstanding American writers as Faith Baldwin, Mildred Cram, Barry Perowne, and Lucian Cary all in productions directed by such big-time experts as James Cruze, Chuck Riesner, and other leading production minds of Hollywood.[24]

Yates was pleased with business at Republic, and, despite what former employees said about him being difficult to work for and with, his staff of executives presented him with an expensive gift in mid-1938. At a banquet in his honor on May 28, 1938, his associates gave him a five hundred dollar watch. The watch was stolen from Yates' table at the event but was returned to the studio four days later.[25]

Republic Pictures' box office receipts for the 1937–1938 season were impressive. Westerns were big money earners, and pictures starring Roy Rogers, the studio's newest cowboy star, were some of the highest grossing films. Rogers made his motion picture debut for Republic in *Under Western Stars* in April 1938, after which he became popularly known as "King of the Cowboys." "Dust," singing cowboy Roy's song in the film, was written by Johnny Marvin and was nominated as Best Original Song. The Academy Award for Best Original Song went to "Thanks for the Memory" from *The Big Broadcast*.

Yates was encouraged by the recognition from the Academy Award nomination a Republic Pictures' film received. He added more westerns to the slate of projects for the 1939-1940 season along with forty-five features. Yates and the company he co-founded were riding a wave of success

FACING PAGE: *Down in Arkansaw* was a comedy released by Republic in 1938.
AUTHOR'S COLLECTION

going into 1939. Taking advantage of his reputation as a shrewd business-man, Yates announced an idea to the industry he believed would make the moviegoing experience even more attractive and ultimately translate into an increase in ticket sales. If accepted by all the studios, the nation would save an estimated fifty million hours a year. An article about the Yates' proposal in the February 5, 1939, edition of the *Akron Beacon Journal* noted,

> Under the present arrangement of things cinematic, audiences must read, sandwiched between film title and opening scene, the names, titles, and state of health of all who had a hand in making the film, from signer of checks to water boy.
>
> Yates plans to announce the names of the cast briefly at the play's beginning. The cameraman, costume makers, writers, sound mixes, et al. heretofore given substantial footage, will be entirely eliminated. These credits will be tacked on at the end of the movie. Then, if the exhibitor wants to give them screen time, he may—or he is allowed to clip them. This can be done with no damage to the film's sound continuity.
>
> Unless the patron is technically inclined, most of the preliminary credits to each picture are a bore. And it seems needless to distress an audience before it sees the picture.
>
> Added convenience is another virtue of the proposal. If interest is to exist in the craft of any of these studio workers, it will be aroused by the picture itself. Then the patron can satisfy his curiosity at the close of the picture, remembering a name he certainly would have forgotten during the run of the film.[26]

Yates' idea was not well received by the majority of the screenwriters, cameramen, and supporting film crew members. No other studio, apart from Republic, agreed to go along with the change.[27]

Four years after Republic Pictures was formed, Herbert Yates announced that the studio would be abandoning the Jubilee films that had initially brought them into prominence and made them the leading independent movie company. Yates viewed Republic as now fully capable of making nothing but feature films. All lower-budget (or quickie) movies were to be thrown out. Republic would join the league of major companies. Yates added one million dollars to the slate of motion pictures to be produced in 1939–1940.[28]

On March 12, 1939, Yates purchased the old Mack Sennett studio for five hundred thousand dollars. He was serious about Republic Pictures being a big-time operation and decided the company needed additional property to realize the venture. The purchase was made with help from the Guaranty Liquidating Corporation and involved a substantial cash payment with the balance to be paid within a short time. Yates told Hollywood reporters that Republic Pictures was contemplating a considerable building program on the 19.5 acres acquired and thirty acres adjoining, which the studio already owned.[29]

Republic Pictures did well in 1939–1940. Owing to three popular movie cowboys, the earnings were impressive. Roy Rogers' trio of pictures *Young Buffalo Bill*, *The Arizona Kid*, and *Days of Jesse James*; Gene Autry's westerns *Blue Montana Skies* and *Mexican Rose*; and John Wayne's feature *Dark Command* made the most money for the studio. *Dark Command* received two Academy Award nominations as well—one for Best Original Score and one for Best Art Direction.

Before Yates could move forward with any big plans for Republic, he had to settle yet another lawsuit involving a horse. This time it was the cowboy actor Buck Jones' ride, Silver.[30] Buck Jones brought a $250,000 suit against the studio for "illegally borrowing" from him and his white horse the movie character he helped create. According to the May 16, 1939, edition of the *St. Louis Star and Times*, Jones insisted that Silver and the

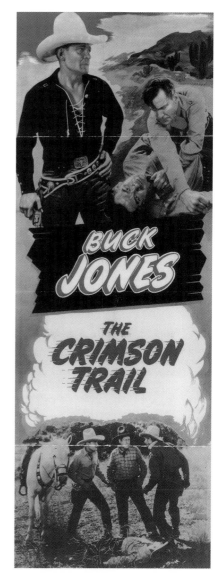

Cowboy actor Buck Jones and his horse Silver were stars at Republic Pictures.
AUTHOR'S COLLECTION

phrase "Hiyo, Silver" were exclusively his and that although Republic Pictures produced the Buck Jones serials, they could not use any item associated with his on-screen persona. Republic's serial *The Lone Ranger* used both the horse's name and the catch phrase.[31]

"I always called Silver by yelling 'Hiyo, Silver' in every picture," Jones told the court. "I have been doing that for twelve years. I was the original yodler [sic] of the phrase."[32]

Republic attorneys contended the only similarities between *The Lone Ranger* series and the Jones pictures were the common use of the white horse known as Silver. They maintained that the name Silver could not be copyrighted. The court ruled in Republic's favor. A federal judge declared it a nonsuit and noted that Jones had no evidence to support the claim that he alone had the right to sing out "Hiyo, Silver."[33]

When the Buck Jones case concluded, Herbert Yates focused on the big budget pictures he hoped would rival films released by major studios. One of the first such projects was a movie entitled *Man of Conquest*, a biopic of the politician and defender of the Alamo, Sam Houston.[34] Yates staked one million dollars on the epic, which featured the recreation of the Battle of San Jacinto. The battle, fought on April 21, 1836, was one of the most decisive battles between Houston's Texas volunteers and Santa Ana's troops. Eight cameras were used to catch the action as the movie troops battled, and two running cameras accompanied the charge itself.[35]

The end result was a critically acclaimed motion picture that was nominated for three Academy Awards: Best Art Direction, Best Sound Recording, and Best Original Score.

Herbert Yates stood tall among the executives from United Artists, RKO, and Universal Pictures who attended the Oscar ceremonies in 1939 and 1940. The little film company had worked hard to win a spot at the prestigious event, and Yates was proud to receive the accolades showered on Republic Pictures.

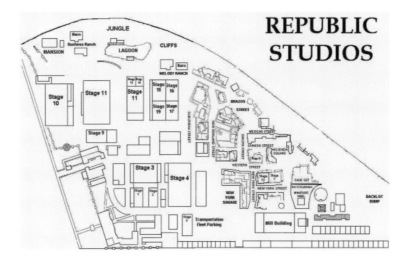

In less than ten years, Herbert Yates grew Republic Pictures from a small production company to a sprawling motion picture studio. AUTHOR'S COLLECTION

Just when it seemed Republic had taken its place in the "major" field, Yates broadcast a decision that had potential to halt any momentum the studio had gained. War was brewing in Europe, and it seemed certain the United States would be involved. Major film companies were clamoring for material based around the subject of war. In an interview with reporters from the *New York Herald Telegraph*, Yates made it clear that Republic would focus on "escape films" and with the exception of one serial and one feature film the studio would veer away from heavy dramatics or pictures of war. Yates believed the public wouldn't be interested in a steady diet of war films. Republic would provide moviegoers with pictures that took their minds off such a weighty subject. The studio had become a solvent company using the "escape" formula, and Yates saw no need to deviate from the philosophy of the studio.[36]

At a subsequent press conference held at Republic on October 2, 1939, Yates assured reporters that the studio would continue to deliver superior pictures like *Dark Command* and *Man of Conquest* regardless of the threat of war. "War would bring no curtailment either as to the amount or the quality of Republic productions during the coming years," Yates stated.

AUTHOR'S COLLECTION

"Out of the fifty-two pictures scheduled in the near future for the studio, eleven have been finished, five are in production, and ten more are set to be completed soon."[37]

Yates saw the future of Republic as full of promise. He desired to continue to grow the company and to expand Consolidated Film Industries as well. Yates wanted his legacy to be that of an industry leader with a slate of memorable films to his credit. He would enjoy the success of a handful of classic pictures but would be remembered mostly for jeopardizing everything he had built for the love and affection of a Russian skater named Vera Ralston.

CHAPTER 2

The Making of a Cowboy

Silence, intense and oppressive, gripped the moonlit expanse of the plains. The slight mist that rose from the ground gave vague and uncertain outlines to the rocks that studded the terrain like stolid sentinels. There was no breeze—no sound or motion of any sort to mar the perfect stillness. No sound, that is, except the steady clump of hoofs as a solitary rider moved through the night.

The rider was Gene Autry. He sat easily in the saddle, but the muscles of his tall body were tensed and his eyes warily alert. He couldn't shake off an eerie feeling of impending trouble. Neither could he account for his anxiety.

Gene's horse, a dark sorrel named Champion, seemed to share his rider's disquiet. Champion trotted smoothly and swiftly through the night, but his ears were twin points and his nostrils quivered.

"What's gotten into us, Champion?" Gene asked in a low voice as he leaned forward to pat the horse's neck. "We're as nervous as a couple of colts. Everything certainly looks peaceful. There's not a living critter in sight anywhere."

It was the first time Gene had ever felt the uneasiness. He had traveled countless miles in the dark of night with only Champion and the stars for companions. Because he had spent half his life in the saddle, complete solitude and trackless country were nothing new to him.

Gene had been a cowboy for as long as he could remember. He loved the wild, free life of the plains. He had tamed broncs, hazed cattle, ridden point on trail drives, bulldogged the toughest of steers, and won a dozen rodeo championships.

He knew the mountains and plains in all kinds of weather. He was familiar with every detail of the country through which he traveled. He could identify the call of every creature of the West, and he knew the name of every tree and shrub. He was completely at home in the moonlit silence of the night.

There was no explanation for the feeling of depression that had fallen over him like a shroud. He hadn't felt that way at sunset. What was there about the darkness of this particular night that disturbed him?

Gene was heading for country where oil had recently been discovered. A week before, he had run into an old prospector just in from the oil fields. As he listened to the old man's stories of the excitement of prospecting for oil, the suspense of drilling down through the sun-baked earth, and the thrill of watching the stream of "black gold" gush upward toward the sky, Gene decided to take a look at this new world of derricks and machines and grim-faced men.

Now, as he rode toward the oil fields, Gene Autry was on the way to greater excitement and adventure than he had ever known.

He started to whistle, but the tune quickly died away.

"Hang it all," he muttered. "I can't shake this mood. I guess I've been in the saddle too long. It's about time to pitch camp and turn in."

Ahead loomed a clump of trees, silhouetted as a patch of black against the sky. Though it was early evening, the rider decided to camp somewhere among those trees. As Champion brought him near the wooded area, Gene heard the sound of running water. Champion's ears cocked forward at the rippling sound and Gene grinned in the darkness.

"That's all you need to hear, eh, Champion? I can let the reins fall and you'll head for that stream," he said to the sorrel.

Cool leaves of low branches brushed Gene's face and the broad brim of his hat. Then Champion stopped abruptly, his strong muscles quivering.

Gene glanced sharply ahead and gasped in surprise as his eyes met those of another man on a level with his own. The moonlight, slanting through an opening of the trees, fell full upon the other man's face. For a moment, Gene Autry could only stare in disbelief. Then he realized the man in front of him was dead, suspended from the branches overhead by a noose about his neck. His feet dangled several inches off the ground.

Gene nudged Champion ahead until he reached the dead man. Then, supporting the stranger with an arm about the waist, he whipped out his sheath knife and cut the rope, lowering the unconscious form to the ground as he dismounted.

The boys and girls who filled the audience of the average movie theater across the country on Saturday afternoon stared wide-eyed at the screen anxiously watching Gene Autry handle the everyday occurrences of the Wild West. There was no doubt the singing cowboy hero would be victorious in his efforts to bring law and order to the territory. Once he met up with his partner Smiley Burnette at the next town, reported the injustice, and sang a song or two, all would be right.

The motion picture studio with the most success at making westerns that featured heroes with the ability to enforce the law and the talent for singing was Republic Pictures. Republic was the number one producer of westerns from 1935 to 1950.

The western film genre is more than 110 years old. During that period of time it has undergone continual changes of emphasis to appeal to a juvenile audience in one era and an adult audience in another. It has had to adjust to technological changes within the film industry and reshape itself to fight off rising production costs.

The western has played an important role in American art and culture. It's as integral a part of American folklore as the *Odyssey* is to the Greeks; to the American audiences, the western, whatever its form,

humble "B" features, grade-scale epic in color and wide-screen, was for years a reliable staple of movie entertainment.

Republic Pictures perfected the assembly line process of making westerns. The plots of the movies were formulaic and motivated by straightforward villainy. A number of Republic's westerns were set in the immediate post–Civil War period with corrupt politicians and guerrillas legally taking over defeated territories and plundering them. Several centered around the trials and tribulations of running stagecoach or freight lines, of getting a contract to supply horses to the army, and the horses of the good guys and those of the villains. Those themes were solid money makers for Republic. Even if the film scripts were stereotypical, the product value of a Republic production was anything but that. The studio's production values were high, featuring razor sharp cinematography, stirring musical scores, and thrilling stunt work.

Gene Autry, a veteran country-and-western singer who had made a name for himself in film starring in Mascot Pictures' bizarre western/sci-fi serial *The Phantom Empire*, was one of Republic Pictures' first cowboy super stars. He made his debut at Republic in the movie *Tumbling Tumbleweeds*. When Gene Autry rode onto the scene, the introduction of musical numbers in western pictures was new. Autry introduced cowboy songs on the screen that made his radio and stage career popular.[1]

Autry was the hero of *Tumbling Tumbleweeds*. His character turned detective when his father was murdered over a water grant because he set a trap to catch the murderer who walked accommodatingly into it. Autry sang a number of songs in the movie, which contained a thrilling scene with the runaway of a four-horse team attached to a medicine wagon in which several men are fighting.[2]

The budget for the fifty-minute production was $12,500, and it grossed more than one million dollars. Critics noted that Autry's "ability to collect a crowd by the vigor of his voice was his main asset."[3]

Gene Autry was born on September 29, 1907, near the little town of Tioga, Texas, which had a population of one thousand on Saturday nights. While still a young boy, he was taken by his family to the Oklahoma side of the Red River where they had bought a farm near Ravia.

His father was a cattle buyer, and according to Autry's autobiography *Back in the Saddle Again*, his earliest recollections were of working at such man-sized chores as rounding up cattle and helping to brand and dip them. His family struggled to eke out more than the merest existence from the land.

Gene was eleven years old before he managed to save a dollar. He immediately invested his dollar as a down payment on a mail-order guitar. The payments were to be fifty cents a month, and to keep them up he took a summer job with a traveling medicine show that came through the country dispensing corn plasters, household articles, and rainbow-colored cure-alls.

The young boy who sang cowboy ballads and plucked his five-dollar guitar became a hit of the Fields Brothers Marvelous Medicine Show, and it was sad parting for everyone concerned when school time rolled around in the fall and Gene had to return to his books.

His summer travels, however, had instilled in him a bad case of wanderlust, and he found it hard to keep his mind on school work. He started spending every spare moment at the local railroad depot helping the station manager with the baggage just so he could be on hand when the twice-daily trains came through.[4]

The years spent at the railroad station led to a job offer as a relief telegraph operator on the Frisco Railway. Gene was grateful for the invitation to join the company but didn't want to commit at the time. He wanted to find out if he could be successful pursuing his other passion, which was baseball.

He had always been a fan of the Oklahoma City Indians, attending as many practice games as he could. It wasn't until the job offer at the railroad that he had enough courage to ask for a tryout. The club owner was impressed with Gene's ability and offered to sign him to a one-year contract. Now he had two opportunities in front of him. After weighing his options, Gene chose the railroad job because it paid better, but he never lost his love for the game.

While working at a railroad office in Sapulpa, Oklahoma, he met fellow employee Jimmy Long. The pair not only shared an interest in the rails but in music as well. They soon formed a duo, and, as news of their talents spread through the area, they were in demand for local parties and entertainments. The pair wrote many western ballads together among them "That Silver Haired Daddy of Mine." Autry would later record that song, and it became one of the biggest selling records of all time.

Will Rogers heard Gene and Jimmy playing at the station one day and was impressed with their sound. He encouraged the pair to travel to New York and try to break into radio. Gene took the advice to heart and traveled to the big city hoping for instant success. He soon realized he wasn't ready for the big time and returned to Oklahoma. All was not lost, however; he managed to talk his way into a fifteen-minute daily program on a station in Tulsa. Billed as "Oklahoma's Yodeling Cowboy," Gene built up an audience and within a year attracted the attention of an executive at Columbia Records. The executive arranged for Gene to be a short-term regular on WLS in Chicago performing for the Farm and Home Hour. That short term lasted more than four years, and it led to a record deal.

The first record Gene made for Columbia was "Silver Haired Daddy of Mine." The song was extremely popular, and soon he began turning out hit after hit. Gene's personal life was successful, too. He married Ina Spivey on April 1, 1932, and the pair made Chicago their home.[5]

In 1934, the Legion of Decency started cracking down on Hollywood movies, demanding that the industry start turning out clean, wholesome pictures instead of the sexy films that had become vogue of the day. Sensing that a new type of singing western might be the answer to the industry's dilemma, the Columbia executive who signed Gene to a recording contract persuaded Herbert Yates to take a chance on the cowboy yodeler.

Gene's first appearance consisted of a musical spot in a Ken Maynard picture. Ken was a former trick rider with Buffalo Bill Cody's Wild West show who turned stuntman and actor and wore a white cowboy hat, fancy shirt, and a pair of six-shooters. He was quite famous and difficult to work with. Although Gene only sang one song, the fan mail response was overwhelming and Yates immediately agreed to star him in a serial.

Gene made several films in the first year with Republic Pictures. *Tumbling Tumbleweeds* gave way to seven additional movies, and each broke box office records. In December 1935, Gene was named the top box office star of westerns. By 1939, his pictures were showing all over the world, and he was planning to do a musical throughout Europe.

Autry was extremely popular, but critics could not understand why. His voice was pleasant, and at least one of the six songs he sang in each film he made for Republic Pictures played regularly on the radio. He was a capable horseman and a "no frills" type of actor. He delivered his lines clearly, but his acting range was limited. He played the same warm and friendly hero of the cowboys in every film. He was dependable. At a time in history when much was in question—the economy was in a state of recovery from gangsters like Lucky Luciano, Ma Barker and her brood were on the loose, and a world war was looming on the horizon—moviegoers needed dependability, and Gene Autry was it.

Autry not only became the top-ranking Hollywood star but also the biggest money-making western hero. Gene was sought to perform in concerts, print, and radio advertisements as well as appear for his work outside the studio, a fact no one seemed to mind until Nat Levine left the studio. Nat argued that Republic wasn't entitled to any of the money earned outside the company, but Herbert Yates disagreed. When Nat left Republic, there was no one at the studio to make a case for Autry.[6]

The conflict between Gene Autry and Herbert Yates began in the fall of 1937. Yates resented Autry's fame because it overshadowed his own. Yates felt he was responsible for Autry's fame. He reasoned that he owned the studio and paid Autry's salary and therefore he was entitled to credit for the creation. Yates didn't feel Autry was grateful enough to him for his success and decided it was time to remind Gene, and any other budding star at the studio, who was in charge.[7]

The feud between the singing cowboy and the film boss became fodder for newspaper columnists. According to the January 26, 1931, edition of the *Hollywood Reporter*, a good old-fashioned battle was being planned at Republic Pictures, and both Autry and Yates claimed grievances. Reporter Louella Parsons wrote,

> Autry's grievances came to this desk yesterday in a wire. He says Republic is doing him wrong by not paying him enough and forcing exhibitors to take inferior pictures in order to get the Autry westerns. Now on personal appearances, Autry says he learned all this by talking to theatre owners, and furthermore, that his pictures rate high in box office surveys and are not losing money as Republic declares.
>
> Yates answered by denying all of the cowboy's allegations, adding that Gene was given two raises and at the time of the last increase he agreed not to mention money again. Yates further states that the studio has spent $500,000 to develop their singing cowboy, who was unknown when they took him.

He will seek an injunction to prevent Gene from continuing the tour. I still don't know what Autry is being paid since Yates refused to say and Autry made no mention of it in his wire.[8]

Leonard Slye peered through the black bars on the giant gate leading onto the Republic Pictures lot. He watched actors, stagehands, wardrobe people, and technicians scurrying from one studio to the next. It was organized chaos, and the young entertainer from Ohio wanted to be a part of it. The year was 1937.

He glanced down at his watch—past lunchtime. He'd been standing at the entrance of the studio since early that morning. He didn't have a scheduled appointment, and no amount of persuasion could entice the dour guard to let him pass. Leonard stared down at his cowboy boots, desperately trying to think of a way to get past the strict sentry. At that very moment, he knew acting hopefuls were competing to be Republic's newest singing cowboy.

Leonard had heard about the search the day before while he was at a hat shop in Glendale, California. A frantic man had burst into the store in search of a John Wayne–style Stetson. When Leonard asked him what he was so excited about, the anxious thespian had filled him in on Republic's quest. Gene Autry was the studio's current singing cowboy star, but it was common knowledge there were contract issues that called into question future pictures with the actor. Republic executives were looking for a possible replacement.

At this point in his career, Leonard Slye was calling himself Dick Weston. He thought the name sounded a bit more rugged than the one his parents had given him, and he needed a rugged handle if he was to be taken seriously as a western entertainer. He was no stranger to the motion-picture business, having performed musically in a number of films with the Sons of the Pioneers. In addition to singing, he had played minor roles in a couple movies, acting alongside Bing Crosby and Joan Davis. Universal even granted Dick Weston a screen test at one time, but he didn't get the job with the studio. Executives felt he photographed too young. Leonard hoped the executives at Republic Pictures would see him differently.

The guard shot the desperate actor a stern look. Leonard smiled a pleading smile then, realizing it was having no effect, turned away. In the middle distance, he spotted a group of studio employees returning from lunch. As they neared the gate, he decided to join them on their way in. Pulling his collar up and his hat down low, he slipped past the guard. The dedicated attendant spotted Leonard ten yards from the guardhouse and called out for him to stop. Leonard did as he was told. Just as he had resigned himself to being thrown off the premises, he heard a friendly voice calling his name. Producer Sol Siegel hurried over to him and shook his hand. The guard returned to his post when the producer waved him off.

Siegel produced many Gene Autry movies and had cast Leonard in minor roles in some of them. Leonard removed his hat and told Sol he had heard they were testing for singing cowboys. The producer nodded. "I've tested seventeen men already," he told Leonard. "And I don't feel good about any of them. If you have your guitar, come on in and give it a try."

Leonard serenaded Siegel with "Tumbling Tumbleweeds" and a fast-paced yodeling tune called "Haddie Brown." The producer was impressed and offered Leonard a screen test. Leonard floated out of the studio on a cloud, his hopes high that he might be offered a contract. He wasn't disappointed.

On October 13, 1937, Leonard Slye signed a long-term contract with Republic Pictures. He would be making seventy-five dollars a week. The young boy from Duck Run, Ohio, had arrived.

Immediately, the studio set out to transform Leonard into "something the movie going public would like." After executives determined his upper body was undersized, he was placed on an exercise program that included one hundred handstands a day. Executives found a problem with Leonard's eyes, too. "They're too squinty," he was told. For a time, he used drops to relax the eye muscle and dilate the pupils. Then he received his first name change. Leonard Slye became known as Dick Weston, making his solo singing film debut under that name in 1937 in *Wild Horse Rodeo*, starring The Three Mesquiteers. Dick Weston also appeared in another film, *The Old Barn Dance*, opposite Gene Autry.

Leonard was grateful for the work and the chance to work alongside the Republic veteran. His weekly paychecks helped him and his bride Arlene purchase a home. The newlyweds were confident his big break was about to come.

In the meantime, however, another name change and image enhancement project was in the works at the studio. Herbert Yates and Sol Siegel decided to call him Roy Rogers. *Rogers*, after Will Rogers, and *Roy* because it was a name that rolled easily off the tongue. Behind the scenes, the publicity department was creating the quintessential cowboy biography for their newest acquisition.

Leonard Slye was amazed at all Roy Rogers had done. According to Republic Pictures, Roy Rogers was born in Cody, Wyoming, and grew up on a large cattle ranch. He was an expert horseback rider, bronc buster, and top hand with a gun and rope. After time spent in New Mexico, he headed even farther west, parking his spurs at Republic Studios. The publicity department assured the reserved singing cowboy that altering history was what B westerns were all about.

For weeks, Roy Rogers sat around the studio lot waiting for his chance to be used in a picture. Six months after Republic completed filming *The Old Barn Dance*, production got under way for another Autry picture, *Under Western Stars*. Gene and Herbert Yates had been at odds with each other for more than six months. Until their differences could be resolved and a new contract between them drawn up, Autry refused

FACING PAGE: Young *Buffalo Bill* starring Roy Rogers was released in 1940.
AUTHOR'S COLLECTION

A **Republic** PICTURE

"YOUNG BUFFALO BILL"

to show up for filming. Yates suspended the actor, and Roy Rogers was summoned to take his place.

Roy would be a good guy in this picture, starring opposite Carol Hughes and Smiley Burnette. The story revolved around a cowboy who took on Congress to help save poor, starving farmers and ranchers during the Depression. Roy had learned to ride as a boy and was a natural for the role that called for an experienced horseman who would sport a white hat and ride a golden palomino named Golden Cloud. Smiley Burnette referred to the animal as Trigger in reference to his speed and style, and Roy instantly took to the beautiful horse with his flaxen mane and tail and proud, arched neck. Trigger was four years old when Roy rode him for the first time. He had already appeared in one other movie, *The Adventures of Robin Hood*. He had an easy lope and fast gallop. Roy and he would become inseparable.

Under Western Stars premiered at the Capitol Theatre in Dallas, Texas, in April 1938. Roy, his costar Smiley Burnette, and the Sons of the Pioneers, a group he helped form, were on hand for the event.

In its review of April 12, 1938, the *Dallas Morning News* wrote,

> "Under Western Stars" introduces young Mister Rogers as a new cowboy hero, real out west and not drugstore variety. This lad isn't the pretty boy type, but a clean cut youngster who looks as if he had grown up on the prairies, not backstage with a mail order cowboy suit. An engaging smile, a good voice and an easy manner ought to put him out in front before very long.[9]

Things were going well for Roy Rogers, and it was then he realized he needed to make an important purchase. Trigger was owned by Hudkins Stables in Los Angeles, and Roy decided he had to have the horse for his own. "I knew they couldn't make anything better than this one," he told the handler. Roy paid twenty-five hundred dollars for his gold-colored

FACING PAGE: Roy Rogers's films made at Republic Pictures were distributed all over the world. AUTHOR'S COLLECTION

costar. "It seemed a lot of money at the time," Roy later confessed. "But I can tell you for sure and certain it was the best twenty-five hundred dollars I ever spent."[10]

Roy and Trigger's success in *Under Western Stars* was overwhelming. They were inundated with cards and letters. Roy's wife Arlene helped him respond to the mountain of fan letters he received every day. The people who wrote him varied in age from eight to sixty-eight. Keeping up with the incoming mail was an expensive chore—one Roy paid for out of his own earnings.

The singing cowboy believed if someone was thoughtful enough to sit down and write him a letter, he had an obligation to answer.

Roy was eventually spending more in postage than his salary. He appealed to Herbert Yates to help him pay for stamps and possibly hire a secretary to help him respond to the writers. Yates declined, suggesting that Roy do what other stars did and throw the letters in the trash. Roy refused to do that.

To supplement his income, Roy arranged a series of one-night appearances. Theaters paid $150 for an evening performance. In between giving musical programs across the country, Roy continued to make movies for Republic, starring in films such as *Billy the Kid Returns*, *Days of Jesse James*, and *Red River Valley*. The fan mail increased as his fame grew. Still, Yates refused to help Roy with the letters.

Frustrated with his apathetic boss, Roy rented a five-ton dump truck, filled it with fan mail, and drove over to the studio. He backed the vehicle up in front of Yates' office and dumped the letters on the lawn. Roy's actions prompted little response from the stubborn executive. He increased the star's pay by twenty-five dollars a week but steadfastly refused to do more.

After two years with Republic, Roy Rogers was making $150 a week and spending most of that salary responding to fan mail. Agents sought out the entertainer, but it wasn't until he met Art Rush that he decided to trust his career to someone other than himself. Rush represented such talent as Nelson Eddy and Benny Goodman. He had grown up in Ohio and seemed to Roy to be a decent and honorable man. Rush arranged public appearances for Roy at rodeos and got him steady work on a radio show called *Manhattan Cowboy*. In no time, under Rush's direction, Roy was earning ten times what his Republic acting job paid for his other appearances.

In April 1943, Republic Pictures' executives officially named Roy Rogers the King of the Cowboys. Yates decided to pair Roy with actress and singer Dale Evans for the film *The Cowboy and the Senorita*. Their on-screen chemistry was so special, Yates signed the duo to do three more films together. Roy, Dale, and their costar Gabby Hayes followed up their hit *The Cowboy and the Senorita* with *Song of Nevada*. Republic Pictures' screenwriters duplicated the formula from the pair's first film, writing Dale's parts to serve as a contrast to Roy's country ways. In *Song of Nevada* Dale played an uppity woman from the east traveling west to see her deceased father's ranch and winding up crossing paths with a down-to-earth ranch hand played by Roy.

Audiences couldn't get enough of the on-screen mix of Dale's sass and Roy's patience. In one year, Republic Pictures turned out seven of the popular westerns featuring their new stars. By the end of 1945, Herbert Yates proclaimed that not only did Roy Rogers continue to be King of the Cowboys, but Dale Evans was now the Queen of the West.

By mid-1947, Roy Rogers was again among his field's top ten box office money makers. Dale Evans made the list as well. The cowboy duo signed new contracts with Republic Pictures in early 1948. Roy received a 100 percent increase in pay, and studio executives were anxious for the pair to start to work on another series of westerns.

In early 1951, Republic Pictures decided to edit the films Roy and Dale had made and sell them to one of the three new television networks.

Republic would profit from the venture but was offering nothing to the stars. According to the June 20, 1951, edition of *Variety*, the top price quoted for old Roy Rogers features was thirty thousand dollars for the first-run or twenty-five thousand dollars for each of two runs. Gene Autry films were knocked down at twenty thousand dollars for first-run or $17,500 for each of two runs. On other features to be made available for television, the price was based on the basic, class A, hourly rate per run. In the works were fifty-two Autry and Rogers pictures. However, due to an exclusivity clause in Roy Rogers' contract, which stated he retained the rights to his name, voice, and likeness for all commercial ventures, the sale of the pictures to television was temporarily blocked. When Roy's contract was up with Republic, the studio decided not to re-sign the actor. The debate over who had the last say over the B westerns being shown on television had been transferred to court.[11]

With Roy immersed in a heated battle with Republic and subsequently freed from making any future films with the company, Paramount Studios offered him a part in a picture starring Bob Hope and Jane Russell entitled *Son of Paleface*.

As the 1940s drew to a close, Roy Rogers' popularity was at its highest point ever. Hollywood reporters like Louella Parsons boasted, "If children were allowed to vote, Roy Rogers would be President." To celebrate their popularity with young moviegoers, Roy's handprints and Trigger's hoofprints were cast in cement in front of Grauman's Chinese Theater.

In the early 1950s, Roy Rogers' agent, Art Rush, decided it was time the celebrated star had his own television show. Roy agreed it was an idea whose time had come and gave his agent the go-ahead to set something up with a network. Talent and crew were assembled, and production began on a thirty-minute pilot movie to be taken to potential sponsors. Roy decided early on that "Happy Trails" would be the theme of the series he hoped to bring to television. If the court case that Roy had pending

FACING PAGE: The fame achieved in doing films with Republic Pictures enabled Roy Rogers to work for other studios. AUTHOR'S COLLECTION

BOB · JANE · ROY AND
HOPE · RUSSELL · ROGERS · TRIGGER

IN SON OF PALEFACE

Produced by ROBERT L. WELCH
Directed by FRANK TASHLIN

Written by Frank Tashlin, Robert L. Welch
and Joseph Quillan A Paramount Picture

Color by Technicolor

against Republic ended in his favor, the *Roy Rogers Show* was ready to go on the air as soon as possible. The format for the series would closely follow the storylines used in the B westerns. Roy's home, the Double D Ranch, would serve as the primary location for the program.

In November 1951, a Los Angeles judge determined that Herbert Yates and Republic Pictures had no legal right to sell Roy Rogers' films to television. A restraining order was handed down permanently barring the studio from releasing any of the movies for that purpose. With the case over and the way cleared for the television series to go forward, a deal was quickly made with NBC to broadcast the program. The *Roy Rogers Show* debuted on December 30, 1951.

Herbert Yates took Roy's actions against the studio personally. He believed he was in large part responsible for the singing cowboy's success and deserved consideration for his efforts. He further contended that Roy had made the films as a contract employee and they were, therefore, the property of the studio to do with as the studio chose. Neither Roy Rogers nor Gene Autry agreed with Yates' assessment. John Wayne, another popular Republic Pictures actor, also argued against the release of the crude productions he did for the studio to television. He felt it might injure his reputation if the amateurish pictures were brought to the vast, television field. Yates disregarded the notion and moved ahead with the business decision. It wasn't the first time he and John Wayne didn't see eye to eye on a matter. Yates and Wayne had had issues before, but this would mark the beginning of the end of the actor's relationship with Republic Pictures.[12]

Herbert Yates' association with John Wayne began in 1935 when the motion picture mogul bought Mascot and Monogram Pictures. Wayne, a former University of Southern California football player who began his career in motion pictures in 1926 in the property department at Fox, appeared in more than two dozen westerns for the studio. Among those westerns was the film *Riders of Destiny* in which Wayne became one of

FACING PAGE: Republic Pictures solidified John Wayne's iconic status as America's most popular motion picture cowboy. AUTHOR'S COLLECTION

the first singing cowboys on screen. He portrayed a cowboy crooner and secret service agent named Singing Sandy Saunders. Wayne was embarrassed by the role. Yates agreed with the hard-working actor and gave him a chance to prove his worth by starring him in a series of eight westerns beginning with a feature entitled *Westward Ho.* The film contained a generous amount of music, but Wayne did not warble a note. The singing was left to his costars, members of the group of men he led called "The Singing Riders." Wayne and his riders fought bandits in saloons and Indians on the open range.[13]

Not only was he convincing as a tough vigilante, but the gentle side he showed opposite the movie's love interest was equally satisfying to fans. Wayne's talent for playing the tempestuous cowhand with a softer side made him appealing to women as well as men. Unlike other popular cowboy stars, he wasn't afraid his image would be tarnished if he kissed the girl.[14]

The Dawn Rider was Wayne's follow-up picture to *Westward Ho.* Once again moviegoers could see him chasing after outlaws that killed his family. He was teamed with stuntman and rider Yakima Canutt, and the two matched each other evenly in screen stunts. Canutt would playfully boast to friends and coworkers on the set that he taught Wayne everything he knew.[15]

In 1938, Wayne's representatives negotiated a new five-year, eight western film contract between the actor and Republic Pictures. In addition to making more westerns for the company, he would now be loaned out to other studios. It was a move that would be mutually beneficial to the actor and the executive. Yates would receive a fee for loaning the cowboy star to competing studios, and Wayne would be able to participate in projects he felt would further advance his career. Yates also promised Wayne he could star in a film about Sam Houston. Yates would later renege on that promise, making the picture instead with Richard Dix

FACING PAGE: John Wayne starred in eight Three Mesquiteers movies alongside Wayne Corrigan and Max Terhune. L. TOM PERRY SPECIAL COLLECTIONS, BRIGHAM YOUNG UNIVERSITY, PROVO, UTAH

in the starring role. When Wayne asked Yates why he went back on his word, Yates told the actor he wasn't "strong enough" to take on the role.[16]

One of the most influential films Wayne was allowed to make outside of Republic was *Stagecoach*. John Wayne was thirty-one years old and a veteran of more than sixty films when he made *Stagecoach*. He had twirled six-shooters, tossed rope, busted broncos, and foiled cattle rustlers in B westerns for five different studios. He was a battle-scarred graduate of the sagebrush school of screen drama, but he was still not as well-known as stars like Gene Autry and Roy Rogers who had fewer films behind them. The 1939 release of *Stagecoach*, directed by John Ford and starring Thomas Mitchell, Claire Trevor, and John Carradine, brought Wayne into the limelight.

Yates took full advantage of Wayne's rising star status and cast him in Republic's ongoing western series, *Three Mesquiteers*. Based loosely on a series of pulp novels by William Colt MacDonald, the films capitalized on Wayne's box office success, but did little to challenge his skill as an actor. In the Mesquiteers films, he was one of three main players who together rode the range and were always getting themselves in and out of trouble. The hastily made, inexpensive pictures were big hits at the box office, but Wayne believed the films were helping to convince the minds of other film executives that he was nothing more than a B player. Wayne wanted more for himself. He wanted more of what he experienced working on *Stagecoach*.

By 1940, Republic had ventured timidly into the A picture business, and Herbert Yates cast Wayne in a film he hoped would put the studio in a different light. The movie was *Dark Command*. Directed by Raoul Walsh, the cast included Claire Trevor, George "Gabby" Hayes, Roy Rogers, and Walter Pidgeon, with stunts by Yakima Canutt. Set in Kansas during the Civil War, opposing pro-Union and pro-Confederate camps clash, and Bob Seton runs afoul of William Cantrell's Raiders while visiting Texas. *Dark Command* was the most expensive and most successful film of Republic's

FACING PAGE: Bob Steele and Ray Corrigan were two of the actors who made up the Three Mesquiteers. John Wayne was the most well known of the trio. L. TOM PERRY SPECIAL COLLECTIONS, BRIGHAM YOUNG UNIVERSITY, PROVO, UTAH.

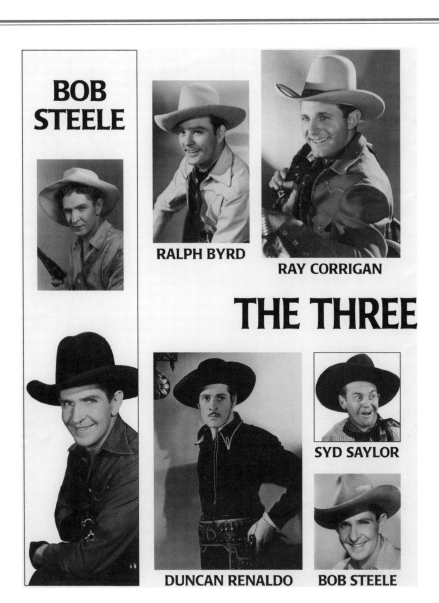

BOB STEELE

RALPH BYRD

RAY CORRIGAN

THE THREE

SYD SAYLOR

DUNCAN RENALDO   BOB STEELE

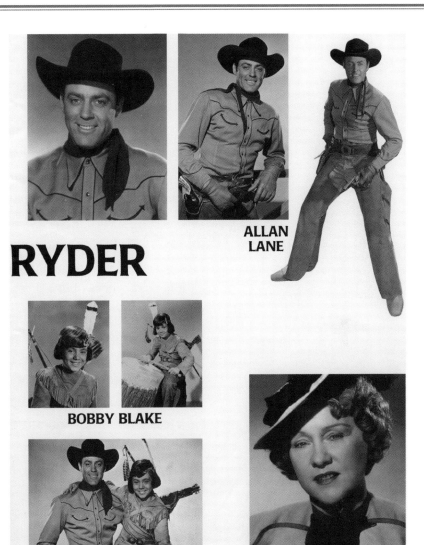

RYDER

ALLAN LANE

BOBBY BLAKE

MARTHA WENTWORTH

early years. The picture was nominated for two Academy Awards: one for Best Original Score and the other for Best Art Direction. John Wayne received special attention from reviewers, most of whom were unfamiliar with his earlier work at Republic and other studios. All were impressed with his ability.[17]

"At Republic we don't attempt to develop personalities," Herbert Yates said in 1939. He was content instead to farm out his best talent and let other studios "do the experimenting." John Wayne's rise followed Yates' strategy. Yates loaned Wayne out to rival studios to do *The Long Voyage Home*, *Seven Sinners*, and *Shepherd of the Hills*. Each film further enhanced Wayne's popularity and made him a box office commodity. Yates reaped financial benefits from the Republic Pictures that starred Wayne after his talent and name was tried and tested. Wayne was grateful to Yates and the studio for the years of steady employment given to him during his early days in front of the camera. He had learned a great deal and was fiercely loyal to Republic for standing behind him. Between 1940 and 1952, he made more than a dozen films for Republic Pictures. From *Lady in the Night* with Joan Blondell, to *Sands of Iwo Jima* with John Agar, and *The Quiet Man* with Maureen O'Hara, Wayne delivered standout performances that brought respect and dignity to Yates' company.[18]

John Wayne's decision to break ties with Republic Pictures and Yates came in 1951. It had been building for several years, and the reason, in part, was Yates' wife, figure skater Vera Ralston.

Herbert Yates first met the Olympic ice skater, Vera Hruba, in 1941 after attending a performance of the *Ice Vanities*. Yates was interested in making a series of ice pictures and was looking for a young talent to be his star. Vera would be his protégé. Not only did Yates sign her to appear in a number of Republic films, but took on the role of managing her career. She adopted the name Ralston after the breakfast cereal. Yates cast Vera in a film entitled *Ice Capades* and set about to find projects for her that he believed would make her a star. He teamed her with a number of leading actors at the studio, not the least of which was John Wayne.[19]

Between 1941 and 1945, Vera made a dozen movies at Republic, and only two of those films turned a profit—those which paired her with John Wayne. The pictures were *The Fighting Kentuckian* and *Dakota*.

FACING PAGE: John Wayne and Yakima Canutt revolutionized the art of screen fighting working for Republic Pictures. AUTHOR'S COLLECTION

Wayne didn't dislike Vera; she simply did not fit the films in which Yates cast her. "She didn't have the experience, and she didn't have the right accent," Wayne is quoted as saying. Yates sensed Wayne's reluctance to commit to appearing in the film *Dakota* with her. When he approached the actor about the project, he offered Wayne a deal he couldn't turn down. He promised to give him a percentage of the profits from the next movie in which he starred. That movie was *Wake of the Red Witch*, released in 1948. The film was a huge success, and Wayne became a millionaire from the deal struck with Yates.[20]

Wayne tolerated Yates' insistence to use his ingénue in more of the films he was to make, but finally reached his limit. He wanted to be free to make his own decisions about whom he would work with and what projects he would do. By 1952, Wayne was working for himself on a motion picture he had wanted to make for a long time, *The Alamo*.

News that Wayne and Republic Pictures had parted ways reached the newspapers in mid-November 1952. An article in the November 13, 1952, edition of the *Hollywood Reporter* announced that Wayne had come to an impasse with the head of Republic and that their falling out meant the end of a picture-making partnership that went back to the early days of Wayne's twenty-year acting career.[21]

"Yates will have to make me a damned good offer to get me to make another picture with him," Wayne said. "I'm fed up." He added that his difficulties with Yates arose over the proposed filming of *The Alamo*. The picture was originally slated to be made under the banner of Wayne's own production company for Republic Pictures.[22]

"Yates said that I should give up my company and make the picture for Republic," said the actor. "He said I owed it to Republic. I don't owe Republic anything. I've made a lot of money for the studio." Asked for a rebuttal, Yates cited the great mental strain and personal problems John "Duke" Wayne had had during the past year:

FACING PAGE: John Wayne received a portion of the box office receipts for the film *Wake of the Red Witch* and was able to launch his own production company with his earnings. Wayne and his costar Gail Russell were good friends as well as coworkers. L. TOM PERRY SPECIAL COLLECTIONS, BRIGHAM YOUNG UNIVERSITY, PROVO, UTAH

John Wayne and Herbert Yates, seen here with director John Ford, made numerous westerns for the studio along with the monster hit *The Quiet Man*.

AUTHOR'S COLLECTION

Duke was employed at Republic on May 11, 1955, when the going in our industry was rough. I have always found Duke a gentleman, a friend, always willing to cooperate, and he has beyond any doubt been helpful in establishing the success of Republic, the same as many hundreds of our employees.

At no time have I, as president of Republic attempted to take any credit for Duke's success; however, what Republic has spent in publicizing and establishing his name throughout the world must have been a contributing factor to his success. Republic has gambled millions of dollars on the pictures Duke appeared in, and the box office quality of these pictures must have been a major factor in influencing those who rated him No. 1 star in our industry.

If Duke decided to leave Republic, although his contract with Republic calls for three additional pictures, I and all of his old friends at Republic wish him continued success and prosperity.[23]

In a five-year time period, Herbert Yates had lost all three of his top box office stars—Gene Autry, Roy Rogers, and finally John Wayne. Their departure signaled the beginning of the end for the company. By the end of the 1950s Republic Picture would be out of the moviemaking business.[24]

CHAPTER 3

Ghouls, Freaks of Nature, and the Walking Dead

A dark figure weaves through a forest of imposing, leafless trees toward a weathered cabin in a clearing. An eerie mist blankets the ground, and a lone wolf howls in the distance. Inside the cabin, two men dressed in business suits and fedoras discuss plans to steal a counter atomic bomb device called the Cyclotrode. Their conversation is interrupted when the door of the structure is flung open and a madman wearing a skull mask and crimson robe enters. This is the Crimson Ghost, and the men deliberating over the robbery work for him. The Crimson Ghost is determined to get his hands on the Cyclotrode. The Cyclotrode cannot only stop nuclear missiles, but it can also cripple transportation and communications. The Crimson Ghost wants the invention for his own nefarious plans, including selling the device to foreign powers.

Two people know of the Crimson Ghost's dangerous ambitions, and they are criminologist Duncan Richards and Diana Farnsworth, secretary for the professor who created the Cyclotrode. The duo is determined to stop the villain and his henchmen from taking the contraption and destroying lives.

Throughout the twelve-part serial named after the blackguard the Crimson Ghost, the duo matched wits and fists with the miscreant and his aides in an attempt to keep the Cyclotrode from being used for mass destruction. Duncan and

Diana were threatened with death by explosion, poison gas, deadly slave collars, and death rays. Each of the episodes in the serial ended with a cliffhanger: a car plummeting over a cliff, a fire started leaving the heroes only moments to save the day, if at all, or a train bearing down on innocent parties.

The Crimson Ghost was just one of several "cliffhanger" serials produced by Republic Pictures that enticed audiences to return to the theater again and again to see if the heroes of the story won out or if the bad guy succeeded in thwarting attempts to put a stop to his diabolical intentions to obliterate mankind.

Republic's stock and trade were cliffhanger serials—science fiction, mysteries, and the ever popular horror genre. Nat Levine, founder of Mascot Pictures and later a much-maligned executive working for Herbert Yates, is credited with the production of a cliffhanger. Writer, journalist, and film historian Ephraim Katz defines a cliffhanger as an adventure serial consisting of several episodes, each of which ends on a suspenseful note to hold the audience in expectation of the next.

Levine made a number of silent-film chapter plays that brought return business to the movie houses. One of the first was *Isle of Sunken Gold*. Produced in 1927, the adventure picture was about a sea captain who had half a map leading to a treasure buried on an island in the South Sea. The ruler of the island, a beautiful princess, had the other half of the map, and the two joined forces to battle a gang of pirates and a group of islanders who didn't want anyone to get the treasure.

At Republic, Levine continued to create cliffhangers that excited and confounded moviegoers.

Bat Men of Africa (a.k.a. *Darkest Africa*), directed by Joseph Kane, was the first fifteen-episode serial produced by Republic. World famous big game hunter and lion tamer Clyde Beatty starred in the chapter play portraying an adventurer on safari in East Africa. While in the Dark Continent,

FACING PAGE: *The Crimson Ghost* was introduced to moviegoers in 1946. AUTHOR'S COLLECTION

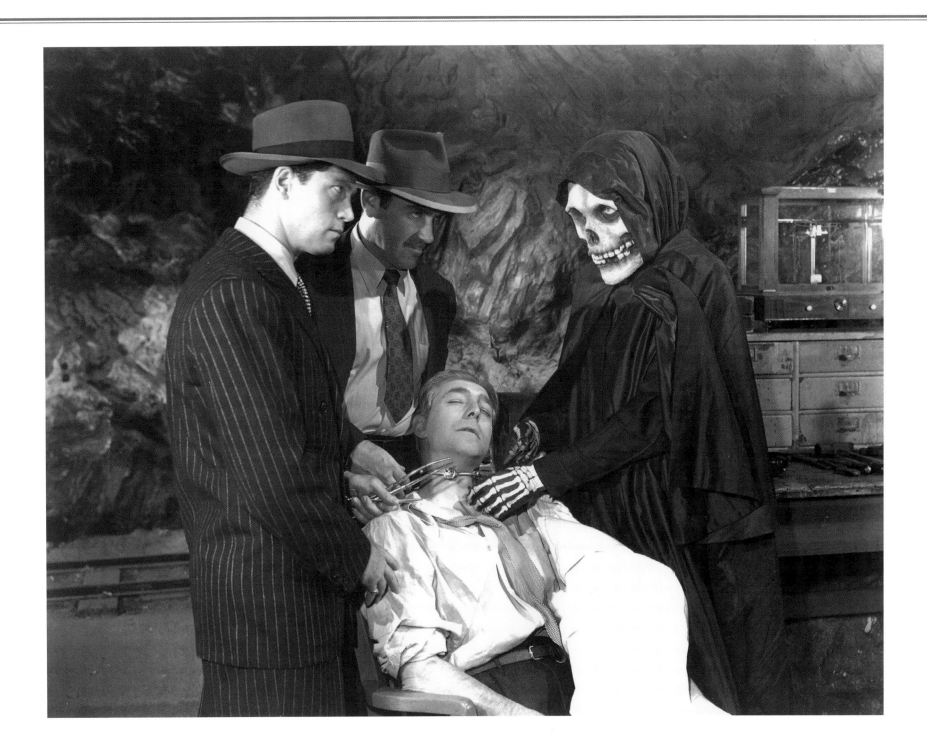

he meets and befriends a loincloth-wearing boy and his pet ape. The boy reveals that he has escaped from the lost city of Joba, King Solomon's sacred city of the Golden Bat, but that his sister, Valerie, remains there. Clyde agrees to help his new friend rescue Valerie and treks through the dangerous Valley of Lost Souls to get to her. Meanwhile, a pair of unscrupulous treasure hunters notices a green diamond the young boy is wearing, and they decide to follow the trio to plunder the city of Joba.

Among the cliffhangers in the picture are volcanic eruptions, a patrol of Bat-men–type creatures attacking the trio from the air, a landslide, and a fall down a mineshaft. At a cost of $119,343, *Bat Men of Africa* was the most expensive Republic serial of 1936.

What Republic serials were lacking in story and character development, they more than made up for in special effects and musical scores. Film enthusiasts at that time considered the plot to such Republic chapter series films like *The Vampire's Ghost* and *The Catman of Paris* of minor importance. The pictures were edge-of-your-seat fun and wall-to-wall excitement. Avid movie fans flocked to the theaters to see a Republic Pictures serial with the sure knowledge they would be thoroughly entertained, and whether that entertainment came from the studio's most expensive serial *Bat Men of Africa* or from what some film historians refer to as Republic's last truly great serial, *The Crimson Ghost*, audiences knew it would be worth the price of admission.[1]

Moviegoers throughout the 1930s and 1940s enjoyed film adventures, from heroes on exotic animals to those in spacecrafts. Such was the case with *The Purple Monster Strikes*, the original Republic Martian invader serial. *The Purple Monster* was actually not a monster at all, nor was he purple. The villainous character was in reality a Caucasian, Martian space soldier. He was part of the advance guard preparing a vast invasion of earth, dressed in a blue, tight-fitting outfit, trimmed with scaly gold metallic material, and wearing a matching gilded hood. Among the

FACING PAGE: Popular Republic Pictures' serial *The Catman of Paris* was released in 1946. AUTHOR'S COLLECTION

The cast of *The Vampire's Ghost* included John Abbott, Charles Jordan, Peggy Stewart, and Adele Mara. L. TOM PERRY SPECIAL COLLECTIONS, BRIGHAM YOUNG UNIVERSITY, PROVO, UTAH

Purple Monster's alien abilities was the power to become a transparent phantom and enter the body of another, controlling his actions, thereby donning the ultimate disguise.

The Purple Monster Strikes was the first post-war serial of 1945. Republic was prohibited from using the term "rocket ship" when referring to the spacecraft the Purple Monster used in the film. Universal Studios had a copyright on the word which was used quite extensively in their serial *Flash Gordon*.

Billed as 1941's "sensational serial surprise," Republic introduced a chapter play that combined monsters designed to take over space with earthly fiends. Entitled *The Mysterious Doctor Satan*, the villain is a mad scientist who wants to rule the world and planets from other galaxies with an army of mechanical monsters. Audiences were treated to fifteen shivering, shuddering, surprising episodes of Dr. Satan manipulating the hideous robots he creates to rob and terrorize the nation into submission. Dr. Satan's sworn enemy is a beefy man in a copper mask appropriately known as Copperhead. Copperhead assumes the identity from his deceased father who was a fugitive from crooked justice in the Old West. The misunderstood hero is determined to protect society from the depredations of Dr.

FACING PAGE: Republic Pictures' chapter play *Mysterious Doctor Satan* was billed as a "sensational serial surprise." AUTHOR'S COLLECTION

Satan, and, at the same time, wipe out the stigma attached to the name Copperhead.

According to Jack Mathis' book *Valley of the Cliffhangers*, *The Mysterious Doctor Satan* was intended to be a series that would feature Superman as the fighter against evil. At the last moment, DC Comics, the owners of the Superman character, refused to let Republic use the radio and comic series star. Instead of abandoning the project, the writers replaced Superman with Copperhead, a character of their own creation.[2]

A popular character Republic Pictures was allowed to introduce in one of its chapter plays was Captain Marvel. Also known as Shazam, the superhero was created in 1939 by artist C. C. Beck and writer Bill Parker for Fawcett Comics. Captain Marvel was the most popular comic book superhero of the 1940s. He was also the first to be adapted into film. The film was entitled *Adventures of Captain Marvel*.

In an interdepartmental memo passed from various executives at Republic to Herbert Yates, the project was touted as having "massive potential to be a box office hit." The twelve-part series premiered in March 1941.

The plot of the chapter play was described in the following way:

To a remote section of Siam, jealously guarded by unconquered native tribes, comes the unwelcome Malcolm Scientific Expedition seeking knowledge of the ancient Scorpion Dynasty. Billy Batson, assistant to a radio expert, is the only one of the party who does not enter a forbidden chamber. As a result he is awarded the power to transform himself into a superman, Captain Marvel, upon uttering the word "Shazam."

After a dozen spine-tingling chapters, Billy is bound and gagged so he cannot utter the word. He tricks the Scorpion into releasing the gag in order, as he pretends, to explain to him the secret of his invulnerability. Once released, he cries, "Shazam"

REPUBLIC PICTURES presents "ADVENTURES OF CAPTAIN MARVEL" with
TOM TYLER and FRANK COGHLAN, Jr.

PRINTED IN U.S.A.

and becomes Captain Marvel. He is able to free himself and his friends and expose the Scorpion once and for all.

Adventures of Captain Marvel was a huge success for Republic Pictures. Critics called the production "roaring good entertainment." Many film aficionados consider the serial to be the best ever made.[3]

The collaboration between Republic Pictures and Fawcett Comics continued after the release of the Captain Marvel serial. In 1942, the two entities brought the character Spy Smasher to the screen. Spy Smasher is a costumed vigilante and freelance agent who battles a Nazi villain known as the Mask. The Mask heads a gang of saboteurs determined to spread destruction across America. According to author and film historian Alan G. Barbour, the Mask was the first in a long line of stereotypes that pictured hard-faced Nazis as propagandist tyrants.[4]

Spy Smasher was a twelve-part serial that was shot in thirty-eight days. Production began on December 22, 1941, just a few days after the Japanese bombing of Pearl Harbor. The Spy Smasher wore a cape, leaped from bridges onto fast-moving cars, outgunned Nazi devils, and escaped from all types of death traps, from burning tunnels to compartments slowly filling with water.[5] Spy Smasher used a number of gadgets, among them being various laser beams and his fire-resistant cape, to foil the Nazis' plans.

Daredevils of the Red Circle was a twelve-part serial that included a cape-wearing villain. The suspenseful, spine-tingling, mystery film told the tale of diabolical mastermind Harry Crowel, a.k.a. Prisoner 39013. Crowel escapes from prison and, aided by a seemingly endless supply of henchmen, sets out to destroy all holdings of industrialist Horace Granville, the man who put him in prison. One target is an amusement park, home of three Daredevils of the Red Circle who perform death-defying stunts. When head Daredevil Gene's kid brother is killed in Crowel's attack, the three heroes swear to capture Prisoner 39013. Unbeknownst to them, he is holding the real Granville captive and, with a near perfect disguise, has taken his place. A mysterious cloaked figure known as the Red Circle aides the daredevils in their crusade.[6]

Shot in five weeks on a budget of $175, *Daredevils of the Red Circle*, directed by William Witney, who was one of Republic Pictures' best directors, consistently appears on lists of all-time greatest serials.

Between 1936 and 1956, Republic released a string of unique horror serials that promised audiences they would quake with fear when they came face to face with the studio's terrifying lineup of ghouls, freaks of nature, and the walking dead.

Drums of Fu Manchu premiered in the spring of 1940. The creepy chapter play featured a race of bald-headed, fanged slaves known as "Dacoits" who had been lobotomized into doing the bidding of the immortal and insidious Doctor Fu Manchu. Fu Manchu hopes to conquer Asia and subsequently the world but needs specific artifacts from the tomb of Genghis Khan to achieve his goal. In Los Angeles, California, he convenes a meeting of the S-Far, an international conspiracy group that helps him draw up his plans. When archeologist Dr. James Parker is killed so Fu Manchu can obtain rare scrolls in his possession, his son Allan joins forces with

Daredevils of the Red Circle was a twelve-part serial released in 1939. AUTHOR'S COLLECTION

William Witney was one of Republic's best directors. AUTHOR'S COLLECTION

Sir Denis Nayland Smith of the British Foreign Office to avenge his father's death.

The sixteen frightful-looking "Dacoits" who contributed many of the thrills to *Drums of Fu Manchu* were a product of the makeup artist Bob Mark's wizardry. The normal-looking people became grotesque monsters in Mark's hands.

Rubber caps entirely covered their hair, giving them the impression of baldness. These caps, which could be worn only once, were especially manufactured at the cost of five dollars each. They were fitted tightly over the "Dacoit's" heads, and heavy, theatrical grease paint was applied over them. The scars, which represented the incisions where Dr. Fu Manchu had removed the frontal lobes of their brain, were made of a special rubber composition and were held in place by rubber cement. The makeup of Fu Manchu himself, an elaboration of the "Dacoit's" makeup, took exactly 2.5 hours each day to apply.[7]

The fifteen-part Fu Manchu serial was directed by William Witney. He considered Fu Manchu to be his finest work. Sam Rohmer created the character of the insidious Fu Manchu in 1913 for a series of adventure novels. Rohmer's books were best sellers, and he used a portion of the profit made from the sales to develop a product he believed needed refining—mothballs.[8]

There was a time in 1935 that Republic Pictures' development department believed there was nothing left on dry land to scare the wits out of moviegoers, so they decided to seek out stories from the depths of the darkest oceans. *Undersea Kingdom* was a 1936 serial thriller that starred Ray "Crash" Corrigan.

Before becoming a costar in a number of Republic westerns, Corrigan was a bit player and stuntman who frequently donned a gorilla costume to act as a crazed ape whenever the studio called for one. Corrigan even had his own gorilla costume.

FACING PAGE: *The Drums of Fu Manchu* premiered in the spring of 1940. AUTHOR'S COLLECTION

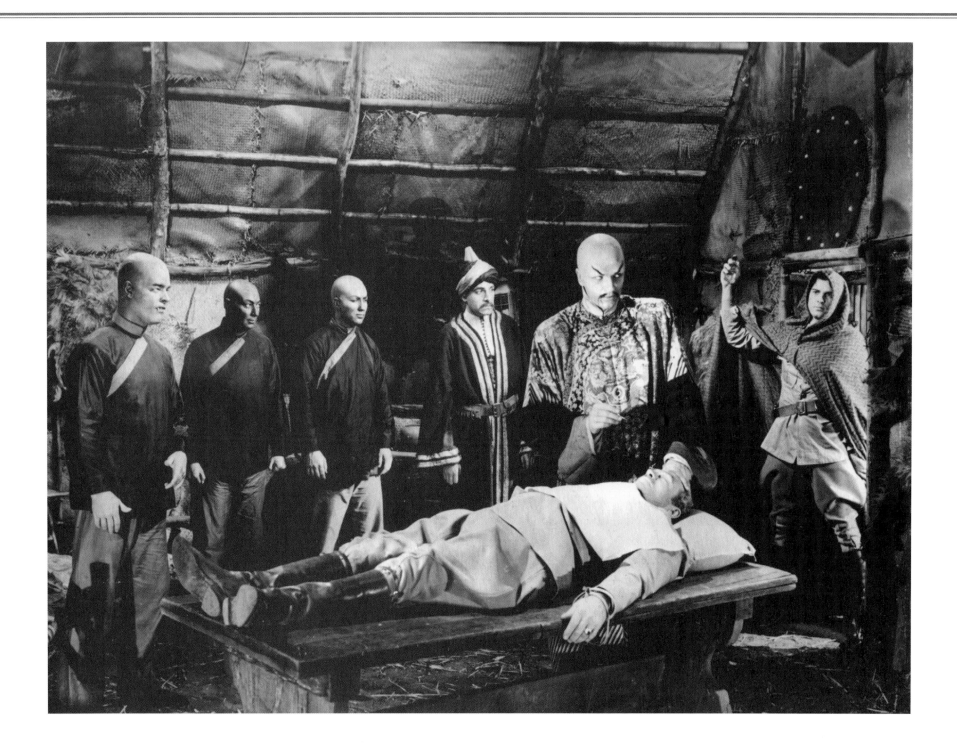

Corrigan's character in *Undersea Kingdom* is a lieutenant right out of Annapolis whose assignment is to stop an evil tyrant ruler from taking over the world. Corrigan's character is recruited for the job when a series of mysterious man-made earthquakes threaten to destroy civilization. He leads an expedition to the ocean floor in a rocket-propelled submarine and discovers the Undersea Kingdom of Atlantis. Soon the explorers find themselves caught between two warring factions led by the peace-loving High Priest of Atlantis and the evil warlord Unga-Khan, whose diabolical plans include conquering the surface of the world.[9]

Corrigan's super-human athletic abilities combined with the genius of the rocket-sub inventor make them targets in an action-packed battle for survival against ray-guns, tanks, and robots.[10]

The filming for *Undersea Kingdom* was completed in twenty-five days, and the entire series cost ninety-nine thousand dollars to produce. It had the lowest budget of any Republic serial.

The tagline for the feature *The Girl Who Dared* was "Out of the fogs of Fear! Storms of Terror!" An old, dark house is the setting of the creepy, who-done-it mystery released in August 1944. Legend has it a ghost appears once a year at the house, and a group of people have been invited to visit the location to learn all about the spook. What begins as a festive weekend of ghost hunting for a handful of friends evolves into a series of gruesome murders.[11]

A story of a pirate ship that capsized near the property have some believing the home is haunted by a desperate soul who was killed trying to bury a treasure there. None of the guests know the identity of the person who invited them, and, in addition to finding out who the specter might be, they each need to solve that puzzle. Bodies start to pile up, and people start blaming one another. Arriving on the scene midway through is an investigator who is pursuing a doctor who absconded with sixty thousand dollars' worth of radium. He suspects one of the guests is in league with the doctor.

Journalist Medora Field wrote the novel upon which *The Girl Who Dared* was based, *Blood on Her Shoes*. Republic optioned the popular book in 1942. Field was best friends with Margaret Mitchell, author of *Gone with the Wind*. Mitchell encouraged Field to submit her book *Who Killed Aunt Maggie* to a New York publisher. It was published in 1939. *Who Killed Aunt Maggie* also takes place at an old house and was adapted to a motion picture in 1940 by Republic.

The motion picture *The Lady and the Monster* was another Republic horror film released in 1944. The press release about the movie issued by the studio noted that *The Lady and the Monster*, starring Austrian actor and director Erich von Stroheim and ice-skater-turned-actress Vera Ralston, made an unforgettable impression on preview audiences. The press release read,

> Seldom has Erich von Stroheim been equaled. In this picture he gives full play to his unfailing knack for sending chills of cold horror down the spine of his audience.
>
> A weird, castle-like mansion in the Southwest is the setting for the eerie tale of a man who preserved a fully functioning brain after death. Von Stroheim, as the diabolical Dr. Mueller, retrieves the brain of a financial genius who crashed to death in an airplane mishap nearby, and carried on a fiendish plot to put this super brain to work for him.
>
> Dr. Mueller's young assistant, played by Richard Arlen, becomes a helpless victim of the plot, and only his love for Janice, Mueller's ward, saves him from an unthinkable fate.
>
> Vera Hruba Ralston makes her debut as a dramatic actress in *The Lady and the Monster* and the lovely blonde Czechoslovakian is undoubtedly the find of the season, cinematically speaking.[12]

Herbert Yates invested more money to produce *The Lady and the Monster* than usual. He was infatuated with Ralston and wanted to make her a star. Prior to *The Lady and the Monster*, Vera's on-screen time had been limited to ice skating performances. She was still learning English when principal photography began on the horror picture. Often her accent was so thick it was difficult to determine what she was saying in the film. That fact was not lost on critics who also found that Vera seemed a bit out of her element in the picture. There were other issues with the film as well that were noted. A review in the May 22, 1944, edition of the *Pittsburgh Post-Gazette* read,

> That widely-acclaimed novel by Mr. Curt Siodmak, *Donovan's Brain*, is the basis of *The Lady and the Monster*, and the title change is unfortunate and so is the casting. However, the premise that a brain, one separated from its parent body and kept alive, may transmit its thought processes to humans via telepathy has a certain fascination. And even if much of Mr. Siodmak's spinal novocaine has been amputated, the picture still bores in satisfactorily. At least it won't put you to sleep.
>
> Mr. Erich von Stroheim fingers the role of the psychopathic scientist with his usual bull-necked ferociousness: Miss Vera Hruba Ralston, the Czech Henie, is just a trifle ill at ease off the ice, and Mr. Richard Arlen keeps his schizophrenia on a time-and-a-half schedule.
>
> *Donovan's Brain* probably deserved a better dish of celluloid but then horror fans seldom read and rarely complain.[13]

Audiences flocked to the theaters to see *The Lady and the Monster*. The picture's performance at the box office validated the studio's interest in making horror projects and confirmed Yates' belief that Vera would someday be a screen legend.

FACING PAGE: *The Lady and the Monster* was ice-skater-turned-actress Vera Ralston's first film role without skates. L. TOM PERRY SPECIAL COLLECTIONS, BRIGHAM YOUNG UNIVERSITY, PROVO, UTAH

The sound of a witch-like cackle can be heard at the start of the frightening film *The Woman Who Came Back*. The story centers on a girl who returns to her ancestral home in New England. While en route to the home, she believes she has been bewitched by a curse put on her by a sorcerer. The woman just so happens to be the last descendant of a witch hunter responsible for condemning fifteen women to be burned at the stake for practicing witchcraft. The stars of the picture, John Loder and Nancy Kelly, play star-crossed lovers who need to find out if Nancy's character is the reincarnation of one of the witches sentenced to death.[14]

The part of the witch who confronts Nancy prior to her returning home was played by Elspeth Dudgeon. Over the course of her twenty-plus years in the business, she portrayed a variety of creepy male and female characters. In her screen debut in James Whale's *The Old Dark House*, released in 1932, she not only played an old man but was also billed as a man.[15]

The Woman Who Came Back was released during the Christmas season in 1945. Moviegoers were elated to see a film about witchcraft. Many devoted Republic Pictures' followers had submitted letters to the studio expressing their desire to honor flicks featuring witches. Herbert Yates answered the call, and it paid off handsomely. *The Woman Who Came Back* had a respectable showing next to other horror films in 1945. Some of those films were *The Picture of Dorian Gray*, *Leave Her to Heaven*, *Spellbound*, and *Dead of Night*.

In April 1946, thrill seekers were looking forward to the release of *The Catman of Paris*. The gruesome mystery melodrama involved a man suffering from a loss of memory who was accused of being a feline killer operating in Paris.

The tagline read: "Walks like a man. Attacks like a cat. Who is the Catman of Paris." The plot involved author Charles Regnier returning to 1896 Paris after exotic travels, having written a best seller that the

Ministry of Justice would like to ban. That very night, an official is killed on the dark streets . . . clawed to death! The prefect of police suspects a type of cat, but Inspector Severen thinks there is nothing supernatural about the crime and thinks Regnier is responsible for the murder. Regnier denies he had anything to do with the crime but begins to doubt himself when he has a hallucinatory blackout during a second killing.

Vienna-born stage actor Carl Esmond played the troubled author Regnier. Lenore Aubert, the female lead in the movie, was also from Vienna. The press packet Republic Pictures circulated to theaters and media across the country contained plenty of information about the film as well as background information about the picture's stars. Aubert's story of how she made it from Vienna to Hollywood could have been a movie on its own.

According to the November 8, 1946, edition of the *Mount Carmel Item*, the actress had just finished making her third movie when the Nazis occupied her homeland. She and her mother fled to France where they hoped to begin a new life. There she continued studying and acting for a year until the downfall of Paris.[16]

"The experience Miss Aubert underwent in getting from France, through Portugal, to Spain would alone defeat most people," the *Mount Carmel Item* article read. "However, Miss Aubert realized her one hope for happiness could be found in America. After six months of ceaseless efforts, she was able to get a priority on a Portuguese boat."[17]

Critics were complimentary of Aubert's performance and the film itself, calling both "satisfying" and "entertaining."[18]

Chills, thrills, suspense, and murder awaited moviegoers who dared to see *Valley of the Zombies* starring Republic's contract players Robert Livingston and Lorna Gray. Debuting in May 1946, the film was about a prominent brain surgeon who is killed; law enforcement suspects the culprit was his associate Dr. Terry Evans. Doctor Evans and his

Valley of the Zombies starred Republic contract players Robert Livingston and Lorna Gray. L. TOM PERRY SPECIAL COLLECTIONS, BRIGHAM YOUNG UNIVERSITY, PROVO, UTAH

sweetheart nurse embark on a quest to prove his innocence. In trying to clear himself, the doctor and his girlfriend visit hospitals, morgues, embalming establishments, and an eerie estate where a few more murders have been committed for good measure. While searching the estate, the doctor and nurse happen onto a gruesome figure that is a zombie. The zombie's condition can only be reversed with large quantities of blood. The caretakers of the undead individuals traverse the woods and mental hospitals at night looking for unwilling blood donors.[19]

Directed by Philip Ford, nephew of award-winning western director John Ford, *Valley of the Zombies* was void of any valleys and, apart from one undead creature, any zombies. It was a picture that was produced quickly to cash in on the zombie craze.

Republic's 1952 chapter play *Zombies of the Stratosphere* was lacking zombies as well. There wasn't a single zombie in the film. There was, as always in Republic Pictures' serials of this nature, a reluctant hero in a flying jacket and helmet who

FACING PAGE: *Valley of the Zombies* was an example of a film that was hastily produced to capitalize on the zombie craze of the late 1940s. L. TOM PERRY SPECIAL COLLECTIONS, BRIGHAM YOUNG UNIVERSITY, PROVO, UTAH

was tasked with preventing any Martian invaders from using a hydrogen bomb to blow earth out of its orbit so the Martians could move a dying Mars closer to the Sun.[20]

Star Trek's Leonard Nimoy made his screen debut in *Zombies of the Stratosphere* playing a Martian. Republic Pictures, known for using footage from other movies produced at the studio, continued its tradition with this science fiction serial. They didn't limit themselves to other films in the same genre, however. Footage from one of Roy Rogers' films was used to show what the aliens were doing on earth.[21]

Zombies of the Stratosphere was one of three movies Republic produced dealing with a Mars invasion. Another profitable serial the studio made was *Panther Girl of the Kongo*. When wildlife photographer Jean Evans discovers a giant crab-like creature in the jungles of southern Africa, she sends word to a big game hunter and friend Larry Sanders for help. The pair soon learn these large crustaceans are the work of a mad scientist who wants to scare the population away from the area to operate a diamond mine. Jean, nicknamed the Panther Girl by the tribal locals because she shot a panther that had been terrorizing the village, and Larry are determined to find the mad scientist and stop him. Along the way, the pair must battle oversized sea urchins, wild animals, creepy henchmen, and inclement weather. They must survive gun battles, falls into quicksand, the roaring rapids, poison darts, and angry gorillas.

Panther Girl of the Kongo starring Phyllis Coats was the most expensive serial Republic Pictures produced in the 1950s. A great deal of footage used to make this film had been originally shot in 1941 for the movie *Jungle Girl*. Frances Gifford, the star in *Jungle Girl*, was the first female lead in a Republic serial, and Phyllis Coats was the last female lead in a Republic serial. In fact, Phyllis Coats wore the same outfit in *Panther Girl* that Frances Gifford wore in *Jungle Girl*.[22]

FACING PAGE: Republic Pictures' serial *Jungle Girl* starred Frances Gifford in the title role. AUTHOR'S COLLECTION

Republic Pictures' contract player Linda Sterling portrayed the fearless Tiger Woman. AUTHOR'S COLLECTION

The director of *Jungle Girl* was studio favorite William Witney. From 1935 to 1956, Witney practiced the philosophy Herbert Yates taught which was "make 'em fast and make 'em cheap." Witney was a specialist in outdoor action and stunt direction. He directed or co-directed more Republic serials than any other company hire. He is considered the greatest action director in B movies.[23]

Witney traveled to Los Angeles from Lawton, Oklahoma, to visit his sister and brother-in-law in 1933. His brother-in-law was a director for Mascot Pictures, and he got Witney a job at the studio as an office boy. After Mascot merged with Republic in 1935, Witney was promoted to script clerk and then to film editor.

In 1937, while Witney was working in Utah on a western serial, the director was fired, and twenty-one-year-old Witney was asked to take his place. Witney went on to direct the studio's principal western, science fiction, and horror serials. From the *Drums of Fu Manchu* to the *Mysterious Doctor Satan*, he was able to masterfully put action sequences together for the screen.

FACING PAGE: Characters from the chapter play *The Tiger Woman* work on a formula that will thwart her attempts to save the natives where she rules. L. TOM PERRY SPECIAL COLLECTIONS, BRIGHAM YOUNG UNIVERSITY, PROVO, UTAH

Among Witney's fans are directors Steven Spielberg and Quentin Tarantino. Tarantino gave Witney high praise for his rough and believable action scenes and visual style. Witney's Republic serials served as the inspiration for Spielberg's *Indiana Jones* movies.[24]

Early in his career at Republic, Witney teamed with director John English for various serial projects. Witney concentrated on the outdoor and action scenes while English worked on the interiors. Both men shared such a similar visual approach that it was difficult to determine which sequences belonged to which director in the editing process. They were responsible for creating quality chapter plays during the time film historians call the "Golden Years of the Republic Serials."[25]

CHAPTER 4

The Biggest Little Studio

Republic Pictures was arguably the most important and influential studio in the history of the B movie. During the Golden Age of Hollywood, the studio flourished, and the low-budget commercial movies produced in mass made Republic a profitable concern. Herbert Yates enjoyed the financial reward for the B pictures his studio produced but lacked the respect studio heads like MGM's David O'Selznick or Fox's Darryl Zanuck had. It took a considerable amount of talent and innovation to make a B movie, and Yates employed an exceptional team of cinematographers, stuntmen and stuntwomen, and special effects artists to achieve the finished product. Despite the skill and invention needed to create the product, such films were generally considered inferior. Yates wanted to experience the admiration other film companies such as Paramount Pictures and United Artists received. It drove him to increase Republic's feature film investments.

In the late 1930s, Yates decided to raise the status of the company. He wanted a better product coming out of the studio. He wanted to make an "A" picture. Yates needed a large budget, bankable stars, and a quality script to realize his vision. He believed he could begin gaining the respectability he longed for by developing a project entitled *Man of Conquest*. He poured considerable resources into the project. *Man of Conquest*, the fictionalized action biopic of Sam Houston, was Republic's first A film.

Directed by George Nichols Jr. and starring Richard Dix and Joan Fontaine, the estimated budget for the movie was one million dollars. *Man of Conquest* was inspired by Marquis James' Pulitzer Prize–winning book *The Raven*. New York film critics announced that *Man of Conquest* was a "thrilling drama skillfully splashed across a broad canvas."[1] The April 28, 1939, article found in the *Brooklyn Daily Eagle* praised the direction of the film noting that it "never loses track of its hero or allows its social message to become bigger than its story." William Boehnel, film reviewer for the *New York World Telegram*, wrote that *Man of Conquest* was a "rousing, spectacular blend of Americanism and adventure which not only sounds the clarion call of freedom and democracy in high, resounding notes but related its message of liberty and the right of men to govern himself in a vigorous, colorful, thrilling manner."[2]

Herbert Yates was pleased *Man of Conquest* had done so well. The film was nominated for three Academy Awards: Best Art Direction, Best Sound Recording, and Best Original Score. The nominations were proof that Republic Pictures had what it took to develop a project to rival the bigger studios. Industry leaders acknowledged Yates' effort, and he pledged to produce additional, bigger budget films. Those bigger films were to be done on a limited basis.

Yates was proud of the studio's reputation for being a dominant force in serials. Not only was Republic good at it, but they also made a substantial amount of money, and financial success was even more important to Yates than respectability as an A movie studio.

Yates wanted to continue building the sales organization as well as creating bigger budget films. He believed a healthy balance of both would elevate the status of the company. In early 1939, he hired James Grainger, the former head of distribution for Fox and Universal Studios. Grainger immediately embarked on a series of meetings with theatrical distributors and exhibitors throughout the nation. He authorized the purchase of franchise distributors and established Republic's own theatrical distribution system. Grainger was exceptional at his job. Within a year, he increased the number of exhibitors (theaters) to more than nine thousand. The number of theaters showing Republic Studios' motion pictures grew even higher with each high-budget film and big-name cast member released. By the end of 1939, a mere four years after Herbert Yates founded the company, Republic was showing a profit of $4,742,175. Industry papers such as *Variety* and the *Hollywood Reporter* predicted the studio would "wind up a top flight major."

Executives at Republic trusted that the studio's next big budget film *Dark Command* would continue to raise the respectability of the company. Released on April 15, 1940, the film starred Walter Pidgeon, John Wayne, Claire Trevor, Roy Rogers, Marjoie Main, and George "Gabby" Hayes. Set in a time period immediately following the Civil War, the story involves renegade William Cantrell (presumably intended to be Confederate William Quantrill), the leader of a pillaging band of guerrillas, who continues to launch raids on innocent civilians, looting, burning, and terrorizing in the name of the Confederacy, and the lawman who must stop the mad rebel at all cost. Pidgeon played Cantrell and Wayne played the marshal dedicated to his arrest.

Before principal shooting began on *Dark Command*, there was some debate that the National Board of Decency would be intervening to make sure the movie met its standards. When transforming a book into screen material, there were obstacles screenwriters had to overcome in order to ensure an acceptable movie would be made. The greatest difficulty usually concerned censorship because the screen is more limited in its frank portrayal of stark emotions and philosophy than the material between book covers. *Dark Command* was one of three pictures the National Board of Decency was watching to see how closely studios got to crossing the censorship bridges. The other pictures under scrutiny were *The Grapes of Wrath* and *Of Mice and Men*.[3]

Dark Command's central character ravaged the border country of Kansas and Missouri in a brutal way. Republic Pictures' screenwriters Grover Jones, Lionel Houser, and F. Hugh Herbert had to deal with both a

fictionalized book and the horrible facts of history. In the end, the script writers delivered a product that satisfied both censors and the studio.[4]

Critics were complimentary of the movie, calling it "stirring" and "poignant." The May 11, 1940, edition of *The Indianapolis Star* noted that the "characterization is more interesting than you usually find it, even in the deluxe westerns, with the roles of Cantrell, taken by Walter Pidgeon and his Ma, played by Marjorie Main, particularly striking."[5]

Roy Rogers' performance, as well as Gabby Hayes', was recognized for being strong and unforgettable. Wayne and Claire Trevor were also praised for their work. "Wayne proves again that he is good at the straight acting required in this sort of film," *The Indianapolis Star* review continued. "Miss Claire Trevor is attractive and daring as the town banker's daughter. Raoul Walsh has directed the film, particularly the scenes of far-flung action, forcefully."[6]

Republic Pictures itself received most of the accolades for the film. Hollywood's biggest little studio had demonstrated in *Dark Command* that the majors had no corner on the big-budget western market. An article in the May 10, 1940, edition of the *Pittsburgh Post-Gazette* proclaimed that Republic could "show the cinema's Big Eight a thing or three about the manufacture of elementary melodrama, the kind that shoots straight and labels right and wrong with a branding iron."[7] *Dark Command* was nominated for two Academy Awards: Best Art Direction by John Victor Mackay and Best Music, Original Score by Victor Young.

Herbert Yates took full advantage of the good fortune Republic Pictures was enjoying and authorized construction of two new stages on its forty-acre lot. On the brink of World War II when most major producing companies were tightening their belts in the face of the world film market conditions, Republic launched an extensive expansion program. The soundstage would be furnished with the most up-to-date equipment available and a block of dressing rooms.[8]

An arts and crafts building was also erected that would house paintings, set decorations, and miniatures. A new preview theater, a commissary, an annex to the editing department, scene docks a third of a mile in length, and the modernization of several existing buildings were also part of the upgrades made at the studio. More than four hundred thousand square feet of asphalt paving were laid down carrying the total for all the improvements and additions well past the million dollar mark.

An opening ceremony for the soundstage and building expansion project was held on December 24, 1940. The new addition was dedicated to the memory of Mabel Norman. Norman was a comedienne of the silent movies. Republic was the site of the former Mack Sennett lot where Norman worked at one time. Hollywood studio executives, members of the press, and friends of the great actress were in attendance.

Additions and changes were being made with the executive staff at the studio as well. Executive producer Sol Siegel was leaving Republic to work for Paramount. Siegel had been with the company since its inception; in fact, he helped organize the corporate merger of the four companies that became Republic Pictures. Associate producer Albert J. Cohen took Siegel's place, and Cohen's assistant, Maurice Hanline, was promoted to story editor.[9]

The success and growth of Republic Pictures under Herbert Yates' leadership was the subject of a column by famed Hollywood reporter Louella Parsons. Parsons' story noted:

> Very little has been said about Herbert J. Yates, the head of the lusty five year old motion picture company. I intend to correct that.
>
> The real romance of the motion picture business is not Marlene Dietrich's glamour, Greta Garbo's aloofness, Clark Gable's appeal to the women, nor Errol Flynn's fascinating ways. The real romance, my friends, is in the men who built the great business and who started on a shoe string, so to speak. One such man is Herbert Yates. Mr. Yates makes his home in New York and comes out here [Los Angeles] every six weeks to plan his products. He couldn't stay away longer because movies made by Republic Pictures, with few exceptions, are written, produced and in the can ready for delivery within a few weeks.

Republic turns out some very good pictures and within the last year has probably made more strides than any other company in the business. That is because this studio counts every nickel. There is no waste and no experimenting. When a camera grinds, the story is ready and so is the actor and there is no delay or change in script and idea.

I made up my mind I wanted to talk with Yates, who within five years has built up this amazing Republic movie company before our very eyes. I had tea with him and Albert Cohen, the head of the studio, in style, served by a pretty blonde girl in a Mexican costume. I wouldn't have been human if I hadn't been a little flattered at all the attention they gave me. In fact, I was so impressed at the reception I almost forgot to ask Yates how he felt about the jokes told on his company. Finally, braced by a cup of tea, I said, "You know Mr. Yates, there are many jokes about Republic, one of them is, 'how many pictures did you make today,' and 'I was afraid to answer the telephone for fear when I came back my picture at Republic would be finished.'" Instead of being annoyed, he burst into laughter and said "Just as long as we can turn out the pictures and get them made I don't mind any jokes. I like them."

But I am not so sure that Republic is going to remain in the "quickie" class. Mr. Yates is ambitious. He told me he is now trying to find a leading lady for Gene Autry, their money-making star, "and we don't care what the price is," he said.

"During the lean days," he told me, "we couldn't spend any money, but now we can afford to branch out and we intend to make pictures that will vie with any products sent out by any studio in Hollywood."

A year ago I might have laughed at this, for like many people I thought of Republic as a little spot in the valley where pictures were ground out by the yard and canned much as we can tomatoes and peaches. But don't for a minute think this is true now.

Republic is a very pretentious little studio. Mr. Yates has two secretaries sitting outside his door just like Darryl Zanuck, and he has an inner office telephone such as Louis B. Mayer talks over, and he gives out orders by pulling strings just as I have seen Jack Warner do many times.

Yates is not a newcomer to the films. His biography says he is sixty, but you would never believe it. He is alert, young and ambitious. More importantly, he started in 1912, having come by the way of the tobacco route. He was a cigarette manufacturer. He financed Fatty Arbuckle's first pictures, and he had a return that not only appealed to his imagination but fattened his pocketbook. From then on it was movies and later he became the head of Consolidated Film Industries.

Republic started on its way under another head, but it didn't do very well. Then Yates took over the reins and from then on in it has been one good picture after another. Their *Three Faces West* would have done credit to any movie company. Gene Autry's westerns play in 9,000 theaters. Roy Rogers has the same number of houses.

"You see," said Mr. Yates, "we have no theaters to take our products when they are bad. We have to make good pictures because the picture houses will turn them down if they are not worth-while entertainment. We have never made a propaganda picture nor fought the Nazi battles. We don't believe that is entertainment."

"The war must be affecting you cruelly," I ventured, "just as it did all the other companies."

"No," he replied, "we have no foreign market. We had just started in Europe, so what we didn't have we couldn't lose. In another year it might have been different because we have just begun to build up a foreign market."

In the years that Mr. Yates has headed Republic, he discovered John Wayne, who is one of the top names on the screen. He took Roy Rogers, the shy, hillbilly, singing cowboy, and turned him into a favorite.

Mr. Yates prides himself on his knowledge of what the movie fans like and want. He passes on every production and every contract. He selects the players and purchases the scripts. In other words, he has a finger in every Republic Picture.

He speaks with pride of the fact that he took three or four little struggling quickie companies and combined them all into the new Republic. And well he might, for while other companies are bemoaning their losses he has just had the biggest year in the history of his studio.[10]

Yates spent the next five years after the release of *Dark Command* and the expansion of the studio building capital to invest further in A List pictures. The best indication of Republic's rise as a producing and distributing organization is the fact that the company, in September 1941, accepted an invitation to join the Association of Motion Picture Producers.* This made Republic the tenth full-fledged member of the Hays Office

---

* The Association of Motion Picture Producers was founded in 1924. As the entertainment industry's official collective bargaining representative, the Association of Motion Picture Producers, like the Motion Picture Association of America, is a key trade association for major film and television producers in the United States.

affiliate of which only major studios belonged.*

Republic Pictures celebrated its tenth anniversary in 1945. The company embarked upon its second decade with studio facilities that could meet any production demand; a roster of skilled producers, directors, and other creative artists and technicians; and a policy augmenting its production talent with men and women whose accomplishments had won industry recognition.

The second decade of the motion picture company began with pre-production meetings for its next premiere feature *Specter of the Rose*. Written, directed, and produced by novelist and Academy Award winner Ben Hecht, the film is the story of Andre Sanine, a half-mad ballet dancer suspected

_____

* The Hays Office, formally Motion Picture Producers and Distributors of America, was an American organization that promulgated a moral code for films. In 1922, after a number of scandals involving Hollywood personalities, film industry leaders formed the organization to counteract the threat of government censorship and to create favorable publicity for the industry. Under Will H. Hays, a politically active lawyer, the Hays Office initiated a blacklist, inserted morals clauses into actors' contracts, and in 1930 developed the Production Code, which detailed what was morally acceptable on the screen.

I can't bear to leave him even if he is a monster because sometimes he is Andre—and he still kisses me sometimes . . . And to the end I never knew that it was not love but murder which lay beside me . . . . I have only one memory — the memory of being loved . . . . A glint of evil touched his boyish smile . . . . He was meant to dance, to love—not to kill . . . . I remembered him as something wonderful but mad . . . . We lived together as though we were two people alone on the moon . . . . His eyes were the eyes of a lover who was a rose — a dream—a thing of smoke and magic . . . . He begged me to leave him and save myself from his madness . . . . There were nights of violence . . . . screams and sobs . . . . I know he will kill me because that's what his madness means . . . .

BEN HECHT'S
Specter of the Rose
A REPUBLIC PICTURE
with JUDITH ANDERSON · MICHAEL CHEKHOV
IVAN KIROV · VIOLA ESSEN · LIONEL STANDER
Produced, Written and Directed by
BEN HECHT
who gave you such great screen plays as
"SPELLBOUND", "WUTHERING HEIGHTS"
"NOTHING SACRED", "SCARFACE", "VIVA VILLA"
and other never-to-be-forgotten motion picture entertainments
Co-Producer-Director and Director of Photography — Lee Garmes
Musical Score—GEORGE ANTHEIL · Choreography—TAMARA GEVA

Academy Award–winning writer Ben Hecht wrote and directed Republic's *Specter of the Rose*. AUTHOR'S COLLECTION

of murdering his first wife. Because he is greatly talented and their own fortunes are low, Madame La Sylph, an aged, desperate ballerina, and Max Polikoff, an impresario temporarily out of work as usual, decide to bring Sanine out of his morbid retirement. They succeed with the help of Heidi, an adoring ballerina who marries Sanine and joins him as a premiere ballerina of the new company. The return is a fleeting triumph; Sanine dances brilliantly on tour but is gradually overcome by returning insanity, plunging at last through a hotel window with a great leap and to his death.[11]

The film noir thriller was released on July 5, 1946, and starred acclaimed actor and acting teacher Michael Chekhov, and, as his leading lady, Judith Anderson. Film reviewers called *Specter of the Rose* one of the "most interesting motion pictures of the season." Moviegoers hailed the film as "unique" and "brave."[12]

"*Specter of the Rose* represents progressive Republic Pictures' most auspicious movie made to date," the January 7, 1947, edition of the *Honolulu Star-Bulletin* boasted. "It is the kind of film that critics, their tastes jaded by dozens of mediocre, average pictures, hail with delight."

Ben Hecht's suspense-filled direction, the eerie, fright-evoking quality of photography by co-producer and ace cameraman Lee Garmes, and the dissonant, discordant musical score by George Antheir were recognized by fellow moviemakers as "exceptional work."[13]

Although *Specter of the Rose* was a critical success, it was not a financial success. Hecht openly admitted he cared nothing about box office receipts. "I'm pleased if just 400,000 people go to the theatre to see the film," he told reporters. Herbert Yates did not share Hecht's sentiment. He was disappointed in the showing and vowed to consider the commercial viability of a project more closely in the future.[14]

Republic released fifty-eight features in the 1946-1947 season. Sixteen of those films were in Trucolor. "The world is waiting for color," Yates told reporters at the *Motion Picture Herald*. "Republic will offer what the public wants." According to Yates, switching from black-and-white to color productions was analogous to the change from silent to sound films. Yates informed the *Motion Picture Herald* that experimentation and research at the Consolidated Film Industries had resulted in a process ready to meet an ever-changing demand for color. "The company plants in New York and Hollywood will be ready by July 1 to handle a potential 100,000,000 feet of color film a year," Yates added. "Worldwide distribution of Republic films in Trucolor would be implemented by a policy of establishing an up-to-date release schedule for the foreign market."[15]

Republic was set to expand in other directions, too. A total of two million dollars was allocated for continued studio expansion and $3.5 million for the company's promotional activities.

Some of the promotional funds would be used to publicize Republic's next premier picture *Moonrise*. Adapted from Theodore Strauss' best-selling novel of the same name, *Moonrise* was directed by Frank Borzage, a master at the art of montage. The stars were Dane Clark, Gail Russell, and Ethel Barrymore.

The story concerns Danny Hawkins, played by Dane Clark, whose father is hanged for murder. As a result, Danny is branded a killer's son and becomes involved in more childhood scrapes than the neighborhood bully. Outside a swamp-side dance hall, Danny kills his chief tormentor and drags the body into the woods. He then proceeds to make a play for the dead man's girl, Gilly Johnson, played by Gail Russell. His crime remains undiscovered, although a philosophical sheriff, played by Allyn Joslyn, is on his trail. The body is eventually found, and the sheriff ascertains that Danny is his man. Danny then flees despite Gilly's pleas to give himself up. He beats a path to his grandmother's home, deep in the mountains where he is eventually tracked down.

Moonrise received mixed reviews when it was released in October 1948. Some critics thought it was "perfectly enacted by a superb cast," and others felt it was "too intense and uneven." Movie and theater reviewer Harold Cohen with the *Pittsburgh Post-Gazette* felt the film was "dreary," the dialogue "stuffy and stilted," and the "acting a shambles."[16]

Moonrise was Republic's second premiere film noir picture to be released. It received an Academy Award nomination for Best Sound Recording, and the studio saw a modest return on the investment. Yates was sure the next movie would do even better. *Wake of the Red Witch* also starred Gail Russell, but she was teamed with John Wayne in this seafaring film. Gig Young, Adele Mara, and Paul Fix were also included in the cast.

Greed for gold starkly stands forth as the theme of *Wake of the Red Witch*. Set in the 1860s in the South Pacific, Captain Ralls, skipper of the *Red Witch*, has a series of adventures involving sunken gold bullion, pearls, natives, an unscrupulous ship owner, and a giant octopus. The film cost $1.2 million to make: one hundred thousand dollars was paid for the screen rights for the book by Garland Roark from which the film was adapted. It was the most money the studio had ever paid for a story.[17]

Republic built a full-scale replica of a three-mast sailing vessel on one of its largest soundstages. The schooner, over two hundred feet long, was an exact duplication of the one used in the ocean sequences that were filmed on location in Catalina Island.[18]

Audiences flocked to the movie many referred to as "Wuthering Heights on the water." Moviegoers praised the picture's non-stop action and listed the underwater sequences and John Wayne's battle with the giant octopus among the best moments of the film. *Wake of the Red Witch* performed well at the box office, finishing forty-third on *Variety*'s list of the top money makers in 1949.[19]

Herbert Yates' goal for Republic Pictures to be recognized as a studio that could make artistic, cultured films as well as fast-paced cowboy operas prompted him to strike a deal with celebrated actor and director

FACING PAGE: *Wake of the Red Witch* starred John Wayne, Gail Russell, Gig Young, Paul Fix, and Adele Mara. L. TOM PERRY SPECIAL COLLECTIONS, BRIGHAM YOUNG UNIVERSITY, PROVO, UTAH

LEFT: *Wake of the Red Witch* was billed as a seafaring version of *Wuthering Heights*. L. TOM PERRY SPECIAL COLLECTIONS, BRIGHAM YOUNG UNIVERSITY, PROVO, UTAH

Orson Welles. Welles and his friend, producer Charlie Feldman, met with Yates in early 1948 to discuss the idea for a film they wanted to do. The story was about a duke who receives a prophecy from a trio of witches that one day he will become king of Scotland. Consumed by ambition and spurred to action by his wife, he murders the king and takes the throne for himself. Yates had no idea the tale was Shakespeare's *Macbeth* when he enthusiastically agreed to make the movie. Welles had led him

FACING PAGE: Orson Welles starred in and directed Republic Pictures' film *Macbeth*. L. TOM PERRY SPECIAL COLLECTIONS, BRIGHAM YOUNG UNIVERSITY, PROVO, UTAH

to believe it was an original piece he had written himself and that the production would be as revolutionary to film making as *Citizen Kane* had been.

It wasn't the first time Welles had taken advantage of a studio executive anxious to do business with the cinematic genius. According to a story from the June 29, 1948, edition of the *Hollywood Reporter*, Welles once bamboozled Harry Cohn, the Columbia Studio boss, into advancing him sixty thousand dollars he needed to finance a stage venture. The news article reported that Welles phoned Cohn, gave him some fast talk about a terrific idea for a picture, and got the money instantly. Welles publicly boasted that Cohn was an "easy mark." He thought no less of Herbert Yates.[20]

Yates signed the Welles project agreeing on a budget of $880,000, one of the largest film budgets ever entertained at Republic Studios. Welles' fee for directing and acting in *Macbeth* was one hundred thousand dollars. Yates knew of Welles' reputation for going overbudget and for seldom making a deadline. He inserted a clause in Welles' contract that noted any overspending was to be deducted from his paycheck. Welles was given twenty-three days to shoot *Macbeth*. He did complete the film in that period of time, but he disappeared before the editing of the picture was concluded. He had been offered an action job overseas in the film *Black Magic* and felt that was more important than finishing the *Macbeth* project.[21]

Executives at Republic were furious with the eccentric thespian's behavior. They demanded to see the rough cut of the picture, and, after viewing the work that had been done, they had some concerns with the footage. The Scottish accents many of the actors employed were so thick it was difficult to understand what they were saying. The cast would spend nine months rerecording the dialogue. Welles, who was in Italy working on another movie, waited until he returned to London to record his part.[22]

FACING PAGE: Republic's *Macbeth* was released in 1948 and was a critical and commercial disaster. L. TOM PERRY SPECIAL COLLECTIONS, BRIGHAM YOUNG UNIVERSITY, PROVO, UTAH

Republic Pictures' executives had planned to release *Macbeth* in late 1949, but post-production delays and the question of how to market the project pushed that day out to June 1950. *Macbeth* was a critical and commercial disaster. "In spite of all the grimacing and growling that was going on, there was a good bit of quiet snoozing from the audiences the afternoon that I saw Orson Welles's personalized version of *Macbeth*," a film reviewer with the *Chicago Tribune* noted. "Mr. W not only produced, directed, and starred in the offering, he also spotted his young daughter in the cast for a brief appearance. The net results are a dark and deadly dull film and I prefer my naps at home."[23]

There were a few reviews that congratulated Welles for his "imagination" and applauded Republic Pictures for the daring risk they took to bring Shakespeare's work to the screen. "Here is a *Macbeth* the like of which no one has seen," the critic with the *Courier-Journal* announced. "It is gory, filled with hanging dead bodies and decapitated ones. It has an eerie quality of the storm-swept heath and it is read in solid guttural tones with all the bass stops pulled out. While the picture does not match, in artistic integrity, the work of Laurence Olivier in his *Hamlet* or *Henry V*, it still is a film that exhibits a decided feeling for the macabre."[24]

The poor box office showing for *Macbeth* left Yates pondering whether to produce another of Welles' projects entitled *The Shadow*. Welles had been the voice of the popular radio serial from September 1937 to October 1938. He had hopes of bringing the detective series to the big screen, but Yates was not in a hurry to give the gifted artist a second chance at a big budget project. As a result, the two parted ways. Welles went on to do the classic film *The Third Man*, and Yates turned his attention to John Ford, a director who had never let him down.[25]

The rising popularity of television was of concern for several motion picture studios, not the least of which was Republic. By late summer 1948, the company had experienced a noticeable decrease in ticket sales.

Audiences were choosing to stay home and watch the *Milton Berle Show* and *Kraft Television Theatre* rather than venture out to the cinema. In September 1948, Yates announced the layoff of extraneous personnel in all departments. Only workers essential to ongoing productions were retained. By the end of 1950, it was clear to Yates that he could no longer take a gamble on such arthouse-style projects like *Macbeth*. He would focus on familiar storylines with proven talent both in front and behind the camera. Yates would use the production funds built up between 1941 and 1945 to hire John Ford and John Wayne to make *The Quiet Man*.[26]

Based on the 1933 *Saturday Evening Post* story by Maurice Walsh, *The Quiet Man* was a romantic drama set in Ireland. The tale centered on an Irish-born American who returned to his homeland to reclaim his family's farm and birthplace in Innisfree. John Ford read Walsh's story when it was released and purchased the rights for ten dollars. Walsh was paid another twenty-five hundred dollars when Yates and Republic Pictures joined the quest to bring the story to the screen. Walsh would earn an additional $3,750 when the film was made.[27]

Republic Pictures agreed to finance the film with Maureen O'Hara and John Wayne starring and John Ford directing only if they agreed to first film the western *Rio Grande*. Yates was taking a chance, albeit a small one, backing Ford and Wayne in anything other than a western, and he wanted to hedge his bets. Whatever funds would be used to make *The Quiet Man* must first be made doing the film *Rio Grande* and its subsequent success.

Rio Grande is an almost balletic story of the relationships among a man and his two loves: his wife and the cavalry. John Wayne plays Lieutenant Colonel Kirby York, who finds his son Jeff among his new recruits at his command in the West. Kirby and his wife Kathleen, portrayed by Maureen O'Hara, have been separated since the Civil War, when in the line of duty as a Northern officer he was required to burn her estate. They meet again for the first time in sixteen years when Kathleen comes to the fort to buy Jeff's obligation, which neither father nor son allow her to do.[28]

Based on another story from the *Saturday Evening Post* entitled "Mission With No Record" by James Warner Bellah, *Rio Grande* completes a loose trilogy about Ford's beloved Seventh Cavalry.

In addition to Wayne and O'Hara, *Rio Grande* also featured Ben Johnson, Harry Carey Jr., Chill Wills, Victor McLaglen, and Claude Jarman Jr. Jarman portrayed Trooper Jefferson York, Wayne and O'Hara's son in the picture. It was Jarman's first adult part. He had risen to fame playing Jody in the Academy Award–winning film *The Yearling*. He was twelve when that classic was released. At sixteen, he was six feet, two inches and stood nearly eye to eye with Wayne in the Ford classic.[29]

Rio Grande was popular with moviegoers, and the healthy box office receipts provided Yates with a financial reserve to draw from in case *The Quiet Man* didn't fare well. Reviewers gave the movie high marks for its acting, music, and cinematography. Filmed in Monument Valley, the motion picture was lauded as a "scenic triumph" as well as an exceptional western story. The October 30, 1950, edition of the *Hollywood Reporter* called *Rio Grande* "the year's finest outdoor screen adventure."[30]

On Friday, November 17, 1950, John Ford, Ward Bond, and Herbert Yates flew to Ireland to visit the spot where *The Quiet Man* would be filmed. Movie columnist Louella Parsons wrote about the trip and the preproduction of the picture in her weekly column:

> This morning John Ford traveled with his boss Herbert Yates to see the location in Dublin where principal photography will commence in June 1951 on *The Quiet Man*. Just before John took off I talked to him, and he told me he had signed Richard Llewellyn who wrote the Academy Award winning *How Green Was My Valley* to do the script for *The Quiet Man*.

Republic Pictures' boss Herbert Yates agreed to produce *The Quiet Man* only if John Wayne, John Ford, and Maureen O'Hara made the western *Rio Grande*. AUTHOR'S COLLECTION

I accused him of taking Herbert Yates along to pay the bills. "Well, that would be part of it," John said, "but I really want him to see what his money is buying when we make our picture, the first Technicolor picture to be produced in Ireland."[31]

Yates was struck by the beauty of Ireland, but overcome with worry. He considered the cost to transport a crew and equipment to the picturesque area would be exceedingly more than Ford had calculated. He began to question producing the film at all. The closer it came to the actual shooting taking place, the more nervous he became. Yates convinced himself he was risking too much for an "arthouse movie" and that the project could lead the company into bankruptcy. In an attempt to quell Yates' fears, both Ford and Wayne agreed to waive their standard fees and take a substantial cut in pay. Yates calmed down a bit but demanded to see the daily expenditures while filming was taking place to make sure there was no danger of exceeding the $1.75 million price tag.[32]

It took six weeks to shoot *The Quiet Man*. Only six days of that were sunny. The rest were either rainy or cloudy. The cameras had to be consistently adjusted to accommodate for the everchanging light. Yates wasn't pleased with the footage he was shown. Ford assured him that the final product would be perfect.[33]

The final production was 179 minutes, and that annoyed Yates. He thought the film was too long, that Ireland was too green, that the entire project was overpriced, and he didn't care for the title of the picture either. His opinion abruptly changed at a special screening of the movie. The response was overwhelmingly good, and the distributors in attendance were enthralled with the picture.[34]

The Quiet Man was released on September 14, 1952. Critics praised the film's lush photography, outstanding performances, and sense of humanity. John Wayne and Barry Fitzgerald's performances were singled out for special praise.[35]

FACING PAGE: *The Quiet Man*, directed by John Ford, was one of Republic Pictures' most successful films. L. TOM PERRY SPECIAL COLLECTIONS, BRIGHAM YOUNG UNIVERSITY, PROVO, UTAH

Movie reviewer Wood Soanes wrote in his column *Curtain Calls* on October 16, 1952:

> It's easy to give *The Quiet Man* an unqualified recommendation on a number of counts. The story is excellent, the photography is beautiful, and the acting is in the hands of gifted and proficient people.
>
> Sean Thornton, so the story goes, is a prize fighter who isn't aware of his own strength. As a consequence he has killed a man in the ring and promptly bowed out of his profession.
>
> He decides to return to the village of Innisfree where he was born to live out his life, content that none will know how he has earned his money. So far all well and good, but Innisfree isn't quite the place he has imagined it would be. It is dominated by a wealthy bully who considers it a personal affront that a foreigner should take over a holding that he considers his own.
>
> The bully is further outraged when he discovers that the newcomer has had the audacity to fall in love with his sister— the bully's that is—and he feels that the matter had best be settled by physical combat. It eventually is, but only after the ex-pug has permitted himself to be tabulated as a coward in his efforts to avoid fisticuffs.
>
> Wayne, who manages to do better work under the direction of Ford who "discovered" him than anyone else, is superb as the killer who wants to be nothing more important than a quiet man, a part of the little village he has selected for himself.[36]

The Quiet Man won two Academy Awards at the twenty-fifth annual awards ceremony in March 1953. The film had been nominated for seven statues and took home the prize for Best Director, John Ford, and Best Cinematography (color), Winton C. Hoch and Archie Stout.[37]

The Quiet Man, starring John Wayne and Maureen O'Hara, was released in 1952. L. TOM PERRY SPECIAL COLLECTIONS, BRIGHAM YOUNG UNIVERSITY, PROVO, UTAH

Herbert Yates was elated by the win and at the glowing reviews Republic Pictures was receiving. *The Quiet Man* was not only an award-winning film, but a box office success, finishing twelfth on the *Variety* list of the top-grossing pictures of 1952. Seventeen years after founding the company, Yates felt he'd finally arrived.[38]

John Ford was not among those offering Republic Pictures and Herbert Yates the respectability Yates had so longed for. Ford's experience with the executive during the filming of *The Quiet Man* left him with the opinion that Republic Pictures would never be anything other than a "cheap, poverty row operation."[39]

According to the contract Ford had with Yates, a portion of the profits from the film were to be paid to Ford's production company, but very little of those funds were making it back to the director. Ford believed Yates was pocketing the earnings. A lawsuit filed by Ford's attorneys against Republic brought about an audit that revealed enormous fraud. Yates was ordered to pay Ford more than half a million dollars. The incident permanently severed the relationship between Yates and Ford, and, by extension, the relationship between John Wayne and Yates. Neither of the men felt they could ever be associated with Republic Pictures again.

Wayne's exit played out in all the trade publications. "The long successful association of John Wayne and Republic Studios has apparently hit the rocks," the November 13, 1952, edition of the *Hollywood Reporter* announced. "Wayne, top man on the box office heap for the past two years, indicates that he has come to an impasse with his old friend and boss, Herbert J. Yates, head of Republic. If their falling out becomes permanent, it will mean the end of a picture-making partnership that goes back to the early days of Wayne's 20-year acting career."[40]

When asked for a comment, Yates was calm when expressing his displeasure over Wayne's decision. "Duke leaving Republic is sad indeed," he told the *Hollywood Reporter*. "Although his contract with the studio calls for three additional pictures, I and all of his old friends at Republic wish him continued success and prosperity."[41]

By the end of 1953, Yates' studio had lost one of the most popular movie stars in the world and was the subject of scorn from one of the most celebrated directors in the industry. Clinging to a number of Academy Award nominations and with an impressive slate of premiere pictures to his company's credit, Yates pressed on toward new deals with bigger stars in the burgeoning frontier of television.

CHAPTER 5

The Amazing Lydecker Brothers

In the beginning, long before computer-generated imagery, there were the Lydecker brothers. Using detailed miniatures, scale model vehicles, creative lighting, and camera techniques, the special effects duo revolutionized the moviemaking business and made Republic Pictures a force to reckon with in the film industry. The Lydeckers followed in their father's footsteps. Howard C. Lydecker worked specifically for actor Douglas Fairbanks and was an early practitioner in special effects, including the filming of miniatures and trick photography. Theodore was born in Englewood, New Jersey, in 1908. Howard, also known as "Babe," was born in Havana, Cuba, in 1911.[1]

Theodore and Howard were enamored with the film business and went to work developing their behind the camera artistry in the mid-1930s. Prior to being hired at Republic Studios, the pair worked for a succession of studios including Columbia, Fox, and Mascot. When Herbert Yates acquired Mascot in 1935, the Lydecker brothers were part of the package. The siblings worked under John Coyle learning all they could about forced perspective and visual effects. When Coyle left Republic in 1938, Howard and Theodore assumed leadership of the special effects department.

According to a 1942 memo from studio head Herbert Yates, the brothers were responsible for nine optical effects areas: montages; inserts; some main titles;

added shots; construction of all props for process shots; the gun room; matte and glass shots; special effects including fire, water, rain, snow, smoke, and underwater setups; and miniatures. It was in the creation of miniatures that the Lydeckers excelled.[2]

Howard and Theodore worked together on conceptualizing the small scale sets. Theodore would then draft the plans for the building and oversee the construction. Howard's job was to film the miniature models of towns, spaceships, buildings, trains, automobiles, stagecoaches, and whatever else a script might call for. In a short time, the Lydeckers earned the reputation as the kings of special effects. The approach they took when preparing for a sequence was simple: build large, photograph the subject matter from every possible angle, and always use natural light.

In addition to using detailed models and filming sequences with the miniatures against real location backdrops, Howard Lydecker shot the scenes in slow motion. He realized that during such shoots, film ran through the camera at a higher speed than normal (determined by the scale of the models) and when projected at normal speed, the slow-motion effect gave the end product the right appearance of mass and size. Utilizing all the techniques the Lydecker brothers developed and subsequently perfected, the visual effects on the movies Republic Pictures produced were superior to that of any other studio.

The majority of the time, the special effects geniuses had a small budget to work with and that forced them to be creative. In the case of the first Republic serial *Darkest Africa*, the Lydeckers were tasked with creating an army of batmen that would fly in and terrorize the heroes in the story. Other studios would have been content to build small models and dangle them on the end of a thread and shoot against jiggly rear-screen footage. Howard and Theodore built more than two dozen clay and rubber figurines, each 3.25 inches long with wing spans of six inches. They suspended the figurines on a rigger and rotated them above miniature sets representing the backdrop in the script. For close-ups of the life-sized batmen flying through the air, they sculptured a hollow shell body from papier-mâché. Sheaves were then placed in the reinforced heel and shoulder areas to allow the figurines to slide gracefully along a pair of stretched wires.

The Lydeckers got all their models, from the batmen in *Darkest Africa* to the planes in the *Dick Tracy* serials, to fly by guiding them along supporting lengths of dulled piano wire. Film grains, camera motions, editing, careful lighting, and selective choice takes effectively concealed or obscured the wires.

For the 1938 film *Born to Be Wild* starring Ward Bond and Ralph Byrd, the Lydecker brothers built a large-scale, outdoor, miniature dam from photos of the San Gabriel Dam. They placed miniature trees and brush in the canyon at the base of the dam to complete the look. With a scale of three-quarters of an inch to a foot, the miniature dam was capable of holding thirty gallons of water as the purpose of the construction was to show a runaway semitrailer (in actuality a thirty-inch copper truck) loaded with dynamite hitting the spillway, causing a massive breach in the wall with water flooding onto the valley below. The dramatic footage was reused in *Dick Tracy Returns* and the western serial *King of the Texas Rangers*.

In 1941, Republic Pictures released a twelve-chapter serial entitled *Adventures of Captain Marvel*. Tom Tyler starred in the title role of the meek radio broadcaster and part-time archaeologist granted with powers to become Captain Marvel whenever he said the word "Shazam." Captain Marvel not only had superhuman strength, but could fly also. The flying sequence the Lydecker brothers designed and shot for the serial was groundbreaking. Howard Lydecker constructed a seven-foot dummy of lightweight papier-mâché with outstretched arms and four tiny pulley wheels connected to each shoulder and calf legs. The wires were strung between two mountain ridges and various buildings so that the dummy, dressed as Captain Marvel, moved smoothly along the wires. For upward movement, his cape was weighted down so that he moved backwards, and film was reversed. This particular technique continues to be used in moviemaking today.[3]

The Lydecker brothers have been praised by motion picture effects experts Tony Dyons (*Star Wars*) and Patrick Tatopoulus (*Independence Day*). Most recognize the brothers as pioneers in the field of special effects. As long as the siblings spent little or nothing on their work, Herbert Yates gave them free reign to experiment in creating feats no one had ever seen on the screen. It all began on the first pictures the Lydeckers worked on for Republic. It was a 1935 serial starring Gene Autry entitled *The Phantom Empire*.

The Phantom Empire was a western sci-fi combination. Autry played a cowboy who ran a radio station from his ranch in which he was the singing star on nightly broadcasts. A gang of outlaws covet the radium mine on Autry's property and plan to take it over. Autry chases the bad guys off his land, and, during the pursuit, they literally stumble upon the entrance to an underground city called Murania. Both the crooks and Autry are captured by the Muranians and their slave robot. Autry must find a way to escape and get back to his ranch in time for his next radio show. The plot was silly and the acting lackluster, but the effects employed by the Lydeckers made the chapter series visually entertaining.[4]

Howard and Theodore constructed an underground room and elevator that actually carried ray guns and models of Muranians up and down. The six-foot-high city, robots, living quarters for the Queen of Murania, and her army all contained such rich detail viewers didn't doubt such a location existed. When the queen's atom-smasher misfired, the models were burned to the ground. The melting effect combined with skilled cinematography work enhanced the action.[5]

In 1936, the Lydeckers turned their attention to a film called *The House of a Thousand Candles*. The plot centered on spies and counterspies all trying to get their hands on a document that exposed plans for a major war. Train derailments, explosions, and car chases were featured in the story and expertly executed by Howard and Theodore. Large-scale models of cars placed on carefully constructed, matching scale roadways were used to create the effect of a black sedan plummeting off an embankment. Whenever possible, the vehicle was photographed in natural light against natural background. It added a sense of realism to the sequence of footage and left audiences on the edge of their seats.

Storm Over Bengal, an action adventure picture released in November 1938, included several inventive special effects from the Lydecker brothers. The film is about an Indian rajah who is an ally of the British who dies suddenly. Upon his death, his successor vows to drive the British out of India. Both British and Indian soldiers go to war. The Lydeckers determined that the soldiers in battle scenes should be comprised of hundreds of lifelike rubber dummies all in various poses. Positioned just right in front of a convincing model of the desert, the dummies gave the illusion that vast armies were involved. The footage Howard Lydecker shot for *Storm Over Bengal* would be reused several times in subsequent Republic films.

Howard Lydecker earned his first Academy Award nomination for best visual effects for the 1940 film *Women at War*. *Women at War* is about the nurses of the British Voluntary Aid Detachment during the Battle of France. The burning villages, bombs dropping on buildings, explosions, and aerial attacks on ships were all achieved with the use of life-sized models and miniatures. Lydecker further enhanced the sequences by tilting the miniature sets sideways and placing a downward-aimed camera above. When the fires from the explosions bloomed upward, climbing the miniature environment, it looked as though it was spreading laterally.

The exceptional work Howard Lydecker did on the film *Flying Tigers* starring John Wayne, John Carroll, and Anna Lee did not escape the

attention of the voting members of the Academy Awards in 1942. The director and special effects wizard was once again nominated for an Academy Award.

Wayne plays Captain Jim Gordon, commander of the famed American mercenary fighter group in China. The mission of the *Flying Tigers* is complicated when a reckless hotshot is recruited and routinely disobeys orders.

As the story called for a number of dogfights involving P-40 aircraft, Howard, his brother Theodore, and their special effects crew needed to construct replicas of the fighter planes and choreograph aerial duels so they would look believable. The Lydecker brothers eagerly dove into the challenge.

The majority of the film's exterior scenes were shot in Santa Fe, New Mexico. The film's director, David Miller, wanted that particular location in order to take advantage of the impressive cloud formations that routinely accumulated there. The Lydecker brothers and their special effects crew utilized the picturesque setting as well. The miniature trains, bridges, aircraft, and rugged canyons were all placed in the foreground of the vast New Mexico landscape. The full-sized planes used in the scenes were made from plywood and balsa wood. The aerial combat footage was shot under the same Santa Fe sky, and the miniature aircraft was pulled along on wires off screen.

As the United States was ensconced in World War II at the time *Flying Tigers* was being filmed, the Lydecker brothers took full advantage of visiting the Curtiss-Wright production plant in Buffalo, New York, to get a look at the Curtiss P-40 Tomahawk planes being built to serve in the effort. The brothers then created miniature Curtiss P-40 Tomahawks to use in *Flying Tigers*. The interior of the planes could not be shown for security reasons. Howard, Theodore, and their team designed their own cockpits and instrument panels for the motion picture. The planes were made entirely of wood, cost five hundred dollars each to make, and took two weeks to build.

A crucial scene in the film involved a bomber being shot from the sky by the Japanese and plummeting to the ground, taking out a train crossing a bridge before exploding into pieces. The Lydeckers staged the miniatures and pyrotechnics with expert precision, making the most memorable action scene in the film.

The special effects techniques used to make the sequence possible included the use of a tower rigged with a cable in which the miniature plane was attached. At the proper time, the model aircraft was released and sent sliding down the cable on a carefully predetermined trajectory into the miniature train and bridge. The noise of the planes, engines, battles, collisions, and explosions were all done entirely in the studio.

Howard Lydecker and Daniel Bloomberg were nominated for an Academy Award for Best Visual Effects. Bloomberg received an Academy Award nod for sound and Howard Lydecker for his photographing of the special effect sequences. The pair lost to the special effects team who made *Reap the Wild Wind* starring John Wayne and Ray Milland.

Throughout the course of the Lydecker brothers' careers, they built many miniature scenes for stories set in the 1930s, 1940s, and 1950s only to see those elaborate structures burned to the ground, crushed by an avalanche, destroyed in an earthquake, or blown down by a wind storm. In the 1944 film *Zorro's Black Whip*, the special effects duo constructed a model of the Iverson Grove Relay Station in Chatsworth, California. The motion picture set was the location where many western films had been shot. Iverson's Village, also known as El Paso Street, contained many period buildings: saloons, corrals, general stores, stables, relay stations, etc. The Lydeckers' re-creation included several of those structures. The villains in the Zorro film hoped to kill the story's hero by causing a rock slide that would crush the relay station where Zorro and a beautiful victim were trapped inside. The finished product was a realistic destruction of the building. Audiences had to catch episode ten of the twelve-part chapter play to find out if Zorro and his companion survived the devastation.

No matter how implausible the storyline was for many of the chapter plays Republic Pictures produced, the Lydecker brothers and their skilled recruits could make the unlikely seem possible. Such was the case of the twelve-part serial *Tiger Woman*. Evil oil speculators in South America attempt to drive away a native tribe and their leader, a white woman they call Tiger Woman. Tiger Woman might be the lost heiress of a vast fortune. Who she really is will be uncovered little by little as the story progresses.

There are many perils in the dark jungle, and the tiger woman and her rescuers fall victim to all of them. She is sent plummeting over a raging waterfall in a speedboat, falls hundreds of feet down an open elevator shaft (a jungle elevator no less), and is locked away in an underground cave that is quickly being destroyed by a blazing inferno. The Lydeckers' work was just as much a star of the chapter play as the tiger woman herself. Full-size models were used to recreate each harrowing experience the lead encountered. Cameras fastened to a miniature barge behind the speedboat heading for the water's edge captured the dramatic and realistic image of careening into the falls. Audiences gasped and were compelled to return to the theater week after week to see how the heroine and her cohorts would survive the mortal dangers so brilliantly executed by Republic Pictures' special effects department.[6]

Prior to *Tiger Woman*, there was *Haunted Harbor*. A sea captain is falsely accused of a hideous murder and must escape from the law, find the real killer, and clear his name. The true killer is living on Haunted Harbor. While en route to the dreaded location, the wrongly identified man rescues a beautiful woman shipwrecked near the creepy harbor. Together they combat pirates, killers, and a horrifying sea creature.[7]

Theodore Lydecker created the rubber monster complete with working tentacles. Wires were attached to the massive limbs and were manipulated by crew members off camera. According to film historian Jan Ala Henderson, "the sea creature was filled through its tail with steam and water hoses, and towed via cable along a ramped underwater track to bring it rearing to the surface. Forced perspective photography effectively doubled the enormity of the six foot sea serpent when it was positioned foreground of the actors and their motorboats, rather than behind them where it appeared to be."

Henderson further explained that the sea creature sequence and other aquatic events were staged at a pair of back lot water tanks. Surface filming was done in a small pool approximately 140 by 210 feet. "The pools' slanted perimeter permitted a continuous flow of water to be pumped over the rim," Henderson was quoted as saying, "establishing a seamless horizon line with an expansive sky-cyclorama back piece behind or various scenic groupings arranged in between."

The Lydecker sea creature was the first the brothers ever constructed; over the course of twenty years, it was leased to several other studios for a variety of other films.

The visual tricks and illusions Howard and Theodore created for the bulk of the films they worked on consisted of scale models used for establishing and transitional shots. That's not to imply that the special effects they used on films such as *In Old Sacramento*, *My Pal Trigger*, *The Last Crooked Mile*, and the hundreds of other projects weren't important. The Lydeckers brought a refinement and respectability to Republic Pictures. Other motion picture companies coveted Herbert Yates' special effects and miniature department. Howard and Theodore were admired by industry leaders and moviemakers, and moviegoers were anxious to see what the siblings would do with each project. Some warranted more attention than others; such was the case with the film *The Fighting Seabees*.

The war picture *The Fighting Seabees* starred John Wayne and Susan Hayward. The story was about construction workers in war zones overseas who do battle with the Japanese. The Lydeckers' job included designing miniature military bases, island encampments, and a fleet of ocean vessels called Higgins boats. Artist Lewis Physioc, a former cameraman for Thomas Edison on staff at Republic Pictures' special effects

FACING PAGE: The Lydeckers were pyrotechnic experts. An example of their handiwork can be seen in the film *The Fighting Seabees*. L. TOM PERRY SPECIAL COLLECTIONS, BRIGHAM YOUNG UNIVERSITY, PROVO, UTAH

department, did much of the matte painting for the film. His background paintings included the Washington Monument and the lush landscape of the Japanese island.

Republic productions often featured footage from other films. Such was the case with *The Fighting Seabees*. Stock shots from *Flying Tigers* involving "enemy" aircraft as well as actual footage of the Seabees marching in review before the Secretary of the Navy from Camp Endicott were used to complete sequences in the film.

As usual Howard and Theodore staged the battle scenes to the precise second. Pyrotechnics strategically placed within the full-scale model set looked like a real bombing when the fires erupted. Critics called *The Fighting Seabees* "authentic and thrilling" and cited the film's special effects team for "adding layers of credibility to the motion picture."[8]

Four years after making *The Fighting Seabees* and spending time doing special effects for numerous westerns, screwball comedies, and melodramas, the Lydeckers were once again challenged to stretch their creative abilities. The first of two pictures Republic assigned the brothers to work on was another John Wayne vehicle. *Wake of the Red Witch* was an action adventure film set in the 1860s in the South Pacific. Wayne's character was the captain of a ship called the Red Witch.

Wayne sparred with a wealthy shipping magnate for a treasure of gold bullion and the heart of a beautiful girl. Howard and Theodore built scale model villages, seaports, and schooners and set the miniatures around and in the ocean. They mounted a camera platform on barges to capture sailing scenes and scenes when vessels were destroyed by an explosion. The miniatures the brothers created for use underwater were precise and the footage Howard shot of the action in the ocean highlighted his innovative techniques involving scale, depth of field, and lighting. A rubber dummy clothed in a period diving suit doubled for Wayne when the story called for him to explore the sunken ship. The mechanical legs

FACING PAGE: Another still from *The Fighting Seabees* shows some action around a fighter airplane. The Lydeckers built these models from wood for about $500 each. L. TOM PERRY SPECIAL COLLECTIONS, BRIGHAM YOUNG UNIVERSITY, PROVO, UTAH

moved back and forth as the faux Wayne was submerged. The movement added to the realism.

The Lydeckers' team made the mechanical octopus Wayne does battle with during one of the dives in the film. The impressive sea monster was stolen from the prop department at Republic in 1954 by the eccentric director Edward Wood Jr. He used it in his science fiction/horror film *Bride of the Monsters* starring Bela Lugosi.[9]

Federal Agents vs. Underworld, Inc. was the other picture the Lydeckers and their special effects team were doing in 1948. The project was a twelve-part chapter play about a female leader of an international crime ring who steals a valuable artifact that gives her the power to control men's minds. Federal agents are dispatched to get it back and stop her evil plans.

The Lydeckers built ancient cities in dark, faraway country's tombs and eerie statues of sinister beasts. They created models of massive, archeological excavated plots of earth. In addition to the inventive, other world set constructed, the special effects experts were called upon to re-create car crashes, train derailments, and collapsing bridges. Some film critics insisted that the best part of the *Federal Agents vs. Underworld, Inc.* was the "powerful screen effects utilized in the movie."[10]

Whether working on a chapter serial with an implausible plot and a mechanical sea monster or on classic films with legendary stars, the Lydeckers took great pride in the jobs they were assigned. Howard and Theodore approached every picture as though it had award-winning potential.

The brothers approached the assignment on the film *Johnny Guitar* with the same enthusiasm as *The Invisible Monster. Johnny Guitar* is a western starring Joan Crawford as a strong-willed, saloon-casino owner who squares off against her nemesis, a cattle rancher played by Mercedes McCambridge who wrongly blames Crawford's character for her brother's

The Lydecker brothers were masters at building miniatures. An example of their work is the model town set used in Republic Pictures' film *Johnny Guitar*.

death. *Johnny Guitar* holds a spot on many film critics' list as one of the best westerns ever made. The Lydeckers treated their job on the project as though it would be considered their best work.[11]

Johnny Guitar was filmed on location in 1953 in Sedona, Arizona, among the sandstone buttes and forested valleys and at Red Rock Crossing. Joan Crawford's character's saloon exterior was built especially for

the film and later burned down as part of the action. The Lydeckers' experience in pyrotechnics made them the perfect duo to oversee setting the saloon on fire. The special effects team also created models of a western town and cabins perched atop a high bluff. They also constructed a scale model train line that ran along the outskirts of the western town. The work Howard and Theodore did on *Johnny Guitar* was subtle but impactful.

Crowd scene from *Johnny Guitar*. L. TOM PERRY SPECIAL COLLECTIONS, BRIGHAM YOUNG UNIVERSITY, PROVO, UTAH

Audiences arrived in droves at the theaters to see the movie and eagerly recommended it to others. It was well received by critics, too. "Johnny Guitar is as violent as the deadly bullets which spit from the flaming six-guns of fearless Vienna, the beautiful owner of the frontier saloon and gambling house portrayed by Miss Crawford," the August 5, 1954, edition of the *Rushville Republican* noted. "The suspense is as coldly menacing as Johnny Guitar himself, enacted by Sterling Hayden, whose haunting music can change to the staccato crack of pistols in the nervous hands of a gun-crazy killer."[12]

There was a great deal of strife on the set of *Johnny Guitar*. Joan Crawford didn't get along with anyone in the cast. Crawford detested costar Mercedes McCambridge and threw her costumes onto a road one evening. Sterling Hayden, who portrayed Johnny Guitar, hated Crawford. "There's not enough money in Hollywood to lure me into making another picture with Joan Crawford," Hayden told newspaper reporters shortly after the film premiered. Spared any such drama in the special effects

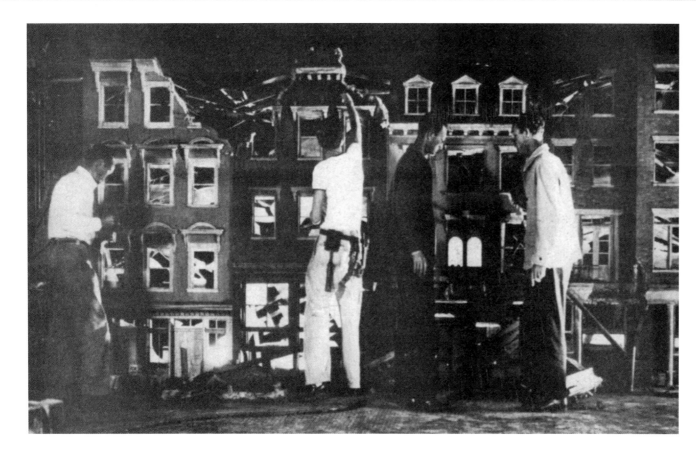

The Lydeckers' earthquake set for the Republic feature *Flame of the Barbary Coast.* AUTHOR'S COLLECTION

department, the Lydecker brothers considered themselves fortunate to be in the line of the motion picture business they were in.[13]

The highly regarded effects wizards' relationship with Republic ended in late 1950. Herbert Yates let the Lydeckers go when the studio could no longer afford to maintain full-time contract players and behind the camera artists. After more than twenty-two years with Republic Pictures, the brothers moved onto other ventures. Howard found employment at 20th Century Fox working with Irwin Allen on the television programs *Voyage to the Bottom of the Sea* and *Lost in Space.* He won an Emmy Award for Individual Achievement in Cinematography for *Voyage*

to the Bottom of the Sea in 1966. Howard died of a cerebral hemorrhage on
September 26, 1969, at the age of fifty-eight.

Theodore Lydecker worked at Disney and Universal Studios. According to film historian Jan Henderson, Theodore created the miniature bird
models Alfred Hitchcock used in his film *The Birds*. Theodore passed away
on May 25, 1990. He was eighty-one years old.

The Academy
Award–nominated
war movie *Flying
Tigers* starred
John Wayne, John
Carroll, and Anna
Lee. L. TOM PERRY
SPECIAL COLLEC-
TIONS, BRIGHAM
YOUNG UNIVERSITY,
PROVO, UTAH

CHAPTER 6

Republic Goes to War

On December 7, 1941, radios buzzed with news that several hundred Japanese planes attacked a US naval base at Pearl Harbor in Hawaii, killing more than twenty-four hundred Americans as well as damaging or destroying eight Navy battleships and more than one hundred planes. Though it would be some time before people learned the full scope of the damage, within days a once distant war in Europe and the Pacific became a central part of life in the United States, affecting politics, business, media, and entertainment.

Hollywood went to war along with the rest of the country. Prominent actors enlisted in the armed forces; actresses joined the Red Cross and volunteered their services to the USO. Notable motion pictures executives took part in the effort, too. Darryl Zanuck from 20th Century Fox got into the Army Signal Corps, and Jack Warner of Warner Brothers was assigned to the Army Air Corps. Studio heads unable to join the military fought the battle from behind their desks, producing films about the scene overseas and the gallant men and women protecting our freedom. By the summer of 1942, more than 125 pictures had been completed, or were in the process of being shot, that reflected war and its various angles or dealt with men in the fighting forces. Those pictures depicted the sterner side of the national and international war scene in not only dramas, features, and short subjects but also in comedies, cartoons, and even musicals.[1]

Hollywood was instrumental in shaping the resolve of the American public during the gloomy days of World War II. President Franklin Roosevelt used Americans' love affair with the movies to keep the public firmly behind the war effort. He was instrumental in creating the Office of War Information. The Office of War Information created campaigns to enhance public understanding of the war at home and abroad; to coordinate government information activities; and to act as a liaison with the press, radio, and motion picture industry. The Office of War Information was heavily involved in regulating Hollywood studios as they churned out war films at breakneck speed. Films like Warner Bros' *Confession of a Nazi Spy* and 20th Century Fox's *The Purple Heart* helped galvanize the American public against two brutal enemies.[2]

Republic Pictures also contributed to the awakening of the country's citizenship as to whom the fight was against and why. Republic's *Flying Tigers*, also known as *Yank Over Singapore*, was released on October 8, 1942. The movie was a tribute to the American Volunteer Group of pilots who battled the Japanese against overwhelming odds long before Pearl Harbor. According to the November 15, 1942, edition of the *Hutchinson News*, "Thrills abound in the picture which is a continuous series of stirring air duels between the outnumbered Americans and the Japanese."[3]

John Wayne has the principal role as leader of the American Volunteer Group. Anna Lee is a nurse in a hospital nearby. Paul Kelly, John Carroll, and Edmund MacDonald are pilots. *The Hutchinson News* noted that "some of the fight and injury scenes are strong medicine."[4]

Flying Tigers was well received in the United States and abroad as well. The February 14, 1944, edition of the Sydney, Australia, newspaper, the *Sydney Morning Herald* called the film "an effective reminder of the part played by the heroic American Volunteer Group." The article cited the cleverly photographed dog-fight sequences and John Wayne's "brilliant performance" as the reason the motion picture was so powerful.[5]

"The recreation of air combats with the Japanese are as dramatic, as detailed, and as spectacular as anything yet turned out by Hollywood's growing host of aircraft pictures," the *Sydney Morning Herald* elaborated.[6]

Flying Tigers was John Wayne's first war film. The movie broke all box office records for Republic Pictures and was one of the top grossing movies of 1942. The picture was nominated for three Academy Awards: Best Sound Recording, Best Special Effects, and Best Musical Score.[7]

In 1944, Republic released two war pictures, *The Fighting Seabees* and *Storm Over Lisbon*. *The Fighting Seabees* tells the story of the formation of the US Navy's Construction Battalion. The work is dangerous, and, after a series of attacks by the Japanese, the Construction Battalion, or CBs, have to both build and be ready to fight. John Wayne starred along with Susan Hayward, Dennis O'Keefe, and William Frawley. Directed by Edward Ludwig, critics called *The Fighting Seabees* "one of the most vivid and entertaining films produced in many years."[8]

Reviewers applauded not only the film's production but also the choice of subject. While other branches of the service were widely publicized in movies and books, the heroic Construction Battalion was not known to most civilians. They were quite literally the men in the front of the man behind the gun. They would land in combat zones ahead of the troops and prepare docks, landing fields, barracks, and everything else the invading troops required.[9]

The picture was dedicated to the sterling work the CBs have done and the traditions they established. Although minor, there was a romantic theme in the film involving Hayward, O'Keefe, and Wayne. The picture was best suited for those who wanted all-out action.

The Fighting Seabees was a high point for Republic. The studio had been edging into the field of premiere, or A, pictures like *The Fighting Seabees* for some time. After specializing for years in westerns and in the application of the western don't-spare-the-gunpowder formula, producing a movie like the Seabees was a step in the right direction.

Spectacular special effects went into *The Fighting Seabees'* battle scenes, particularly that in which a blown oil farm cascades blazing fuel down a valley after the fleeing enemy.

The Fighting Seabees did well financially for Republic. The April 14, 1943, edition of *Variety* reported that the budget for the film was $1.5 million, the highest budget in the history of the studio. The film more than made the money back that was invested in its production and was even nominated for an Academy Award for Best Musical Score.[10]

Storm Over Lisbon was released in October 1944. The spy picture was Republic Pictures' version of *Casablanca*. The film centered on a night club singer who helped track an enemy agent on the trail of an American newsman. Erich von Stroheim, Vera Ralston, Richard Arlen, and Mona Barrie starred. Reviews were mixed, but several critics called the movie "interesting and timely." According to the October 20, 1944, edition of the *Altoona Tribune*, the cast was excellent. "Vera Hruba Ralston, dancer and ice skater, is superb in the role of the night club singer," the article noted.[11]

The story itself was filmed against the background of a fabulous pleasure house. "Deresco's in Lisbon, where refugees awaited transportation from Europe, where diplomats and espionage agents rub shoulders, where plots of international importance are hatched and where whispered words affect the entire world," the *Altoona Tribune* explained about the setting.[12]

George Sherman was the director of *Storm Over Lisbon*, which was one of Republic's high-budget films. The espionage film was also entitled *Inside the Underworld* and was one of Herbert Yates' early attempts to make Vera Ralston a star. Yates was fascinated with the exotic beauty and tried for fifteen years to persuade audiences and Hollywood that Vera was star material.

In the film *G.I. War Brides*, Linda Powell, an English girl, stows away on a ship bound for the United States in order to join the G.I. she loves. She assumes the identity of an English war bride, Joyce Giles, who has

FACING PAGE: *The Fighting Seabees*, released in 1944, starred John Wayne, Dennis O'Keefe, and Susan Hayward.

RIGHT: Released in August 1946, Republic Pictures' *GI War Brides* starred Anna Lee, James Ellison, and Harry Davenport. AUTHOR'S COLLECTION

FACING PAGE: *Storm Over Lisbon*, starring Vera Ralston and Erich Von Stroheim, was Republic Pictures's version of the film Casablanca. AUTHOR'S COLLECTION

decided she no longer loves the American soldier she married and is not going to join him in the United States. Linda arrives to find her soldier no longer wishes to marry her. The post–World War II comedy starred Anna Lee, Harry Davenport, James Ellison, and Doris Lloyd.

On the day *G.I. War Brides* was released, several hundred British war brides and their babies in Southampton, England, boarded the S.S. *Argentina* to sail for America. Not only did the occasion merit front-page

John Agar and John Wayne contemplate the battle ahead in a scene from Republic Pictures' *Sands of Iwo Jima*. L. TOM PERRY SPECIAL COLLECTIONS, BRIGHAM YOUNG UNIVERSITY, PROVO, UTAH

attention all over the world, but it also made the opening of *G.I. War Brides* a timely event.[13]

The most financially successful and critically acclaimed war movie made by Republic Pictures was the *Sands of Iwo Jima* starring John Wayne. This was a vast saga of a Marine platoon whose history was traced from its storming of Iwo Jima's beaches to the historic flag raising episode atop the sandy atoll. It was loaded with the commercial ingredients of blazing action, scope, and spectacle.[14]

Sands of Iwo Jima was producer Edmund Grainger's pet project. Inspired by the famous Joe Rosenthal photograph of a group of Marines planting the American flag at the Summit of Mount Suribachi and with a title for the project, Grainger had writers Harry Brown and James Edward Grant pen a screenplay. World War II was still a popular subject matter in 1948 and Yates knew it. He leapt at the chance to make a motion picture about the valiant Marines.[15]

Republic Pictures' executives initially budgeted one million dollars for the project, and, in the summer of 1949, the studio crew and actors traveled to Camp Pendleton in Oceanside, California, to begin filming.

The celebrated Lydecker brothers, special effects wizards at Republic, built hundreds of models, plaster creations, palm trees, pill boxes, and gun emplacements, and covered their makeshift beaches with sand and mixed oil into the setting so the combination would make the battle location look real. The goal was to make the film as realistic as possible.

The movie cost $2.5 million to make. Released at Christmas 1949, it was Republic's most expensive film to date. Yates never complained about being over budget because he was sure he had a major hit.

Critics called *Sands of Iwo Jima* a "gripping war picture." John Wayne's portrayal as the hard-bitten veteran Marine sergeant John Stryker, who takes a squad of twelve recruits through two major engagements, Tarawa and Iwo Jima, was praised for giving the best performance of his career.

"The battle scenes were fearfully convincing," an article in the December 31, 1949, edition of the *Brooklyn Daily Eagle* read. "There were times when the screen rocked under the simulation blasts of a half dozen different kinds of war munitions."[16]

Henry Ward, film reviewer for the *Pittsburgh Press*, called the movie a "triumph." In the December 30, 1949, edition of the *Pittsburgh Press*, he noted, "There are footprints on the sands of Iwo Jima that neither man nor time can ever erase. Republic Pictures has gone all out in a brave effort to make them immortal."[17]

Gossip columnist and actress Hedda Hopper wrote about *Sands of Iwo Jima* in the August 12, 1949, issue of the *Los Angeles Times*. Actual military personnel were used in the film, and many found the realism of the soundstage backgrounds sobering. "For a moment I felt as though I were back in the South Pacific," Gene Howland, leader of Pacific Operations during the war, shared with Hopper. "It was so real it was frightening."[18]

Sands of Iwo Jima received four Academy Award nominations: Best Editing, Best Sound Recording, Best Screenplay, and John Wayne for Best Actor. *Sands of Iwo Jima* was one of the highest grossing films of the 1949-1950 motion picture season.

Herbert Yates was pleased the handful of war pictures Republic produced did well. His decision to not make as many war films as his competitors was a calculated one. Yates believed the effects of World War II were so pervasive in the lives of American audiences they needed to see films that took their minds off the hardship and loss. He was convinced the studio should focus on making the chapter plays that had always attracted audiences and consistently made money. The war presented the necessity for change in the plots of the serials, but it was a change Yates was willing to allow as long as Captain Marvel, telepathic monsters, or singing cowboys were the heroes fighting against Nazis and Japanese villains.[19]

Republic began its battle against enemy villainy with *Spy Smasher*, a 1942 adventure starring Kane Richmond as the costumed comic book hero who battled a Nazi menace called the Mask. *Spy Smasher* was filled with acrobatic fight sequences and inventive chapter endings that found the hero being trapped in a tunnel by burning oil, locked in a flooded submarine compartment, and nearly being cremated in a pottery kiln.[20]

Spy Smasher had a twin brother who was in love with the daughter of an admiral. The admiral directed a counterespionage unit. That association made for powerful intrigue. The chapter play was popular with audiences thirteen and under. Fans of the serial could register to become members of the Spy Smasher Victory Club. Members received a special identification card and a button denoting membership.[21]

For those movie fans who liked heroes they could relate to who dressed in official uniforms, there was the twelve-part serial *King of the Mounties*. In this 1942 Republic production, theatergoers found Canada being bombed mercilessly by a mysterious enemy plane called the Falcon, under the supervision of Admiral Yamata, Count Baroni, and Marshal von Horst, chiefs of the Axis Fifth Column in Canada. No one could identify the plane until American inventor Professor Marshall Brent and his daughter Carol arrived with a new type of airplane detector.[22]

FACING PAGE: John Wayne and cast in *Sands of Iwo Jima*. L. TOM PERRY SPECIAL COLLECTIONS, BRIGHAM YOUNG UNIVERSITY, PROVO, UTAH

King of the Mounties was heralded by reviewers as one of the most thrilling and suspenseful chapter plays ever filmed. Popular star Allan Lane starred as Sergeant King of the Royal Canadian Mounted Police Air Patrol, the man who led the fight against the Axis spy ring. Carol Brent played the daughter of the man who created the detector that would help save them all.[23]

Based on the characters western author Zane Grey created for his book *King of the Royal Mounted*, *King of the Mounties* was billed as a "new page of heroic exploits destined to achieve immortal fame in the archives of history."[24]

William Witney, directing veteran of numerous serials for Republic Pictures, was in the director's seat for *King of the Mounties*. Howard and Theodore Lydecker provided the special effects for the series. The experts built full-scale models of planes, boats, trains, buildings, cars, and a volcano to use in the production. The Lydeckers used elaborate, well-timed pyrotechnic effects to destroy the Axis' secret base in the final chapter. "Audiences across the country cheered loudly at that part of the film," an article in the January 19, 1943, edition of *The Evening Times* reported. "It seemed to echo their desire to do away with the Nazi and Japanese forces in much the same manner."

As the war continued, the public had an insatiable appetite for films with secret agents as the protagonists, and Herbert Yates was more than willing to meet their demands. On January 16, 1943, Republic Pictures introduced patrons to the *G-Men vs. the Black Dragon*. It was up to the brave government agents of the allied nations, Rex Bennett (Rod Cameron), Chang Sing (Roland Got), and Vivian Marsh (Constance Worth), to stop the Japanese infiltrators of the Black Dragon Society. The nefarious group of spies led by the cunning Oyama Haruchi (Nino Pipitone) was working to destabilize the United States' war efforts through sabotage.

G-Men vs. the Black Dragon was a fifteen-part serial filled with non-stop action. There were fistfights, car and boat chases, exploding bridges, train crashes, and collapsing buildings. Studio promotional material let audiences know that each chapter was electric with thrills, that every scene was bursting with action, and that every episode was packed with pulse-pounding tension.

Try as they might, the Japanese spies in *G-Men vs. the Black Dragon* could not subvert America's war effort. That factor helped make the war serial a box office sensation grossing more than one million dollars and breaking the record held by the *Lone Ranger* serial. *G-Men vs. the Black Dragon* was so successful that star Rod Cameron's next serial, *Secret Service in Darkest Africa*, was rewritten as a sequel to *G-Men*.

In the chapter play *Secret Service in Darkest Africa*, G-Man Rex Bennett tangles mostly with Nazis and Arabs. The villains in the series attempt to control the entire Middle East and defeat the Allies. Nazi agent Baron von Rommler (Lionel Royce) captures and impersonates Sultan Abou Ben Ali, leader of the Arabs. Agent Bennett, British reporter Janet Blake (Joan Marsh), and police captain Pierre LaSalle (Duncan Renaldo) discover the Nazi's plan and work together to stop the enemy.[25]

The writers for *Secret Service in Darkest Africa* realized it would be quite a task crafting a series that rivaled *G-Men vs. the Black Dragon*. A sign on the door of the Republic Studio's serial department where six writers worked reflected their attitude toward the job. It read, "The difficult we do immediately. The impossible takes a little longer."[26]

The wordsmiths set the action in the first episode in Casablanca. Rod Cameron portrayed an American undercover agent who had been serving incognito with the Gestapo in Berlin. Through his connections there he learned, in detail, the Nazis' plans to swing the African Arabs to the Axis' cause, using as persuasion the Dagger of Solomon and a forged scroll purporting to be the words of an ancient Moslem leader.[27]

Audiences were not disappointed with *Secret Service in Darkest Africa*. It was filled with as many explosions and fight sequences as its predecessor.

Secret Service in Darkest Africa was one of the top five most expensive serials produced at Republic. It cost more than $210,000 to produce, but the return on the studio's investment more than made their money back.

The last serial Republic Pictures did focusing on aspects of World War II was called *The Masked Marvel*. In *The Masked Marvel*, released in late 1943, a hero dressed in a business suit and a face mask fought the Japanese saboteur Sakima and his espionage organization. *The Masked Marvel* was a twelve-part series, and the identity of the Masked Marvel was kept a secret until the last chapter. Stuntman Tom Steele was the real Masked Marvel. He did all the action work and wore the hero's mask, but he never received screen credit for the job. Five different actors portrayed the unmasked Masked Marvel. The actors were Bob Barton, Frank Jeffers, Terry Morton, David Bacon, and Jim Arnold.

The series featured a non-stop parade of spectacular destructive fights and explosions. The Lydecker brothers saw to it that the special effects were first rate. At the end of chapter 1, the Lydecker siblings blew up a full-scale model gas tank where the Masked Marvel and enemy agents were fighting.

The Masked Marvel was a hit with young audiences, but a great deal of the publicity surrounding the serial didn't call attention to the production value or the ticket buyers who flocked to the theaters. The promotion material focused on the real-life murder of one of the film's stars. David Bacon, one of the actors who portrayed the Masked Marvel when he wasn't wearing the mask, was found murdered in a bean field in Venice, California, on September 12, 1943. Bacon bled to death when his left lung was punctured with a knife. He was seen erratically driving his vehicle when it slowly came to a stop in the field. Authorities believed Bacon was stabbed prior to getting into his car.

The twenty-nine-year-old actor was practically nude when his body was discovered by police, and he was covered with cuts and bruises. Detectives speculated he was slain by a hitchhiker or chance acquaintance. Bacon was the son of Massachusetts lieutenant governor Gaspar G. Bacon. His murder remains unsolved.[28]

As long as the war lasted, the moviegoing experience remained the central, unifying wartime ritual for millions of Americans. When World War II was officially declared over on September 2, 1945, the era of post-war films was ushered in. Serial scriptwriters at Republic Studios returned to creating projects in which the antagonists were sinister scientists, gruesome ghouls, and other run-of-the-mill matinee villains.

Herbert Yates' Republic Pictures had promoted patriotism and American ideals through the movies that were produced. Studio executives were pleased to have had a part in the United States' crusade against tyranny and oppression.

The year 1946 proved to be one of the most profitable years in Republic Pictures' history, and, although many of the actors and key personnel at the studio celebrated their good fortune, they couldn't completely let down their guard. Another battle loomed on the horizon, one that would threaten their very existence—television.

Yakima Canutt, considered to be the best stuntman in motion picture history, was head of the stunt department at Republic Studios for a number of years.
AUTHOR'S COLLECTION

CHAPTER 7

The Stuntmen

A pair of frantic, disheveled riders race side by side down a dusty, sun-scorched path. Suddenly they plunge into a wooded area. Branches slap at them, but neither dares slow his mount's gait. They break through the other side, each still jockeying for lead position. The rider barely lagging behind now extends his arm out to grab the young man inches from him. The young man spurs his horse along faster and pulls away from the man trying to catch him. Ahead in the near distance, the crude path ends abruptly, giving way to a rocky cliff with a raging river far below. The two riders continue on fast, unaware of the danger. The young man is the first to leap off the precipice, his horse still under him. The rider behind him doesn't hesitate but pushes his roan harder. The two fly off the cliff with great speed and plummet into the water.

The daring riders find their way to the surface. They're dazed, but alive. The animals are alive as well, and they scramble to the water's edge and hastily step out onto dry land.

After fighting the river's strong current, both men manage to reach a sandy bank and drag themselves out of the water. They are exhausted and drenched. The young man struggles to stand up and, once he finds his footing, hurries off after his horse. The cowboy that was chasing him hasn't any strength left. He lies flat on his back on the bank staring up at the cliff where he dropped, contemplating how he could have survived such a fall.

That particular stunt was executed by legendary rodeo champion turned stunt-man Yakima Canutt for the film *The Devil Horse* starring Harry Carey. Canutt was one of the most well-known members of the group of dedicated men and women who were willing to risk their lives for little pay and no screen credit—the stunt person. When a script called for rough and tumble action such as a fistfight, car crash, or jumping off a seventy-two-foot cliff into a ravine without a net or soft landing pad, a stunt person was required.[1]

Republic Pictures had a stable of daredevils who lived to perform death-defying feats that kept audiences on the edge of their seats. Yakima Canutt and the other stunt staff revolutionized the art and helped make Republic features and serials some of the most exciting and profitable works in the motion picture industry.

Canutt appeared in more than two hundred films during his on-screen career, but he didn't start out wanting to be in the movies. He broke horses and for a while was content with the work. Canutt was born in Colfax, Washington, in 1895. He attended school until he was twelve, and then he went to work full-time on a ranch. He won his first world championship cowboy award in 1917. Canutt became one of the best-known saddle and bareback bronc riders on the rodeo circuit. He was often among the top money winners in what was then the roughest of all competitive sports.[2]

In between rodeos, he managed to break horses for the French government's use in World War I. He then dropped the rodeo circuit temporarily to enter the Navy and served aboard a minesweeper. In 1919, he regained his world championship crown, the second of the five total he earned.[3]

Canutt headed for the movies in 1923. He did forty-eight silent westerns before talkies took over. He didn't have a voice for talkies, so he made the leap to stunt work. He excelled in the field. He and John Wayne developed a way to stage on-screen fights to make them look more realistic. Prior to the development of the choreographed screen brawl, the good guy and the villain threw unrealistic punches at one another and wrestled and flailed around. A Canutt screen fight involved positioning of the camera at angles to the participants, rather than straight on, and the camera would often face one of the participants. That camera angle gave the perception of bone-crushing punches landing on the jaw.[4]

Not only did Canutt perform amazing stunts for the numerous pictures he was in, but he also choreographed stunt sequences for many movies in which he wasn't a part of the on-screen talent. Some of the movies Canutt choreographed stunt sequences for included *Flying Tigers*, *Spy Smasher*, and *Jungle Girl*.

Canutt became a second-unit director in addition to stuntman and stunt coordinator. In that capacity he directed breathtaking action sequences of some of Hollywood's most spectacular films; *Spartacus* and *Ben Hur* were two of those films. He also directed a number of low-budget westerns.

Canutt created and perfected a number of stunts for Republic Pictures, but the feat he is most famous for was used in a film both he and John Wayne appeared in with permission from Herbert Yates. That movie was *Stagecoach*.

In the film, Canutt portrayed a Comanche Indian who attacks the stagecoach in which John Wayne and costars were traveling. The stunt called for Canutt to jump from one team of horses to another while the teams pulled the racing stage. When he reached the lead team, he was "shot" and appeared to fall in front of the horses' slashing hooves. Instead, he grabbed the wagon tongue, swung below it, straightened himself out for a few feet, and then dropped to the ground between the horses. They passed on each side of the stuntman, and the stagecoach went directly over without touching him.[5]

"I had it pretty well figured out how I could do it without getting hurt," Canutt shared in a 1971 interview about performing that stunt. "I wanted to see how fast I could drag on my back without rolling. If I rolled either way, of course, I was dead. So I rigged up a drag on the back of an automobile and found that by relaxing my legs I could get up to fifty miles an hour without rolling. The horses couldn't run that fast."[6]

The stunt department at Republic Pictures was the envy of most of the studios. Canutt headed the department, overseeing the individuals who made the harrowing acts look real.

Tumbling champion Dave Sharpe was one of the studio's great work-horses. He doubled for many of Republic's talent. Sharpe performed his best in serials, providing unbelievable stunts with cars, wagons, and horses. Known as the Crown Prince of Daredevils or Little Dave Sharpe, he had a trim build and was only five feet, eight inches tall, which enabled him to double for female stars as well as men.

Sharpe appeared in several thousand films and serials including *Jungle Girl*, *Pals of the Pecos*, and *King of the Royal Mounted*. Some of the most daring work Sharpe did occurred when he was doubling for Tom Tyler in the serial *The Adventures of Captain Marvel*. In the performance of many stunts, Sharpe did such a good job of concealment that many of the movie audience never realized it was he.

While working on the western serial *The Adventures of Red Ryder*, Sharpe would do a variety of thrilling stunts. The horse transfer was the most common feat in Republic westerns. The gag, a term used to refer to a particular stunt, involved jumping from one horse to another at a dead run. He would also perform a horse-to-horse bulldog. That's when one horseman, generally the horseman playing the hero, is chasing another, generally the bad guy. When the hero catches up to the bad guy in the film, he jumps from his horse, grabs the other rider by the shoulders, and both go to the ground.[7]

The Running W was another popular gag used in the *Red Ryder* serials. In this particular act, wires or cuffs were attached to a horse's

Stuntman David Sharpe suits up to perform death-defying work for another Republic serial. AUTHOR'S COLLECTION

forelegs and run through slip rings on the saddle cinch underneath the animal. The wire was anchored to the ground via a stake, and, when the wire went taut as the horse galloped along, the legs pulled up toward his belly causing him to tumble. The rider on the animal had to tumble off the horse at just the right time. This type of Running W was banned in late 1930 because dozens of horses died while taking part in the gag. The stunt was replaced with horses that were trained to trip and fall without any apparatus. It required a skilled rider or stunt person to help pull off the effect.[8]

Sharpe had a reputation for making his stunts look seamless. His background in gymnastics aided his ability to perform the gags with ease. In episode twelve of *The Adventures of Red Ryder*, Sharpe performed a somersault while falling from a wagon. In an episode of *Buck Rogers*, he crashed through a window, did a somersault, and punched the bad guy in the jaw in one fluid motion.

Stunt work came easy for college football legend Dale Van Sickel. The All-American football player for the University of Florida began his career in motion pictures in 1933 performing stunts alongside the Marx Brothers in the film *Duck Soup*. The handsome, five-foot, ten-inch athlete was hired on at Republic Pictures in early 1936 and appeared in more than 140 movies and serials for the studio including *Haunted Harbor*, *Manhunt on Mystery Island*, *Canadian Mounties vs Atomic Invaders*, and *Captain America*.[9]

Van Sickel often played a heavy who got into fistfights with the hero of the film. He was famous for literally launching himself off a wall, then "flying" directly into the actor he was battling. Whenever he worked opposite fellow stuntman Tom Steele, the two would plan out the fight sequences in detail. One gag that went into most every brawl was that either Van Sickel or Steele would toss the other over his shoulder, turn him upside down, and flip him onto a bookcase or fireplace mantel.[10]

Although Van Sickel was more than capable in fistfights, he excelled in car and motorcycle stunts. In chapter 4 of the *Captain Marvel* serial entitled *Preview of Murder*, the stuntman, dressed in superhero garb, leaped onto a motorcycle to quickly pursue a robot-controlled truck. Van Sickel as Captain America then dumped the motorcycle, rushed to a hilltop, and leaped onto the truck as it sped along the road. Grasping the roof of the truck as it skidded and squealed along the winding mountain road, Captain America managed to get inside just before the driverless vehicle crashed into a building and exploded in a blinding flare of fire and smoke.

The work Van Sickel did for Republic prepared him to take part in notable films such as *Spartacus*, *North by Northwest*, and Steven Spielberg's *Duel*.

In July 1975, Van Sickel was seriously injured while filming an attempted stunt. He was driving a car that was supposed to go off the end of an oil-slicked wharf in a Walt Disney production. The car skidded into an abutment, and doctors said the stuntman suffered brain damage. He died on January 25, 1977, from further complications resulting from the accident.[11]

One of Republic Pictures' most capable and rugged stuntmen was Kenneth Jones Terrell. Terrell was with Republic Pictures longer than any other stuntman in the history of the studio, from 1939 to 1954. A former body builder, Terrell got his start as a model and then in vaudeville where he was a part of a juggling and tumbling act. He moved from New York to Los Angeles in 1937 and quickly landed a role in an RKO film entitled *Living on Love*. Work as a stunt person came more frequently than acting, and Ken decided to continue in that line. He made the move to Republic Studios in mid-1939 where he appeared in hundreds of serials and motion pictures.

Among the more than fifteen hundred stunts he performed in popular serials such as *Spy Smasher*, *Mysterious Doctor Satan*, and *Drums of Fu Manchu* were knife and sword fights, high dives, long swims, and Ju

Dale Harrison Van Sickel was one of Republic's best stuntmen. AUTHOR'S COLLECTION

Jitsu–style fights. Terrell specialized in fights that took place on catwalks, ladders, and rooftops. He had great upper body strength and could swing from fixtures and beams over open spaces.[12]

Terrell performed in a few projects after leaving Republic Studios. His most notable role was that of the butler in the 1958 film *Attack of the 50 Foot Woman*. The same year the movie was released, Terrell broke his ankle acting out a stunt in a Chevrolet commercial. He never fully recovered from the injury, and his career suffered as a result. He died on March 8, 1966, at the age of sixty-one.

Second only to Yakima Canutt, Tom Steele is probably the most recognizable name in the history of stuntmen at Republic Pictures. Born in Scotland as Thomas Skeoch and transplanted in America at an early age, Steele was an expert equestrian who played professional polo. He entered the motion picture industry in 1930 after laboring in a steel mill for a number of years. The country was struggling with a depression when he decided to try his hand at acting and made the move from northern California to Hollywood. He changed his name to Steele when he arrived in Los Angeles because he believed it would help him land a part in a film.[13]

Steele found work quickly making his screen debut in the western *The Lone Star Ranger*. Apart from that role, acting jobs were few and far between. Perhaps that was because Steele's voice didn't seem to fit his persona. In the series *The Masked Marvel*, in which Steele was the star, radio actor Gayne Whitman spoke for him, and Steele mouthed the words. Acting jobs might have been hard to come by, but the call for Steele to do stunt work was steady, so he decided to focus on the latter.[14]

Steele went to work for Republic in 1935. He was the only stuntman ever actually under contract with the studio. Herbert Yates believed Steele had the perfect leading man look and insisted film directors at Republic cast their serial heroes based in part on their resemblance to the stuntman. Steele usually played the man behind the mask, portraying

FACING PAGE: Stuntman and actor Tom Steele as the Masked Marvel defends himself against one of the many villains in the chapter play. AUTHOR'S COLLECTION

numerous parts in one serial. In a couple of Republic chapter plays, *Undersea Kingdom* and *Mysterious Doctor Satan*, he even played mechanical robots.

Steele became the head of the studio's stunt department in the 1940s, and he stayed with the company until its glory days ended in the late 1950s. His most notable role at Republic came when he was cast as the Masked Marvel. He played the part entirely wearing a thin, black mask that fit over his eyes and down his cheeks. He not only performed all his own stunts in the serial but also doubled for other actors doing all their gags as well. Steele received no on-screen credits.

Steele was good at fistfights and falls but was noted for gags that called for him to be set on fire. In 1951, he performed one of the first full-body burns in the film *The Thing From Another World*. He wore an asbestos suit with a special fiberglass helmet with an oxygen supply underneath.

Tom Steele's career continued long after his time at Republic had ended. He went on to do stunts in many films including *McLintock!*, *Cat Ballou*, and *Our Man Flint*. He was eighty-one when he died on October 30, 1990.[15]

One of the hardest working stuntmen at Republic was Cliff "Tex" Lyons. He regularly stood in for western actors Buck Jones, Tom Mix, and Ken Maynard. Born in South Dakota in 1901, Lyons traveled the country as a rodeo rider. When he reached Los Angeles in 1922 he decided to pursue a career as an actor. He had moderate success in silent, western pictures, proving himself to be versatile enough to play both the hero and the heavy. Like others who tried to make the transition from silent films to talkies, Lyons' voice was lacking, and he was relegated to only small roles.

Lyons was an agile stuntman, and what he lacked in acting jobs he more than made up for working as a double for lead talent. One of the men he doubled for was John Wayne. The two were not only work colleagues but also friends off the set. Lyons not only worked with Wayne at

Republic Studios but also was hired to coordinate stunts for films made at Wayne's production company. *The Green Berets*, *Big Jake*, and *The Alamo* were just a few of the pictures Lyons worked on for Wayne.

Among the gags that Lyons was called on to perform in many Republic serials was transferring from a galloping horse onto the back of a stage, riding a bucking horse that needed to be broken, and scooping heroines into his arms as he rode by them at a full gallop. Lyons worked behind the camera, too, as a second unit director on such films as *The War Wagon* and *Chisum*.

The last film Lyons did was *The Train Robbers* in 1973. He passed away on January 6, 1974.

It was a given that stuntmen needed to be daring to attempt the gags directors asked them to perform. The most responsible stuntmen planned each gag with precision, anticipating what could go wrong and making allowances. Stuntman Duke Green wasn't detail oriented. He wasn't reckless, but he wasn't as cautious as others. He executed falls and leaps so fantastic his cohorts referred to him as "Crazy Duke." His career began in 1925 when he doubled for John Barrymore in *The Sea Beast*. He was born in Los Angeles and was a tumbler, competitive swimmer, and fancy diver. His diving talent came in handy when it came to stunt work. He often made leaps off buildings, ships, or mountain ledges. In 1941, he was paid eight hundred dollars to fight atop a power pole for the movie *Man Power*.[16]

While performing a difficult stunt on the set of *The Flame and the Arrow*, Green broke his neck. The stunt called for his foot to be trapped in a snare and for the stuntman to then be whipped off the ground. The rigging holding Green in place broke, and he was dropped head first into the ground, breaking his neck. He never fully recovered from the injury. He passed away in 1984 at eighty-four years old.

One of the highest paid stuntmen in Hollywood began his career at

Cliff Lyons was recognized as the hardest working stuntman at Republic Pictures. AUTHOR'S COLLECTION

Republic Pictures in the mid-1930s. Eddie Parker moved to California from Minnesota in 1931 to try his hand at acting. He did appear in front of the camera in movies such as *The Star Packer* and *The Trail Beyond* with John Wayne. He had promise as an actor, but stunt work turned out to be his true passion.

Parker, a former vaudeville dancer and weight lifter, was a big man standing six feet, four inches and weighing more than two hundred pounds. He was the perfect double for John Wayne and actor Ray Corrigan. He portrayed a henchman in many Republic productions such as *Undersea Kingdom*, *The Three Mesquiteers*, and *Radar Patrol vs. Spy King*. Parker's specialty was fistfights and barroom brawls.

Parker amassed a staggering number of credits in his career at Republic and elsewhere. He was recognized by movie studios outside Republic as one of the most reliable stuntmen in the business. Audience members didn't recognize Parker in his most successful stunt performances. That's because he was wearing costumes in a series of horror films. He was the wrapped protagonist in *Abbott and Costello Meet the Mummy* and the giant monster in *Frankenstein Meets the Wolfman*. He was also Mr. Hyde to Boris Karloff's Mr. Jekyll in *Abbott and Costello Meet Dr. Jekyll and Mr. Hyde*. Parker broke his ankle in that particular film jumping from rooftop to rooftop. He wore a cast during the completion of the shooting of the film. He walked with a limp but that only added to the sinister countenance of Mr. Hyde.[17]

Parker died of a heart attack in 1960 at the age of fifty-nine. He was rehearsing a fight sequence for a television program when he collapsed.

Minor league baseball player Charles "Fred" Graham entered the motion picture industry with the help of the actors Robert Young and Nat Pendleton. Graham was hired by MGM to train the actors for their roles in the film *Death on the Diamond*. The three men became fast friends, and Young and Pendleton encouraged the athletic Graham to pursue a career as actor and stuntman. He had a variety of bit parts before deciding to focus solely on stunting. While with Republic Pictures, he appeared in more than fifty westerns and twenty-two serials. He traded on-screen punches with Roy Rogers, Rex Allen, and Monte Hale. Graham was known as one of the best fight men in the industry. He could expertly act out the power and intensity of a punch he delivered and use the same acting skill when taking a punch. Graham was good at "selling the blow," as stuntmen referred to it. The technique he employed to show the impact of a punch he would take consisted of using head movements to register the blow, keeping the lips loose, and letting the body go temporarily limp before spinning out of control.[18]

Like all the other stuntmen in Republic Studios' stable of stunt performers, Graham played many roles within a single chapter play. In the western *Silver City Kid*, he can be seen in one saloon brawl as three different characters.

Graham retired from motion pictures in the late 1960s and moved to Scottsdale, Arizona, where he was appointed the first director of the Arizona Film Commission.[19]

When a Republic Pictures' script called for rough and tumble action, the studios had the finest stunt people in the business to take on the job. Herbert Yates and his executives needed the talents of Yakima Canutt and his crew to preserve the illusion that the star of a picture was really being hit with a fist, falling off a cliff, or pushed off a moving stagecoach. Republic serials and movies were successful because theatergoers weren't able to detect where the actor left off and the stuntman took over.

John Wayne and Shaila Mannors strike a pose in the film *Westward Ho*. Mt. Whitney looms in the background. AUTHOR'S COLLECTION

CHAPTER 8

The Second Hollywood

About two hundred miles north of Hollywood is the small town of Lone Pine. Almost at the dawn of motion picture making, the Eastern Sierra hamlet became a popular outpost for location filming. It offered scenery ranging from Sierra peaks to sand dunes. The mountain scenery there could double for the Himalayas, and the desert landscape could double for Salt Lake Valley. Lone Pine has proven to be as versatile as some of the most gifted actors performing on screen.

Movie cowboys from Hopalong Cassidy to John Wayne and Gene Autry to Rex Allen chased innumerable bad guys in the hills around Lone Pine. The cry of "Hi-Yo, Silver, Away!" still echoes through the canyon where the masked marvel and his sidekick Tonto rode. The songs sung by Roy Rogers can still be heard in the hills on quiet nights, and the report from shotguns fired by hundreds of celluloid outlaws ricochet off the ancient rocks.

Films requiring a foreign country's rocky, desert landscape have been shot at Lone Pine. Even films depicting lunar landscapes have been shot on location there. Lone Pine has served as a supporting player of sorts for more than fifty studios for more than ninety years.

The first movie production came to Lone Pine in 1914. It was a William S. Hart western, but the name of the project has been lost to time. Historical records note that the town's elders recalled only that it involved "a lot of riding and shooting" and that practically every able-bodied male in the community was pressed into service to portray either a law-abiding vigilante or one of the bad men being chased by Hart.

Mount Whitney, the highest summit in the contiguous United States and Sierra Nevada, was the backdrop to numerous Republic Pictures films.
AUTHOR'S COLLECTION

The 1920 silent film *The Roundup*, starring Rosco "Fatty" Arbuckle and Wallace Beery, was the first commercial production shot at Lone Pine. Locals loaned horses, wagons, and talent to make the movie. Lone Pine evolved from being a mining community when it was founded in 1865 to being one of the most favored spots to shoot motion pictures. Owens Valley in which the community is situated is regarded as one of nature's masterpieces. Surrounded by massive ranges, it is not only one of the most richly endowed scenic areas in the world but also one of the most compelling.[1]

Most of the actual filming at Lone Pine was either done on the desert bed of the valley, which is rimmed on all sides by towering mountains, or in the hills. From Lone Pine itself can be seen seven peaks more than fourteen thousand feet high, with Mt. Whitney reaching 14,496 feet into the sky. Nearby Death Valley, on the other hand, is 287 feet below sea level. There is snow all year on the mountain tops, and Palisade Glacier, the most southerly glacier in the United States, is less than sixty miles away.[2]

Republic Pictures' president Herbert Yates was enamored with Lone Pine and suggested the setting to film John Wayne's first feature for the studio, *Westward Ho*. Wayne plays a character named John Wyatt who, at a young age, saw his parents killed and his brother kidnapped. Wayne's character is leading a wagon train west when he meets up with his brother now working for the people who murdered their mother and father. The movie received high marks, and one of the reasons cited is that it was filmed on location and not on the studio's backlot.

An article in the September 6, 1935, edition of *The Times Recorder* noted:

A saga of the Old West filled with wagon trains, herds of cattle, marauding bandits, and singing vigilantes, *Westward Ho* has all the ingredients needed for a successful outdoor, action picture. The story deals with a group of "Singing Riders" led by a young Westerner who protects the slow moving covered wagons against the onslaught of vicious desperados. Romance has its full share of the plot of *Westward Ho*. John Wayne, as the leader of the "Singing Riders," fights successfully against terrific odds, but succumbs to the charms of lovely Sheila Manners.

The photography of Archie Stout and the direction of R. N. Bradbury are outstanding. So too is the landscape where the magnificent film was made. Long after the movie has ended theatergoers will want to seek this idyllic spot out and linger in its beauty.[3]

Many scenes from *Westward Ho* were filmed with the Alabama Hills as the backdrop. The Alabama Hills were named in the 1860s during the Civil War by Southern sympathizers in honor of the Confederate warship CSS *Alabama*. There are three thousand acres associated with the Alabama Hills and hundreds of natural rock arches. It was the perfect area for Wayne's character to capture the villain Black Bart and his gang.

Republic Pictures wasted no time in utilizing both Wayne and the Alabama Hills in its next picture *The New Frontier*. In Wayne's second outing for the studio, he's once again on the hunt for a man who killed his parents. Following in his father's footsteps, he takes the job of sheriff in the town where he had died. Actor Warner Richmond is the saloon-keeper, the villain who has a razor-edged brim to his black hat; actor Al Bridge is the good outlaw who, with his gang, comes to Wayne's aid and kills Richmond at the cost of his own life.

The Alabama Hills were regularly used as the setting for many westerns. AUTHOR'S COLLECTION

Several sequences in *The New Frontier* aren't new at all; it's stock footage of the Cherokee strip land rush and footage from Ken Maynard's silent film, *The Red Raiders*.

In addition to the magnificent rocks scattered about the Alabama Hills that are used in abundance in this feature, the director, Carl Pierson, included shots of the snow-covered Sierra Nevada and Mount Whitney. The lofty, snow-capped mountains, deep canyons, and vast expanses of glacially carved terrain loomed large and beautiful in the scenes where Wayne was pursuing desperadoes across the plains. The trouble was that the setting for the story was Kansas, and there are no snow-covered mountain ranges in the state.

The panoramic scenery around Lone Pine served as the backdrop for another Republic film set in the Midwest in 1938. *Under Western Stars*, directed by Joseph Kane, starred Roy Rogers and Smiley Burnette. Rogers portrayed a principled man elected to Congress to bring the misery of the dustbowl of the 1930s to the attention of Washington politicians. Kane was much more selective about the terrain he included in the film, limiting himself solely to the Alabama Hills. The result was a motion picture that moved audiences and once again brought attention to the hazard of deep plowing in dry lands.

In 2009, *Under Western Stars* was selected for the National Film Registry by the Library of Congress for being "culturally, historically or aesthetically" significant and will be preserved for all time. As noted by

FACING PAGE: Republic's 1938 picture *Storm Over Bengal* was filmed in the Alabama Hills at Lone Pine, California. L. TOM PERRY SPECIAL COLLECTIONS, BRIGHAM YOUNG UNIVERSITY, PROVO, UTAH

Howard Kazanjian and Chris Enss in *Under Western Stars: An Essay for the National Film Registry*:

King of the Cowboys Roy Rogers made his starring motion picture debut in Republic Studio's engaging, western musical *Under Western Stars*. Released in 1938, the charming, affable Rogers portrayed the most colorful congressman ever to walk up the steps of the nation's capital. Rogers' character, a fearless, two-gun cowboy and ranger from the western town of Sageville, is elected to office to try to win legislation favorable to dust bowl residents.

Rogers represents a group of ranchers whose land has dried up when a water company controlling the only dam decides to keep the coveted liquid from the hard-working cattlemen. Spurred on by his secretary and publicity manager Frog Millhouse, played by Smiley Burnette, Rogers campaigns for office. The portly Burnette provides much of the film's comic relief and goes to extremes to get his friend elected. His tactics include pasting stickers on the backs of unsuspecting citizens he engages in conversation and helping to organize a square dance to highlight Rogers' skill and dedication to solving the constituents' crisis. Using his knowledge of land and livestock and his talent for singing and yodeling, Rogers wins a seat in Congress.

The sweep of this picture, which moves rapidly from physical action on the western plains to diplomatic action in Washington and back again, is distinctively thrilling. The surging climax in the dust-stricken cattle country makes for one of the most refreshing films of its kind. The politicians Rogers appeals to about the drought are not convinced the situation is as serious as they are led to believe and decide to inspect the scene for themselves. The investigation committee is eventually trapped in a real dust storm. The shots of the storm and the devastation left in its wake are spectacular.

Roy Rogers came to Hollywood from Duck Run, Ohio. He made a name for himself as a member of the successful singing group the Sons of the Pioneers. Reigning box office cowboy Gene Autry's difficulties with Herbert Yates, head of Republic Studios, paved the way for Rogers to ride into the leading role in *Under Western Stars*. Yates felt he alone was responsible for creating Autry's success in films and wanted a portion of the revenue he made from the image he helped create. Yates demanded a percentage of any commercial, product endorsement, merchandising, and personal appearance Autry made. Autry did not believe Yates was entitled to the money he earned outside the movies made for Republic Studios. He refused to include Yates in the profits and threatened to leave the studio if Yates did not reconsider. Autry was also demanding a raise in pay.

Yates decided it was time to begin grooming another talent to take Autry's place should the need arise. Rogers was a contract player with the studio making seventy-five dollars a week. Billed as Leonard Slye, he appeared in a handful of films with Gene Autry singing along with the Sons of the Pioneers. Rogers even had a part as a bad guy in one of Autry's films. When Autry caught up with Rogers in the picture, instead of taking him to jail he demanded the wily character yodel his way out of his troubles.

Yates had been looking for a musical actor to go boot-to-boot with Autry, and Rogers was to be the heir apparent. His sweet, pure voice and wholesome image made him a natural for the hero in *Under the Western Stars*. Whether regaling the audience with a song about fighting the law entitled "Send Our Mail to the County Jail" or delivering a stump speech via a tune called "Listen to Rhythm of the Range," Rogers makes the most of his leading role.

The Maple City Four, the well-known quartet who made the number "Git Along Little Dogies" popular, added their talents to Rogers' harmonizing on the film's most important song entitled "Dust." Written by Johnny Marvin, a recording artist from Oklahoma, "Dust" was nominated for an Academy Award for Best Original Song. It was the first song from a B western to be Oscar nominated.

According to the February 24, 1938, edition of the *Hollywood Reporter*, "Dust" was purchased by Republic Studios from the composers Gene Autry and Johnny Marvin for use in *Under Western Stars*. A subsequent news item in *Hollywood Reporter* on April 13, 1938, just prior to the film's release noted that Autry was suing the studio for twenty-five thousand dollars for unauthorized use and dramatization of the lyrics with "Dust." According to contemporary sources, the suit over "Dust" was settled out of court, and Johnny Marvin is listed as sole writer of the song.[4]

Audiences made *Under Western Stars* a box office success, and critics called its star "the new Playboy of the Western World."

Director Joseph Kane, Republic's top director of westerns, delivered a film with a slight new slanting to make it different from all other B westerns before it. In addition to the political intrigue in *Under Western Stars*, there is a fair amount of gunfights, fast horses, and unforgettable stunts. What makes Kane's film unique is that the fight is not over horse thieves but the rights of man. Critics at the *Brooklyn Daily Eagle* newspaper cited Kane's "sensitive directing eye with giving the horse opera a social consciousness."[5]

Actors Carol Hughes, Guy Usher, Tex Cooper, Kenneth Harlan, Curley Dresden, Bill Wolfe, Jack Ingram, Jack Kirk, Fred Burns, and Tom Chatterton round out the exciting cast of players, and no happy ending would be possible at all if not for Roy's magnificent palomino horse Trigger. Brothers and veteran western writers Dorrell and Stuart McGowan penned the screenplay for *Under Western Stars* along with actress and screenwriter Betty Burbridge.

The film was shot in the Alabama Hills of Lone Pine, California. The scenic location has been used for the backdrop in hundreds of motion pictures and television programs. The high desert surroundings are integral to the storyline of *Under Western Stars* and could be billed as a supporting role in the film.

Roy Rogers' first starring vehicle solidified his place as a rising star in B westerns. Film writer and critic Louella Parsons likened Rogers to "Gary Cooper in personal appeal." According to her report with the *International News Service* on November 29, 1938, she called Rogers an "upstanding young American who made the picture *Under Western Stars* a delight."

According to the May 7, 1938, edition of the *Hollywood Reporter*, *Army Girl*, starring Madge Evans and Preston Foster, was the second largest budgeted picture in Republic Studios' history. The story of *Army Girl* centers on life at several United States' posts. Preston Foster is seen as "Duke" Conger, a tank expert, who is sent out to mechanize various army posts. Conger, somewhat of a ladies' man, meets and falls in love with the daughter of a post commander, played by Madge Evans. Trouble ensues and the plot develops into a minor civil war.[6]

Directed by George Nichols Jr., *Army Girl* offers gigantic and powerfully sweeping scenes depicting military maneuvers between the cavalry and tanks. Those maneuvers, or "tests," had been ordered by army headquarters to determine whether a cavalry regiment near the Mexican border shall be mechanized. The rugged Alabama Hills were used as the setting for the romantic comedy.[7]

Cinematographers Ernest Miller and Harry Wild beautifully filmed the landscape of Lone Pine for the picture. Once the movie was released, audiences and filmmakers expressed an enthusiastic interest in the area. Fans everywhere wrote letters to Republic Pictures inquiring about the "scenic beauty" in the film.[8]

Harry Sherman Productions, a competing film company that made the *Hopalong Cassidy* features, was also being bombarded with notes about the area. Producer Harry Sherman decided to give feature billing to the place in which the movies were filmed. On-screen at the beginning of the *Hopalong* pictures appeared the announcement: Filmed at Lone Pine, California.[9]

One of the most famous serials of all time was filmed in Alabama Hills in 1938. *The Lone Ranger* rode through the picturesque rock formation near the eastern slope of the Sierra Nevada on his faithful steed Silver, fighting bandits alongside his friend Ponto.* The fifteen-part chapter play, based on the radio program of the same name, was the first serial Republic Pictures produced. Lee Powell portrayed the masked hero in the inaugural introduction of the character.

Born in Long Beach, California, in 1908, Powell attended the University of Montana where he studied dramatics, and when he graduated he tried his luck in Hollywood. *The Lone Ranger* was the second film he ever made. A smart studio manager practically blueprinted what the Lone Ranger as an individual should look like, then set about finding a man who filled all the specifications in the blueprint. Powell was selected.[10]

---

* The name Ponto was used first in the film because Tonto in Spanish means stupid.

Powell portrayed the Lone Ranger on screen, but when the Lone Ranger calls out "Hi-Yo, Silver, Away!" it's not Powell's voice that is heard. It's the voice of Earle W. Grasher, the radio's Lone Ranger.[11]

In *The Lone Ranger*, movie audiences find the Lone Ranger and Ponto coming to the assistance of five lawmen struggling to foil a gang of outlaws planning to take over the State of Texas at the end of the Civil War. Tightly filmed with heart-stopping action, talented Republic Pictures' camera crews maneuvered around rocky outcroppings of the Alabama Hills in an effort to convey to the audience a great sense of urgency in many of the action-packed scenes.

Numerous Republic Pictures cowboys rode after outlaws traveling through Turtle Canyon. AUTHOR'S COLLECTION

Filming of *The Lone Ranger* took place from November 28, 1937, to December 31, 1937. The budget only permitted seven days of shooting in the Alabama Hills. It cost $168,777 to make and grossed more than $650,000. It was the most financially successful serial in Republic Pictures history.[12]

Preparations to film the Gene Autry picture *In Old Monterey* at Lone Pine were being made as the shooting for *The Lone Ranger* was wrapping up. Autry plays an army attaché assigned to buy out-of-the-way land for use as a practice bombing range. The villains in the movie are un-American types trying to make a quick buck buying land and selling it to the Army at inflated prices.[13]

In Old Monterey was one of several films Autry made at Lone Pine. According to the biography *Public Cowboy No. 1: The Life and Times of Gene Autry*, Autry always enjoyed his time at Lone Pine and spoke fondly of it. He had a great appreciation for the otherworldly landscape of the foothills.[14]

Movies Autry had previously made in Lone Pine, such as *Oh, Susanna*, helped to increase tourism. Filmed in 1936, *Oh, Susanna* featured a modern-day dude ranch setting, the fictitious Mineral Springs Ranch, set in the exquisite scenery of the eastern Sierra Nevada. The idyllic surroundings highlighted in the picture prompted moviegoers to make the pilgrimage to the area, which in turn stimulated economic growth.

In 1939, Roy Rogers visited the Alabama Hills again to film the movie *Saga of Death Valley*. The picture was Rogers' twelfth western made at Republic. Principal photography included not only shots of the Lone Pine's most photographed chunks of granite but also parts of Death Valley, too, ninety miles east of Lone Pine. "That was the benefit of making a movie in Lone Pine," Republic Pictures' director Joseph Kane noted in an interview about the Rogers' film. "There's a variety of terrain available that suits the scripts most popular at Republic."

In *Saga of Death Valley*, Rogers once again takes on a water baron who uses control of water rights to drive local ranchers into poverty. That theme worked well in the film *Under Western Stars*, so the studio decided to reuse the plot. Roy galloped to the rescue apprehending the bad guys in the nick of time. Critics called *Saga of Death Valley* a "sure-fire hit for all ages."[15]

Filmed in the Alabama Hills, *Wagons Westward* starred Buck Jones and Chester Morris and was released in 1940. The film is noticeable for cowboy hero Jones being cast against type as a cold-blooded, evil sheriff, but little else about the movie is memorable. Morris plays twin brothers: one good, one bad. He impersonates his worse half to capture characters played by Guinn Williams and Douglas Fowley, only to have dance-hall girl Louise mistake him for his brother and demand the marriage she has been promised.

Herbert Yates initially wanted John Wayne to play the lead, but director Lew Landors was able to convince the studio boss that Wayne wasn't the dual brother type. According to the August 5, 1947, edition of the *Lubbock Evening Journal*, Landors, one of the industry's most prolific directors, enjoyed working in Lone Pine. "The rock formations change color depending on the time of day one films in the hills," he is reported to have shared.[16] "There's plenty of open space to work with, too. It is a grand frontier." A review of *Wagons Westward* in the October 11, 1940, edition of *The Plain Speaker* echoed Landors' sentiments. "It's an unforgettable epic of the Old West," the article noted. "A story of the last frontier before our territories were cut up into pieces; made all the more satisfying because it was filmed on the vast, scenic frontier near Mount Whitney."[17]

Proving the versatility of the Lone Pine region, Republic Pictures shot a film calling for a North African backdrop at the location. Entitled *Perils of Nyoka*, the story centers on an expedition into the hills of Libya where a professor obtains a papyrus that might reveal the hiding place of the Golden Tablets of Hippocrates, containing lost medical secrets. The movie stars Kay Aldridge as Nyoka the Jungle Girl. Nyoka's job is to help the benevolent expedition team reach the tablets before the evil Queen Vultura, ruler of the Arabs, and her team. The task isn't easy. Nyoka encounters robed henchmen who chase her through the arid landscape driving chariots, strap her to a sacrificial altar where swinging blades drop slowly from the ceiling inches away from her torso, and force her to the edge of a jagged cliff. Although audiences enjoyed the stirring, adventurous chapters and scenes where Nyoka and Queen Vultura physically fought, they struggled with the production. Moviegoers recognized the hills where the action sequences were filmed. They noticed it looked a great deal like the hills where many B westerns were shot. Instead of paying attention to the on-screen action, audiences were busy naming other movies filmed at the location.[18]

Film enthusiasts would see the same majestic setting in the 1943 film *Song of Texas* starring Roy Rogers. Roy plays a singing rodeo star who helps a man who lost his ranch. He enters a chuck wagon race in order to win back the property. Lone Pine portrayed New Mexico in this western. The opening shot is of Lone Pine Peak in the background and Owens Valley in the foreground. Roy rides through the Alabama Hills to gather friends to assist in his benevolent quest.

An article in the August 21, 1943, edition of *The News Leaders* announced,

> Audiences who have become annoyed with the sameness of the run-of-the-time western pictures have a treat in store for them when they see Republic's big, new Roy Rogers' deluxe production *Song of Texas*. Tired of the same story-lines, scenery and show-downs? This picture has something more. There is a definite, exciting plot that will have audiences on the edge of their chairs.
>
> The old cliff-hanger, western formula was scrapped, and a modern believable story with a prominent female character will be introduced.
>
> The story, built around a modern rodeo circuit has thrill a plenty, action and outstanding production value. Even the way this movie has been photographed is fresh and appealing.[19]

Republic Pictures filmed more than forty movies and serials at Lone Pine. If not for the fact that so many other studios were competing to shoot at the location, Republic might have made more features there. Lone Pine was referred to by many in the motion picture industry as the "second Hollywood." It may not have been known by that name to the average Republic Pictures' fan, but it's certain its terrain was as familiar to them as Gene Autry, Roy Rogers, and John Wayne.

Republic Pictures Movies Filmed at Lone Pine from 1935 to 1957

1935

Lawless Range

The New Frontier

Westward Ho

1936

Comin' Round the Mountain

King of the Pecos

Oh, Susanna!

The Oregon Trail

1937

Boots and Saddles

Gunsmoke Ranch

Rootin' Tootin' Rhythm

Wild Horse Rodeo

1938

Army Girl

The Lone Ranger

The Old Barn Dance

Under Western Stars

Storm Over Bengal

1939

In Old Monterey

Saga of Death Valley

1940

Hi-Yo Silver

Melody Ranch

Three Faces West

Wagons Westward

1941

Down Mexico Way

1942

Perils of Nyoka

1943

Daredevils of the West

The Man from Music Mountain

Song of Texas

1944

Hands Across the Border

1945

Utah

1946

Plainsman and the Lady

1947

Trail to San Antone

1950

Under Mexicali Stars

1957

Gunfire at Indian Gap

Actress Gail Russell

CHAPTER 9

Republic's Leading Ladies

There were many talented female contract players at Republic Pictures. In the mid-1940s, the studio had more than 120 actors in its stable of gifted individuals. Some of those actresses became household names because of their work in front of the camera, and others rose to fame as a result of their off-screen exploits. The following is a look at a few of the studio's most recognizable and popular women thespians, their careers, and the roles that made them stars.

One of Republic Pictures' most popular actresses was one of the motion picture industry's most troubled. Her name was Gail Russell. Russell, a beautiful brunette with dark, blue eyes, was a gifted talent who dreamed of becoming a commercial artist. She was born Elizabeth L. Russell in Chicago on September 21, 1924. Throughout her childhood, she was painfully shy and often hid under her parents' piano whenever guests came to their home. The young girl only felt completely comfortable when she was sketching various people and places in her sphere of influence. She began drawing at the age of five and was considered exceptional by most who saw her sketches and paintings.

When she was in her late teens, her mother, Gladys Russell, encouraged her to set aside her drawing pencils and venture into films. Russell was fourteen when her parents moved to Los Angeles so their daughter could pursue their dream of her becoming a star. She attended Santa Monica High School, and as soon as she graduated, she auditioned for Paramount Pictures and signed a contract with the studio for fifty dollars a week.

Russell's shyness followed her as she began her career. Acting instructors were hired to help her overcome her timidity, but it never completely subsided. It did add to her haunting persona, and she was cast in roles where that part of her personality could be highlighted. As her star rose in the industry, her fear of performing became more pronounced. With each film it took more effort to overcome her lack of self-confidence and commit to the part. While filming *The Uninvited* in 1944, Russell chose to deal with her paralyzing self-doubt by drinking. Alcohol did not quiet her nerves; it merely made her more anxious. By the end of the production, she had become dependent on liquor and was on the brink of a nervous breakdown. *The Uninvited* was a critical success, and the film was nominated for an Academy Award. Russell became even more popular thanks to the film. She went on to work with such stars as Alan Ladd and Joel McCrea, Jane Wyatt and Adolphe Menjou. The work was continuous and the pace grueling. Russell dealt with the frantic schedules the same way she did with her shyness, by drinking.

In 1946 Russell starred in the first of four films she made for Republic Pictures. John Wayne co-produced *Angel and the Badman* and specifically requested Gail Russell to play opposite him in the western written and directed by James Edward Grant. Wayne was moved by her quiet, unassuming personality. He treated her with the respect and kindness she'd not known from many other leading men or producers. The two became good friends while working on the film. Wayne was protective of Russell. He recognized vulnerability in the actress some could have taken advantage of. He was a father figure to Russell, and she considered him to be a fiercely honest individual.[1]

Wayne's second wife, Esperanza "Chata" Baur, was less than enthusiastic with the bond the shy actress and her husband had forged. Wayne and Chata's marriage was strained at this point, and Russell's presence made matters worse. The pair was nothing more than friends, but Chata often accused Wayne of feeling more for Russell than he did.

When filming for *Angel and the Badman* was complete, the cast and crew of the picture celebrated the progress at a restaurant across the street from Republic Studios. The party graduated from the restaurant to a bar. Wayne offered to escort Russell, who had been drinking, to her family's apartment. He drove her car with plans to take a cab back to his home after dropping her off. Along the way, Russell and Wayne stopped to have something to eat. It was late by the time they arrived at the Russells' home. Russell's parents invited Wayne to come in and visit a while. Not wanting to be impolite, he accepted their invitation. It was one in the morning when Russell's brother called a cab for Wayne and even later when Wayne returned to his own home. Chata was furious and not long afterwards filed for divorce.

While Wayne's domestic issues were being covered in various West Coast newspapers, *Angel and the Badman* was released in theaters across the country. The movie was well received. Russell's performance was praised by film critics. A review in the March 3, 1947, edition of the *New York Times* noted that her portrayal of the soft-spoken Quaker Penny Worth was a "haunting mixture of sweetness and sex appeal." Russell was thrilled with the positive response for her work, and she was looking forward to the other film projects that were lined up.[2]

Shortly after the release of *Angel and the Badman*, Russell began work on another Republic Pictures vehicle, a crime drama entitled *Moonrise*, acting opposite Dane Clark, Ethel Barrymore, and Lloyd Bridges. The story involves a man who is despised because of a murder his father committed. Russell portrays the tortured man's love interest. Audiences again applauded her talent and made it known through ticket sales they wanted to see her perform more.[3]

The chemistry Wayne and Russell exhibited on screen in *Angel and the Badman* would be duplicated in another Republic Pictures production titled *Wake of the Red Witch*. In this seafaring adventure, Wayne plays Captain Ralls, who fights a Dutch shipping magnate for the woman he loves, Angelique Desaix played by Russell. Reviews for the pictures were mixed, but all agreed Russell "lent charm and distinction to her role of Angelique."[4]

Just as the actress was basking in the approval of moviegoers and film critics, her name was mentioned in Wayne's divorce case. Chata named Russell as a co-respondent and told the court that she and Wayne were having an affair. Wayne vehemently denied the accusation. Russell was crushed, and the publicity from the scandal caused her to have a nervous breakdown.[5]

Russell spent a month in a sanitarium learning to deal with the humiliation and hurt she experienced from the public divorce proceedings. Once she was released, she resorted to drinking again. On November 26, 1953, Russell was arrested for drunk driving. At her hearing two months later, the troubled actress was placed on two years' probation with the condition she refrain from intoxicants, stay away from places where liquor was sold, and obtain medical treatment. She was also ordered to pay a $150 fine.[6]

Russell's reputation wasn't the only thing that suffered from her alcoholic tendencies; it had taken a toll on her marriage, too. Five years after she married actor Guy Madison, she filed for divorce citing mental cruelty. The truth was that Madison couldn't deal with Russell's constant drinking.[7]

While the terms of the divorce were being decided, Russell appeared in her last project for Republic Pictures, a movie entitled *Studio 57*. She portrayed a lone woman aboard an oil tanker who embarked on a dangerous journey. Shortly after the production was completed, Russell was involved in another drunk driving accident. While traveling in North

Hollywood, the actress failed to stop in time and rear ended a vehicle in front of her. Instead of waiting for the police to arrive, Russell fled the scene. A day later, accompanied by her attorney, she turned herself in to the police.[8]

Russell's career stalled after the second drunk driving incident. Studios felt she was too big a risk to hire. In September 1955, John Wayne came to her rescue and offered her a part in a film he was making under his own company's banner. The movie was 7 *Men from Now*. For a moment it appeared as though the actress was well on her way to a successful comeback. Other film offers began to come in, and, when she wasn't working, she spent time painting and practicing archery. Try as she might, however, she could not overcome the power alcohol had on her.[9]

In the early hours of July 5, 1957, Russell drove her car into a closed coffee shop in West Los Angeles and pinned a janitor under a wheel. At the scene of the accident, she was given a series of sobriety tests, all of which she failed. "I had two drinks. No four. Oh, I don't know how many I had. It's nobody's business," she told the arresting officer. Russell was arraigned on felony drunk driving charges and sued for seventy-five thousand dollars in damages. She was released on one thousand dollars bail.[10]

On August 21, 1957, Russell was found unconscious on her bathroom floor by deputies who came to arrest her for failing to appear in court on the felony drunk driving charge she had received a month prior. According to the August 21, 1957, edition of the *Star-Gazette*, Sergeants H. W. Trail and G. A. Corbett said Miss Russell's mother met them at the front door and said, "Gail's on the bathroom floor. Will you help me get her up?"

The deputies said the actress, barefooted and clad in pajamas, was unconscious. They took her to the prison ward of Los Angeles General Hospital where she was booked on charge of failure to appear for arraignment in Superior Court on the drunk driving accusation. Russell was later fined $420 and placed on three years' probation. She was also ordered to surrender her driver's license for an indefinite period. A thirty-day jail sentence was suspended.

Ashamed of her actions and deeply sorry for the trouble she'd caused, Russell vowed to turn her life around. "When God is going to do something wonderful, He begins with a difficulty," she told a reporter with the *Los Angeles Times* on October 5, 1957. "If it's going to be something very wonderful, He begins with an impossibility."[11]

Producer and director William D. Coates hired Russell to star in a movie entitled *Man from Arizona*. She played the role of the wife of a domineering husband who was a paraplegic. Gail had also committed to doing a play. She hoped establishing herself as a star again would erase doubts Hollywood had about her.[12]

On August 26, 1961, less than four years after her pledge about setting her life on a new course, Gail was found dead in her apartment. She had lost her battle with alcohol. Her body was discovered by neighbors who had stopped by to check on her. Russell was lying on the floor next to an empty bottle of vodka. There were additional bottles of alcohol strewn about her home.[13]

Gail Russell was thirty-six years old when she passed away.

In many of the films actress Anne Jeffreys made for Republic Pictures, she played a damsel in perilous situations. Neither the studio nor the performer could imagine how much those movies would affect the lives of young ticket buyers. A letter from a fan written to the motion picture studio in the summer of 1945 expressed what many males were thinking about the talented Ms. Jeffreys.

"The first time I saw her [Anne Jeffreys] in a movie her lovely image was secured permanently," the admirer wrote. "She was not only staggeringly beautiful, but kind and warm, and understanding. If she only knew how many times I've swept her off a teetering bridge just before it collapsed;

Actress Anne Jeffreys
AUTHOR'S COLLECTION

how many hoodlums I flattened with my powerful fists as they tried to force
you, kicking and screaming, into their black limousine or into a stagecoach,
for God knows what evil purpose; how many times, as you cradled my head

in your arms (after I just saved your life AGAIN) and tearfully asked 'Are you all right?' I've replied: 'It's nothing, just a bullet wound in the chest.'"[14]

Born Anne Carmichael on January 26, 1923, in Goldsboro, North Carolina, Anne was one of Republic Pictures' most versatile leading ladies. She played everything from a mobster's girlfriend to a singing cowgirl. As a child she displayed outstanding musical talent. Her first professional appearance was on a radio program of mixed songs at Durhum when she was ten. Anne's mother was encouraged to take her daughter to New York to audition for various theater companies. There she sang before a number of vocal celebrities; all agreed Anne was an operatic find and offered to finance her further musical education. Anne preferred, however, to pay her own way by becoming a John Powers model.

The young North Carolina girl studied her music diligently, ultimately winning a scholarship with the Municipal Opera Association.

The Metropolitan, goal of all opera singers, seemed just around the corner when Mrs. Jeffreys decided her hardworking child had earned a vacation. Mother and daughter boarded a bus for Hollywood.

Even in a community well peopled with charming blondes, Anne's blonde beauty attracted the attention of cinema talent scouts. Carefully trained by Lillian Albertson, a studio drama coach, Anne Jeffreys began appearing in motion pictures in 1942. In the beginning, she played a number of background characters in such popular Republic Pictures as *Moonlight Masquerade* and *Flying Tigers*. In 1943 Anne finally got her chance to costar in two movies opposite Bill Elliott and Gabby Hayes. The pictures, *Calling Wild Bill Elliott* and *The Man from Thunder River*, were westerns. Newspapers across the country reported on the studio's decision to cast Anne in the films' main female role.[15]

Anne's debut in the Bill Elliott films was applauded by moviegoers everywhere, and Republic Pictures was praised for the decision to use the gifted songstress in such an inventive role.

"Singing cowboys are not new to the Hollywood scene, but blonde and gorgeous Anne Jeffreys can honestly claim the distinction of being the first singing cowgirl," an article in the August 7, 1943, edition of the *Hollywood Reporter* noted. "She is Wild Bill Elliott's leading lady in all his Republic Pictures now. In each of the pictures in the Elliott series, Anne breaks into song at one point or another."[16]

The February 3, 1943, edition of the *Hollywood Reporter* read,

Somebody out at Republic had a revolutionary idea. They'd make a series of pictures without a singing cowboy, by cracky. They'd make 'em with a singing cowgirl!

When I heard that, I got on my hoss and went jingle-jangle-jingle over the pass to see. That's how come I'm reporting today on Miss Anne Jeffreys, a North Carolina girl who always wanted to sing in opera and has made the grade in the hoss variety.

"It's a start," she said, "even if it's horse opera. If I make enough money in pictures, I'm going to take five years off and study and work like mad, and try for the Met."

It was disappointing, sort of, that Miss Anne the Singing Cowgirl wasn't togged out in her ridin'-and-shootin' outfit. She's a beautiful blonde, blue-eyed, and looked more like a glamor-gal than a prairie flower. She had on a fancy, green dress and a fur jacket, and wore gold earrings, gold bracelet, gold wristwatch and a finger ring with a stone an inch square.

"But I can really ride," she said, justifying her new western role. "Back home I had a pony as a child, and out here I love to ride horseback. What I'm afraid of is I won't get to ride a horse at all. I was always a tom-boy, and I always was Tom Mix when we kids played cowboys at home."[17]

There were seven pictures in the Bill Elliott series in addition to *Calling Wild Bill Elliott* and *A Man from Thunder River*; there were *Bordertown Gun Fighters*, *Wagon Trains West*, *Death Valley Manhunt*, *Blazing Action*, and *Hidden Valley Outlaws*. Audiences loved Bill Elliott's leading lady and referred to her as the Diva of the Hoss Opera. The Bill Elliott series contained enough shooting, fighting, hard riding, and singing to meet the demand of the western fans.[18]

Anne and the other major players in the series made personal appearances at parades, rodeos, and department stores. They also traveled the country helping to sell war bonds during World War II.[19]

Anne's time with Republic ended when the Elliott series was concluded. She went on to star in several movies for various Hollywood studios, most without her horse. She made the leap to television in the 1950s, receiving renewed fame in the program *Topper* based on the popular film of the same name. Her husband, Robert Sterling, starred with her in the series. Anne guest starred in numerous television shows and performed on stage in theaters from Broadway to London. From 1984 to 2004 she was a regular on *General Hospital*. Singing cowgirl and spirited heroine of Republic Pictures westerns, Anne Jeffreys died on September 27, 2017, at her home in Los Angeles at the age of ninety-four.[20]

Dale Evans was one of Republic Pictures' most popular western stars. The unlikely celluloid cowgirl and western star starred in tandem with singing cowboy Roy Rogers in most of her thirty-eight films and two television series. The undisputed Queen of the West was born Frances Octavia Smith on October 31, 1912, in Uvalde, Texas. In her words, her upbringing was "idyllic." As the only daughter of Walter and Betty Sue Smith, she was showered with attention, and her musical talents were encouraged with piano and dance lessons.[21]

While still in high school, she married Thomas Fox and had a son, Thomas Jr. The marriage, however, was short-lived. After securing a divorce, she attended a business school in Memphis and worked as a secretary before making her singing debut at a local radio station. In 1931, she changed her name to Dale Evans.[22]

By the mid-1930s, Dale was a highly sought-after, big-band singer performing with orchestras throughout the Midwest. Her stage persona and singing voice earned her a screen test for the 1942 movie *Holiday Inn*. She didn't get the part, but she ended up singing with the nationally broadcast radio program *The Chase and Sanborn Hour* and soon after signed a contract with Republic Studios. She hoped her work in motion pictures would lead to a run on Broadway doing musicals.[23]

In August 1943, two weeks after signing a one-year contract with Republic Studios, Dale began rehearsals for the film *Swing Your Partner*. Although her role in the picture was small, studio executives considered it a promising start. Over the next year, Dale filmed nine other movies for Republic, and in between she continued to record music.[24]

When she wasn't working, Dale spent time with her son, Tom, and her second husband, orchestra director Robert Butts. Her marriage was struggling under the weight of their demanding work schedules, but neither spouse was willing to compromise.[25]

"I was torn between my desire to be a good housekeeper, wife, and mother and my consuming ambition as an entertainer," Dale told the *Los Angeles Daily News* in 1970. "It was like trying to ride two horses at once, and I couldn't seem to control either one of them."[26]

Dale's marriage might have been suffering, but her career was taking off. Republic Studios' president Herbert Yates summoned Dale to a meeting to discuss the next musical the studio would be doing. She took this as a hopeful sign. It was common knowledge around the studio lot that Yates had recently seen a New York stage production of the musical *Oklahoma* and had fallen in love with the story. Dale imagined that the studio president wanted to talk with her about starring in a film version of the play. It was the opportunity she had always envisioned for herself. For a brief moment she was one step closer to Broadway.

Dale Evans dreamed of starring as the lead in the film version of *Oklahoma*, but Republic president Herbert Yates had other plans for the actress. He wanted her to play opposite the studio's star cowboy in the movie *The Cowboy and the Senorita*.

Dale's only experience in westerns had been a small role as a saloon singer in a John Wayne picture, and she was not a skilled rider. She committed herself to doing her very best, however, in the role of the "Senorita," Ysobel Martinez.

The picture was released in 1944 and was a huge success. Theater managers and audiences alike encouraged studio executives at Republic to quickly re-team Dale and Roy in another western.

In between her film jobs, Dale toured military bases in the United States with the USO. She sang to troops on bivouac, from Louisiana to Texas. She was proud to think she was bringing a little sunshine into the hearts of the soldiers.

Dale also brought sunshine into the hearts of moviegoers, and ticket sales were evidence of that. Republic had happened onto the perfect western team. Dale was a sassy, sophisticated, leading lady and the perfect foil for Roy, the patient, singing cowboy.

The Cowboy and the Senorita was a big hit for Republic. The April 1944 edition of *Movie Line Magazine* heaped praise on the film and its stars. "Intrigue and song fill the Old West when America's favorite singing cowboy rides to the rescue of two unfortunate ladies about to be swindled out of their inheritance," the magazine article read:

> In Republic Pictures' latest film *The Cowboy and the Senorita*, Roy Rogers and his sidekick Guinn "Big Boy" Williams amble into a busy frontier burg looking for work and are mistakenly

identified as felons. Roy and Williams' character "Teddy Bear" are accused of kidnapping 17-year-old Chip Martinez, played by Republic Pictures singing sensation, Mary Lee. In truth, Chip has run away from home and her cousin Ysobel, played by talented newcomer Dale Evans, to hunt for a buried treasure.

Roy convinces Ysobel that he had nothing to do with her cousin's disappearance and offers to help find the teenager. Rearing on his famous palomino Trigger, Roy and Teddy Bear comb the countryside until they find Chip. The pair is then hired on to work on the Martinez ranch and to watch over the impetuous Chip. Desperate to get away again, Chip tells the boys she wants to find the treasure buried in a supposedly worthless gold mine she inherited from her father. They agree to lend the young girl a hand in spite of her cousin's objections.

Meanwhile, Ysobel has promised to sell the mine to her boyfriend Craig Allen, played by John Hubbard. Allen is a charming gambler and town boss who has convinced the unsuspecting Ysobel the mine has no value. Allen of course knows differently.

Using a clue left by Chip's father, Roy investigates the mine and discovers a hidden shaft that contains the gold. The boys must outride Allen's men who are determined to stop Rogers and his sidekick at any cost. Our heroes are in a race against time and a posse. They must get ore samples back to town before the ownership of the mine is transferred.

The action in *The Cowboy and the Senorita* is heightened with several song and dance numbers performed by Roy Rogers, the Sons of the Pioneers, and Dale Evans. Songs include the title tune, "Round Her Neck She Wore A Yellow Ribbon," "Bunk House Bugle Boy," and "Enchilada Man." The chemistry between Roy

Rogers and Dale Evans is enchanting and "Big Boy" Williams adds great comic relief as Roy's riding partner.

The King of the Cowboys and Trigger will ride the range again this fall in their next picture *The Yellow Rose of Texas*. Roy will be paired with Dale Evans for a second time in this feature. He'll be playing an insurance investigator working undercover on Dale's showboat. No doubt Rogers' 900,000 fans will flock to the theater to watch him ride to the rescue.[27]

Herbert Yates was quick to capitalize on the success *of The Cowboy and the Senorita* and the chemistry between Roy Rogers and Dale Evans. The motion picture executive decided to star the pair in three more westerns: *Yellow Rose of Texas*, *Lights of Old Santa Fe*, and *San Fernando Valley*.

Audiences flocked to theaters to see Dale Evans opposite Roy and his horse Trigger. She received sacks of mail from fans of all ages complimenting her on her acting and singing and expressing their desire to see her continue starring with Roy in more westerns.

With the exception of the motion picture *The Big Show Off*, Dale's admirers would get their wish.

Republic Pictures' *The Big Show Off* was released in January 1945, and, in addition to Dale Evans, it starred Arthur Lake and Lionel Stander. Dale portrays a nightclub singer being romantically pursued by the piano player at the club. In order to get Dale's attention, the musician disguises himself as a professional wrestler. He is aware of Dale's character's fascination with professional wrestling, and he hopes if he manages to make a name for himself in the ring she will fall in love with him.

Movie critics and fans alike appreciated Dale's work. The actress had "many sides to her talent," the February 15, 1945, edition of the *Hollywood Reporter* noted. "Not only can she dance and sing as well as act, but she also writes her own songs. 'There's Only One You' which she sings in *The Big Show Off* is one of her own compositions."[28]

Dale's departure from westerns was short lived. *Utah*, *Bells of Rosarita*, *Man From Oklahoma*, *Along the Navajo Trail*, *Sunset in El Dorado*, and *Don't Fence Me In* were all released in 1945. Each starred Roy and Dale along with Trigger, and there were many more films to come.

Throughout the 1940s, the careers of Roy Rogers and Dale Evans rode the crest of an incredible wave. Their popularity spanned across the ocean into Europe, and fans who wanted their heroes with them at all times could purchase toothbrushes, hats, dishes, and bed sheets with the pair's names and likenesses on every item. By the late 1940s, Roy Rogers and Dale Evans were second only to Walt Disney in commercial endorsements. They played to record-breaking crowds at rodeos and state fairs.

Roy and Dale were together most of their waking hours. They were good friends who confided in each other and discussed the difficulties of being single parents. Roy's wife had died after giving birth to their son, and Dale had divorced her third husband. They depended on one another and respected each other's talents. Roy was impressed with Dale's on-screen take-charge personality. Dale had a quick, smart-aleck delivery, and she wasn't afraid to get into a fight or two.

In the fall of 1947, Roy proposed to Dale as he sat on Trigger. The pair was performing at a rodeo in Chicago, and, moments before their big entrance, Roy suggested they get married. The date set for the wedding was New Year's Eve. Gossip columnists predicted that Trigger would be the best man and that Dale would wear a red-sequined cowgirl gown. The predictions proved to be false.

Roy and Dale's wedding was a simple affair held at a ranch in Oklahoma, which happened to be the location for the filming of their seventeenth movie *Home in Oklahoma*.

Roy Rogers continued to reign as King of the Cowboys after he and Dale married, but his wife was temporarily dethroned from her honorary role as the Queen of the West. Republic Studios believed the public would not be interested in seeing a married couple teamed together, and a series of new leading ladies took Dale's place on screen. Ticket buyers did not respond well to the new women. It wasn't long before Republic executives decided to reinstate Dale and begin production on another film that would re-team the popular pair.

In between filming their westerns, Roy and Dale kept busy recording some of Dale's compositions for RCA Victor records. Their song "Aha, San Antone" sold more than two hundred thousand copies. Roy and Dale were also doing a radio show, performing at rodeos, and keeping up with personal appearance tours that took them all over the United States.

When Roy Rogers parted company with Republic Pictures in 1951, Dale went with him. The cowboy duo decided they would try their hand at television. Both Roy and Dale were among the top-ten money-making western stars in the industry. Network executives at the National Broadcasting Corporation believed their audience would follow them to the new medium. The Roy Rogers Show ran from 1951 to 1957. The song entitled "Happy Trails," which Dale Evans wrote for the television show, has endured through the decades.[29]

Dale Evans died from congestive heart failure on February 7, 2001. The movies she made with Republic Pictures continue to air on various western channels today and prove she still reigns as Queen of the Cowgirls.[30]

The most influential woman at Republic Pictures from the early 1940s to the studio's demise in the early 1960s was Vera Hruba. Born in Prague, Czechoslovakia, on July 12, 1919, the blonde beauty caught Republic Pictures' president Herbert Yates' attention in 1939 when she toured the United States with an ice-skating show called *Ice Vanities*.[31]

Vera was an exceptional ice skater, having placed seventeenth in the 1936 Olympics behind figure skater Sonja Henie. Yates was captivated

Actress Vera Ralston
AUTHOR'S COLLECTION

with Vera's talent and looks and believed she could be as successful as Ms. Henie, who was one of the leading stars at 20th Century Fox. He cast Vera, and the entire company of the *Ice Vanities*, in a musical film entitled *The Ice Capades*. Critics called the picture "sheer enchantment on ice."

Vera was mentioned along with five other skaters as "spectacular." Yates couldn't have agreed more and in 1943 signed her to a long-term contract with the studio and added Ralston to her name. He added Ralston, a name borrowed from the cereal, because Hruba was difficult for moviegoers to pronounce.[32]

The first movie Vera Hruba Ralston appeared in as a star, minus the skates, was Republic Pictures' 1941 horror film *The Lady and the Monster*. Her costars were Erich von Stroheim and Richard Arlen. Billed as "a picture from out of this world," the plot involves a millionaire whose brain is preserved after his death, and telepathically begins to take control of those around him. Von Stroheim portrays the diabolical Dr. Mueller who retrieves the brain of a financial genius who crashed to his death in an airplane mishap near the laboratory. The doctor carries out a fiendish plot to put the super brain to work for him. Richard Arlen plays the doctor's assistant who falls in love with the doctor's ward, Vera Ralston. The film reviewer for the *Havre Daily News* referred to Ralston's debut as a dramatic actress as "the find of the season."[33]

Most did not agree with the critics who found the foreign ingénue to be a promising star. Many complained that her performance was wooden and that her accent was too thick. Yates ignored every voice but his own and quickly re-teamed von Stroheim and Arlen with his discovery in another feature entitled *Storm Over Lisbon*. In this spy thriller, Ralston plays an allied operative in Lisbon and Arlen an American newspaper man whom she helps get out of Portugal with important information. Audiences found Ralston attractive, but struggled to understand what she was saying.[34]

Yates hired acting instructors and speech coaches for Ralston. While her English and her acting soon improved, she could not lose her strong Czech accent. Yates felt that ticket buyers would eventually see how compelling the stunning blonde's talent truly was and learn to embrace her

way of talking in much the same way they did Marlene Dietrich. In order to help Ralston gain a broader acceptance, he paired her with an actor that had mass appeal—John Wayne.

The western starring Wayne and Ralston was *Dakota*. Wayne and Ralston portray newlyweds who plan to use their nest egg to buy property at a location where a railroad town is rumored to be built. Before the pair has a chance to make a start for themselves, they are robbed of their money, and Wayne sets out to find the crooks and retrieve what's his.

Wayne was hesitant to work with Ralston. None of the pictures she had made for Republic had done well. Yates enticed Wayne into making *Dakota* with the promise of a percentage of the revenue from the next movie he was slated to do for the studio. The film was *Wake of the Red Witch*, and Wayne made a substantial amount from the percentage Yates agreed to give him. It was enough to fund a production company of his own.[35]

Widely released on Christmas Day in 1945, audiences were pleased with the fast-moving film. The movie critic at the *Tallahassee Democrat* called *Dakota* a "rip-snorting, fast-shooting, western drama packed with action."[36] The November 1945 edition of *Variety* wasn't as enthused with the picture as the ticket buyers seemed to be. "Republic has dressed up a familiar land-grab story with sufficient production to give the outdoor epic more than formula values," the article about the movie read. "The action isn't always robust, but there are a number of knock-down fights to help carry it along. Wayne runs through his assignment under Joseph Kane's direction with his customary nonchalance. Vera Hruba Ralston, femme lead, comes through a river dunking, fire, and fights with every hair in place and not a single wrinkle. . . . *Dakota* has draw value in the John Wayne name to aid the action market and returns will prove okay."[37]

Returns were better than okay. *Dakota* was hugely profitable. In terms of box office sales, it would be the most profitable film Vera Hruba Ralston would ever make.

FACING PAGE: Erich Von Stroheim, Vera Ralston, and Richard Arlen in *The Lady and the Monster* AUTHOR'S COLLECTION

Ralston's next project was one written specifically with her in mind. In *Murder in the Music Hall*, she plays Lila Leighton, a lovely ice ballerina, who meets Carl Lang, an ice-show producer who offers her the starring role in his new Music Hall Ice Show. She refuses and shortly thereafter the producer is found dead. Ralston's character is implicated in the killing of the producer and the only hope of clearing her name is to find the murderer herself.

Audiences were impressed with the ice-skating routines but found the mystery commonplace and noted that "*Murder in the Music Hall* isn't nearly as good a mystery as it is a skating spectacle."[38]

In the westerns *The Plainsman and the Lady* and *Wyoming*, Ralston appeared opposite popular cowboy star Bill Elliott. Her performance in both films was praised as "being better than usual." By 1947, Ralston was being referred to in trade publications as the Queen of Republic Pictures. She was known for being in big budget films that could potentially yield big returns. Herbert Yates' preoccupation with making sure Ralston's career at Republic Pictures was secure extended beyond the studio. He hosted lavish parties in her honor to celebrate her talent and to demonstrate his commitment to the actress. Ralston was flattered by the attention. At some point the relationship between Ralston and Yates evolved into a romantic one. Yates separated from his wife Petra in 1948. From that point on Yates and Ralston were inseparable.[39]

Between November 1947 and November 1948, Ralston made four blockbuster films, all of which received poor reviews. In an effort to restore the reputation the actress had at the studio for being a bankable star, Yates re-teamed her with John Wayne in the film *The Fighting Kentuckian*. Directed by George Waggner and coproduced by Wayne, the film was set in Alabama in 1818. Wayne portrayed a bluff trooper romancing an upper-class French woman, played by Ralston, who is exiled to the hills.

FACING PAGE: Herbert Yates tried in vain to establish Vera Ralston as a major star but had better luck convincing the exotic beauty to marry him.
AUTHOR'S COLLECTION

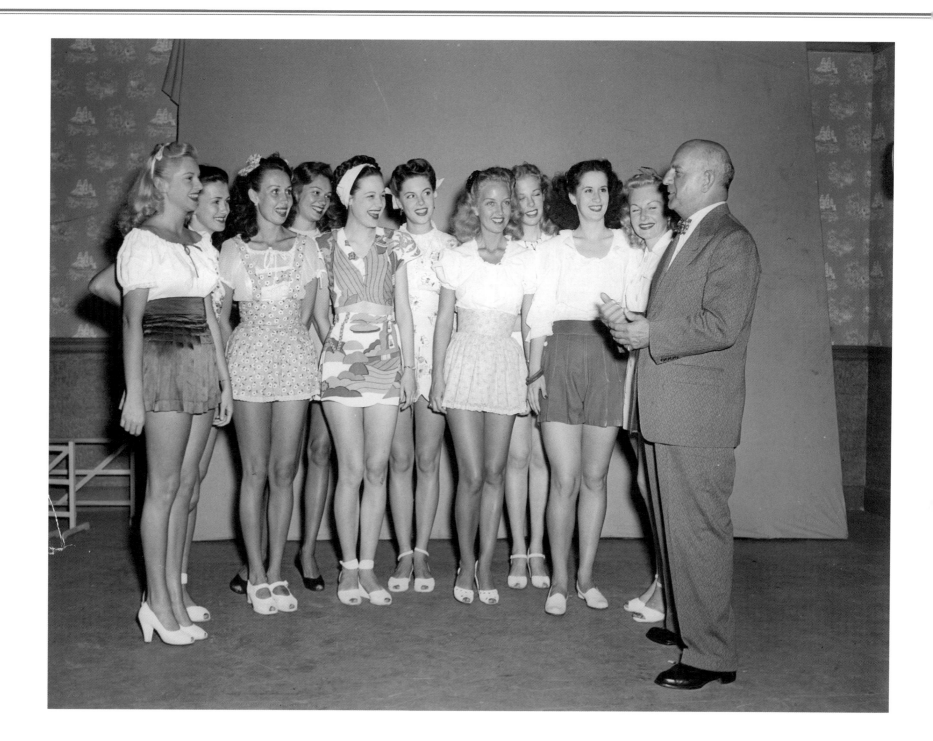

Critics disliked the film. In the October 20, 1949, edition of the *Pittsburgh Post-Gazette*, a reviewer noted in his column,

> No picture has the right to be this bad or punishing. Somewhere there are probably people who will be able to explain what the movie is about, but don't bet on it. Double acrostics are much less complicated, and certainly a lot more exciting.
>
> Apparently it has something to do with the settling in Alabama of a band of Napoleonic exiles and how a gang of real estate thieves switched the boundary lines on them and waited until the land was developed and cultivated, whereupon they intended to move in and grab it. But the heavies reckoned without John Wayne and a regiment of coonskin-capped, Kentucky riflemen, who were passing through on their way home from the war of 1812 and pitching in with the foreigners because by that time John Wayne has had a good look at the French general's lovely daughter.
>
> Of course this could quite possibly be an entirely erroneous synopsis. But then nobody will ever know whether it is or not, particularly so after seeing the movie.[40]

Wayne placed the blame for the poor, critical response to the movie solely on costar Vera Ralston. "Yates made me use Vera," Wayne told colleagues years later. "I've always been mad at Yates about this because we lost the chance to have a damn fine movie."[41]

Undaunted by the comments from reviewers and industry leaders alike, Yates continued to promote Ralston and cast her as the lead in ambitious films Republic Pictures produced. On October 16, 1950, the *Los Angeles Times* announced that Yates' mistress would next be seen in the movie *Surrender*:

James Edward Grant's story of *Surrender* is laid in the fabulous West of the bust-and-bustle period. The shooting is reserved for the last couple of reels. The first part has to do with the naughty machinations of Vera Ralston, whose come-hither eyes lure every man within bird's-eye view of her.

Miss Ralston weds an older man, an elegant thief, and leaves him to wither in jail while she skips out—only to get other men into scrapes in a town near the Mexican border. But gambling house owner John Carroll is tough, and he tosses her about brutally, even though he is in love with her. However, in the end, she proves his ruin, too.

Vera Ralston is a remarkable, convincing siren, so that you can easily believe in her conquests.[42]

Although costars John Carroll and Walter Brennan were cited for their standout performances, it wasn't enough to earn the film a great deal of money.

None of the four films Vera Ralston made between January 1951 and March 1953 performed well at the box office. Yates helped take the actress' mind off the box office woes during this time with a trip to the county clerk's office to obtain a marriage license.[43] The seventy-two-year-old Yates and thirty-one-year-old Ralston wed on March 16, 1952. It was Ralston's first marriage and Yates' second. The pair was too busy to honeymoon after the wedding and chose to get away to celebrate their nuptials once Ralston finished filming the action-adventure movie *Fair Wind to Java* opposite Fred MacMurray.[44]

Hollywood gossip columnist Louella Parsons caught up with the new bride shortly after she and Yates returned from a trip to Europe. Parsons asked Ralston about her life with the studio president, her work, and her future endeavors:

One of the few completely honest persons in our town is Vera Ralston, in private life Mrs. Herbert J. Yates. Born in Czechoslovakia, she says she walked out of Prague as Hitler walked in.

When Vera walked into my house I'd never have known her. Her blonde hair is now jet black. She had been blonde ever since she arrived in Hollywood after appearing as a skater at the Olympic Games.

And when I asked her how come a brunette she said: "I read the script of *Fair Wind to Java* and wanted to play the half-cast slave girl. Herb said, 'If you want the part you'll have to have dark hair because the girl in the story is part Japanese.' I tried dozens of wigs, but I get pretty rough treatment from Fred MacMurray in the picture and the wigs would slip off. Besides, they looked phony. So Herb said, 'Unless you dye your hair I can't let you have the role.' After I dyed my hair I cried my eyes out, then when he saw me he said, 'I like it,' so I kept it dark for my next picture *Perilous Voyage*. Now he wants me to stay a brunette, which is a complete new departure since I was born a blonde."

Vera has a good philosophy on life. She never asks anyone to deny anything that's written about her, but she said she was surprised to read one of the columnists who said that she and Herb had left the Venice film festival in a huff. "You know what really happened," she said, "we left to avoid a bad rainstorm because I was wearing one of the queen's dresses."

"The queen's dresses," I repeated, "what do you mean?"

Vera laughed and said, "Ex-King Farouk couldn't pay for five gorgeous gowns he bought for Narriman, so they went up for sale. I saw them in Venice and went out of my mind about them. Besides, I needed an evening dress for the festival. We had left for Venice an hour after I finished my picture and I hadn't had time to shop.

"Well, the king begged the couturier not to sell them, but he had to have his money, so he offered to sell all five of them at 20 percent off. I bought all of them, and they're simply beautiful. It seems that I'm always leaving town five minutes after I finish a picture. I went on my honeymoon the day after I made my last scene in *Fair Wind to Java*, with no time for shopping for our European trip. *Perilous Voyage* was finished three days before Christmas and we went to New York for the holidays," she said.

Vera said that being married to a studio owner has made no difference in her career—she's always worked hard "because I had a lot to learn." She's eager about *Fair Wind to Java* because she has her first good character part.

Fair Wind to Java was panned by critics. Costar Fred MacMurray agreed with the poor reviews. Later in his career, he would refer to the film as the worst he ever made. The balance of the motion pictures Ralston appeared in for Republic Studios received the same dismal response from reviewers.[45]

At times the stress of making one bad picture after another affected the Yates' marriage. Ralston would become despondent and want to give up, but Yates would insist she carry on. The couple separated in May 1961. It had been three years since Ralston's last picture, and Yates was no longer a part of Republic Pictures. Their lives had changed dramatically. The Yateses reconciled their differences the day they appeared in Superior Court in Santa Monica to argue Ralston's plea for fifty-five hundred dollars in monthly, temporary alimony. After they emerged from a conference, Ralston said of her eighty-two-year-old film executive husband,

"I love him and he loves me." The two decided then to take a second honeymoon to Italy.[46]

Herbert Yates died on February 3, 1966. Vera Ralston died on February 9, 2003. She had been battling cancer and passed away at her home in Santa Barbara.

She began her career in motion pictures as Republic's answer to 20th Century Fox's Olympic gold medalist turned actress, Sonja Henie, and ended up the Queen of the Bs for a Poverty Row Studio.[47]

Vera Ralston was seventy-nine when she passed away. She was laid to rest at the Santa Barbara Cemetery in Montecito, California. The headstone on her grave reads, "A Champion in the Beginning. A Champion in the End."[48]

CHAPTER 10

Fade to Black

On August 17, 1958, Herbert Yates stormed out of a meeting with the principal shareholders of Republic Pictures and headed into the streets of New York. He was too mad to talk and hoped he could walk off some of his fury. Studio executives and stockholders had gathered in the city, 2,917 miles from the capital of the motion picture industry, to discuss the financial affairs of the company. The situation was dismal, and the blame for the current state of affairs was placed squarely in Yates' lap. In fact, the frustrated executives accused the head of the studio of running the business for the private enrichment of himself and his family. Insulted by the claim, but unable to refute it, Yates slammed his fists on the boardroom table and stomped out of the room.

Abraham Meltzer, one of the studio's backers who owned more than 540 shares of the company's stock, contacted the state supreme court when Yates left and informed them of the board's findings. Meltzer and the others were seeking an order to place Republic Pictures into receivership. The executives charged Yates with misappropriation of funds. According to Meltzer, Yates drew fifty thousand dollars a year for five years plus bonuses. That was in addition to his $150,000 a year salary. He further accused Yates of bringing Republic's business to a standstill and trying to unload his shareholdings for a premium over the marketplace.[1]

The studio executives also blamed the troubles Republic was encountering on Yates' preoccupation with producing films to star Vera Ralston. The head of Republic Pictures had greenlit twenty films featuring the Czechoslovakian skater, and all but two were commercial failures. Yates had let his personal feelings for Ralston cloud his judgment, and the stockholders and the courts were compelled to make him answer for it.

A short twelve years prior to Yates' confrontation with Meltzer and the other shareholders, the studio leader and Republic Pictures were the talk of the industry. Under Herbert Yates' management, the company had brought comic book characters to life and sent them soaring through the skies. Daring cowboys thundered across the plains and brought evildoers to justice. Airplanes dropped down from the clouds and careened into buildings and bridges in spectacular explosions. Ticket buyers craving action and adventure found satisfaction in Republic Pictures' productions. *The New York Times* proclaimed Yates' studio the "little acorn that grew" and predicted the motion picture company would soon be an industry giant.[2]

The February 2, 1941, edition of *The New York Times* read,

A far cry from those struggling days when it was the film industry's stepchild and Hollywood's flea circus, little independent Republic is today the happiest of picture companies. Republic is in the chips; its spacious lawn is rapidly disappearing under the hammering of carpenters busily building new sound stages, projection and recording rooms and other studio appurtenances. These improvements are being paid for by the substantial profit Republic tucked away in its bank account last year. Considering that Republic has been in business only five years and that the odds against its success were great, the fact that the company has a bank account of substantial size and description bears investigation.

More than just a knack is required to successfully manufacture low-cost movies. Good management in the executive department and showmanship in the productive division are the prime requisites.

FACING PAGE: *Along the Oregon Trail*, starring Monte Hale, was one of Republic Pictures' first movies filmed in Trucolor. AUTHOR'S COLLECTION

Republic has risen out of the talents of entertainers such as Autry, Canova, Rogers, and Burnette and on the strength of their perennial popularity which will endure for always.[3]

Herbert Yates was dedicated to making sure Republic Pictures would endure always. In an interview with the *Motion Picture Herald* on June 22, 1946, he proclaimed that very sentiment. "Republic will continue to make its mark on the industry. There is a great demand for our product," Yates proudly stated. "To meet the demand Republic will release fifty-eight features budgeted at $25,500.00 during the 1946-47 season. The world is waiting for color and so sixteen of Republic's features will be filmed in Trucolor. The switch from black-and-white to color production was analogous to the change from silent to sound films."[4]

Republic Pictures was doing so well in 1946 an expansion program was introduced. A second western street was constructed, and the music facilities received major improvements. The slate of films produced that year, including *In Old Sacramento*, *Calendar Girl*, and *Angel and the Badman*, were predicted to do well, and the profits were earmarked for further building at Republic Studios and Consolidated Film Industries.[5]

Herbert Yates and Republic Pictures seemed poised to move into the next decade as a force to be reckoned with. A slate of projects to be filmed overseas were planned, new distribution deals with British companies were negotiated, and accomplished actors such as Rex Allen and Esperanza "Chata" Baur (John Wayne's second wife) were added to the list of the studio's contract players.[6]

For a while it seemed as though Republic Pictures could do no wrong, but then the tide turned.

Much publicized battles between Yates and cowboy superstar Roy Rogers over money and actor John Wayne over Vera Ralston contributed to the ultimate demise of the one-time burgeoning motion picture company. Yates struggled to keep order. In addition to the issues at work, he had to contend with personal matters outside the office. In 1948, he left his wife, Elsie Petra, of thirty-six years and in 1949 filed for divorce. Vera Ralston was cited as the reason for the marriage ending.

When Yates became romantically involved with actress Vera Ralston is unknown. Almost from the moment he met the Olympic skater in 1941, he began a campaign to launch her film career. Ralston was attractive, but her beauty could not override her lack of acting talent. Had any other of his stars consistently failed to win over the public and lose revenue, Yates would have released them from their contract. Ralston was the exception, and his inability to recognize her failure to capture the public's attention cast doubt on his decision-making process. Not only were Ralston's films losing money, but Yates hired her brother to be part of the production team. He had even less experience in the industry than Ralston. It wasn't until the stockholders meeting in the summer of 1958 that the shareholders realized Ralston's brother had been on the payroll.

Poor business decisions and the popularity of television took its toll on Republic Pictures. Failure to dedicate a large portion of funds to the television market and capitalize on developing programming for the at-home audiences also had an effect on the studio's bottom line. Republic Pictures' sales managers and staff tried to enlighten Yates, but he maintained that the decline in motion picture ticket sales was temporary. An article that appeared in the November 24, 1951, edition of the *Motion Picture Herald* expressed his optimism for the future of films at Republic.[7] The *Motion Picture Herald* reported,

> "Republic Pictures is investing more than $15,000,000 in production during the next twelve months," Herbert Yates told a meeting of studio executives last weekend. The Republic president conveyed his confidence in the future of the industry, outlined

Republic Pictures' president Herbert Yates cast his wife, Vera Ralston, in a number of movies, but *Dakota* was her only financially successful film.
AUTHOR'S COLLECTION

Republic products now in release or soon due to reach theaters, and voiced his determination to make Republic films more attractive through the use of top stars.

"Enthusiasm is the life blood of our business," Mr. Yates declared. "I have always prided myself on being an optimist and I am backing this optimism with greatest appropriation of productions dollars since our company was founded in 1935, every dollar of which must find its way to the screen."[8]

Yates' positive outlook about the studio and the action he was taking to increase revenue spilled over into his personal life. The action he employed to improve his social status was to finally divorce his wife and marry Vera Ralston. The two were wed on March 15, 1952. Yates was more than forty years older than his bride. Prior to traveling to Europe for their honeymoon, Yates announced that his new wife would be starring in the movie *Fair Wind to Java*. The trip abroad was to be both for business and pleasure.[9]

The news of Yates and Ralston's nuptials and of another project starring Ralston prompted Republic Pictures' stockholders to schedule an emergency meeting in the spring of 1952. According to *Variety* magazine, Yates was unable to attend the conference and was represented by James Grainger, sales manager for the studio. Shareholders had three issues they wanted addressed. They wanted two of the company's officials to take a pay cut, and they also wanted to know which, if any, of Vera Ralston's films had shown a profit.[10]

Variety reported,

In view of the company's poor earnings record, a demand was voiced at the stockholder's meeting for President Herbert J. Yates to cut his annual $175,000 salary to $75,000. A call was also sounded for James Grainger's salary to be reduced from $75,000 to $25,000.

Walter L. Schulman, representing H. Hentz and Company brokerage firm, holding two-hundred Republic common shares, asked for a breakdown of the profit or loss of each of ten films in which Miss Ralston appeared since 1945. Louis Atz, Republic accountant, replied that it was against company policy to disclose earnings of individual pictures.[11]

Grainger's report back to Yates about the meeting made it clear to the studio president that although he might have been optimistic about the future of the company, the stockholders were not.

On the heels of the stockholder's meeting came word that Yates had been offered an undisclosed amount of money to buy controlling interest in Republic Studios. *Variety* caught up with Yates on April 11, 1952, to ask about the reported sale. The studio head refused to confirm or deny he had received a bid for the company. A spokesman from the Wall Street brokerage firm of J. W. Sparks and Company, holder of six thousand shares of Republic Pictures common stock, asked in writing about the news. Yates responded with a note that he viewed the question to be inappropriate. "This is a strictly personal matter," he added, declining to give any further comment on the matter.[12]

The studio chief did offer his assurance to shareholders that Republic Pictures would reap hefty earnings from the television industry, Consolidated Film Industries' business, and the foreign market. He announced that Republic had invested $1.5 million in special television stages and equipment. The idea was that producers of television programs would need a place to create their shows. Yates wanted Republic to be ready to provide the location and materials for the production of those shows. "We plan to take from T.V. what T.V. has taken from us," Yates proclaimed.[13]

If shareholders' anxieties about the future of the studio were put to rest after Yates' assurances, it was a short rest. In May 1952, executives held their breath waiting for the federal court to rule on the cases Gene Autry and Roy Rogers had pending against the studio. Both cowboy actors were hoping to get a ruling in their favor to stop Republic Pictures from releasing the films they starred in to television. The judge in the case ruled against the singing cowboys, noting that it was clear from the contracts they signed with the company that Republic had absolute ownership of the product and as such could do with it what they wanted.[14]

On July 22, 1952, Herbert Yates announced that Republic Pictures would double its production budget for the 1952-1953 season. Yates believed his ambitious plan was the best way to fight "box office doldrums." Commenting on his lofty plans, Yates declared, "It is my opinion, after a most exhaustive grass roots study of conditions now and in the immediate future, that there is great hope for our industry. There have been enough indications in recent weeks by the results achieved by our pictures to convince me that the theater business, while depleted, is certainly not in the critical state many observers would lead us to believe." Yates added that the continued success of the studio was not only in the films they produced but in the stars that were featured. He was pleased with the talent under contract with Republic.[15]

When one of Republic Pictures' major stars decided to move on in November 1952, stockholders once again became nervous about the future of the company. John Wayne moved his furniture out and closed his office at Republic in early November 1952. According to gossip columnist Sheilah Graham, Wayne's decision to leave the studio was based on the fact that Yates failed to honor his promise to back a film about the Alamo that Wayne wanted to make.[16]

An article in the November 13, 1952, edition of *The Times* confirmed the end of the motion picture making partnership. "Yates will have to make me a darned good offer to get me to make another movie with him," Wayne told *The Times*. "I'm fed up." When asked for a rebuttal, Yates cited

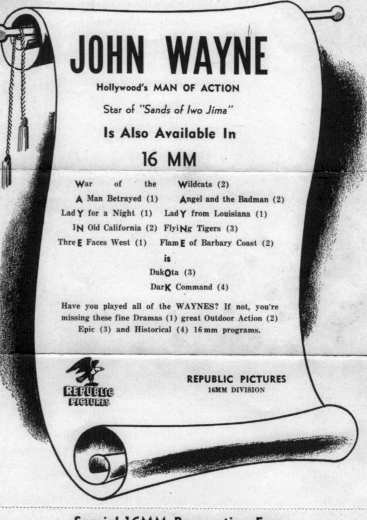

the "great mental strain and personal problems Duke Wayne has had during the past year." He continued, "Duke was employed at Republic on May 11, 1935, when the going in our industry was rough. . . . I have always found Duke a gentleman, a friend, always willing to cooperate and he has beyond any doubt been helpful in establishing the success of Republic, the same as many hundreds of our employees have also been helpful."[17]

Circumstances at the studio didn't fully improve when 1953 began. James Grainger, at this point vice president in charge of sales and distribution for Republic Pictures, chose to leave the company to become head of RKO Pictures. Howard Hughes personally selected Grainger for the position. Yates quickly made major executive changes at Republic that included naming his son as assistant director of sales, another move the company stockholders found questionable. Some shareholders contemplated discussing the subject of nepotism at the next board meeting but decided to table the talk after Yates announced that the net profit for the fiscal year was $759,603,000, one million dollars more than the previous fiscal year.[18]

Yates successfully moved to use the funds on a substantial expansion program to meet the challenge of rapidly advancing motion picture techniques. By mid-summer 1953, construction on four new soundstages of the newest design and technical innovations had begun.[19] The new construction would bring the number of soundstages on the studio lot to eighteen. Yates' plan was to rent the studio space to the growing number of production companies creating television programming. The venture turned out to be extremely profitable for Republic Pictures.[20]

Shareholders who felt Yates should be removed as head of the company because they believed he would eventually bankrupt the studio maneuvered to buy out his controlling interest in the business. Their every attempt was thwarted, however. Yates aligned himself with other lesser, but important stockholders, in a move that would prevent a sellout by them.[21]

FACING PAGE: Republic Pictures issued order forms to movie theaters for films like *I'll Always Love You* and the entire catalog of films John Wayne made at the studio. AUTHOR'S COLLECTION

The behind-the-scenes wrangling did not distract Yates from his goals for his company. He reflected on how well Republic Pictures had done in the first eleven years of its existence as well as the impact the studio had made with its chapter plays and feature films, and he was convinced the company could be a force in television as well. At the annual stockholders meeting in April 1955, Yates proposed the company stop producing theatrical releases and devote its resources to its laboratories and television.

The majority of the stockholders were opposed to a retreat from the theatrical field. They remained unconvinced that television would generate the same income as motion pictures. Yates explained to the board that heads of competing studios and theater chains were complaining that given the current state of motion pictures it was impossible to make a profit. Republic was not signing anymore talent contracts, Yates disclosed, and the company would be free of existing contracts by the year's end.

Yates also let the executives know that television studio rentals of more than one million dollars were earned by Republic in 1954 from the lease of some eighteen stages in regular use.[22]

Stockholders queried Yates again about his salary, and he divulged that he was paid $168,000 annually but that he hadn't collected his pay in full for several years and that the studio owed him one hundred thousand dollars.

While Yates was encouraging stockholders to focus more of Republic Pictures' interests on television, at home he and Ralston were discussing making the film *The Spanish Lady*. In the spring of 1955, the couple flew to Europe to hunt for locations. *The Spanish Lady*, based on the novel of the same name, was written by Maurice Walsh. Walsh authored *The Quiet Man*, which won John Ford an Academy Award.[23]

The Spanish Lady is the gripping story about the tragic life of Henry VIII's first wife, Catherine of Aragon. Vera wanted to see the novel made into a movie from the moment she read the material. Yates was sure he could convince his executives to move forward with the project. It was a dream that would never become a reality.

Another of Yates' pet projects that would never make it to development was the film adaption of a Robert F. Mirvish novel entitled *The Long Watch*. Yates paid one hundred thousand dollars for the novel and had even inspected possible film location spots in the Philippines, Egypt, Hong Kong, and New York.[24]

Between 1955 and 1958, numerous film companies leased studio space at Republic. The company was still making a limited number of low-budget pictures, but the bulk of the funds stemmed from the rental of studios exclusively owned by Republic.

Columnist Sheilah Graham mentioned the revenue Republic Pictures was accumulating with the move in the November 23, 1957, edition of the *Hollywood Reporter.* "Herbert Yates is making $824,000 a year from his Republic Studio in North Hollywood," the column reported. "Herb merely rents the twenty-four stages of what was the very first studio here, originally owned by Mack Sennett for his bathing beauty pictures with Mabel Normand, Gloria Swanson, etc. Today, Republic is the busiest place in Hollywood with more stars and famous directors buzzing in and out in one day than during a month at any of the major movie studios."[25]

Republic Pictures was making fewer and fewer films, and by July 1958 the company was entirely out of the business of making movies for theatrical release. "The fact that the motion picture end of Republic's business was sustaining losses is what has led to the liquidation of this phase of its operations," Yates told reporters at the *Los Angeles Times*. Republic also closed all but two of its foreign distribution branches.[26]

"The news came as not a great surprise in Hollywood circles," the *Los Angeles Times* article continued. "Actually, Republic Pictures suspended developing new projects more than two years ago," the report revealed.[27]

A month prior to the public announcement that Republic Pictures would no longer produce motion pictures, Herbert Yates was taken to St. Joseph Hospital in Burbank for immediate surgery. The film executive's physician told the press the operation was necessary to "correct a recurring ailment." Company stockholders suspected the seventy-eight-year-old leader of the studio was suffering from heart issues.

One month after news broke about Republic Pictures' future, Vera Ralston Yates was in the news as a victim of theft. The actress reported that twenty thousand dollars in jewels was stolen from her hotel at the Ojai Valley Inn in Ojai.

The May 19, 1958, edition of the *Press-Courier* read,

Police are continuing the investigations today of the mysterious disappearance of between $20,000 to $50,000 in jewels belonging to movie star Vera Ralston Yates. Six months ago Mrs. Yates told police a $1,000 mink stole was taken while she was a guest at the inn.

Ojai police have questioned all the employees at the inn without finding a suspect in the reported burglary. Mrs. Yates valued the loss at $50,000. Police Chief James Alcorn said he has other reports setting the value at $20,000. He believes the loss was insured.

Mrs. Yates said that the theft occurred Saturday while she and her husband, Herbert Yates, were taking a tour of the inn. Mr. Yates is president of Republic Pictures. Two large police dogs were left to guard the couple's cottage.

The loss included a diamond and platinum bracelet, two diamond rings, two diamond and pearl earrings and two diamond clips.[28]

Life for Herbert Yates would not improve in 1958. Not only was his wife's jewelry never recovered, but a notice of death for Republic Pictures that initially appeared in the April 8, 1958, edition of the *Hollywood Reporter* was reprinted in newspapers across the United States for a period of two months:

> There are few things sadder than writing an obituary for a movie studio. That's my unpleasant chore now that the death of Republic as a movie producer and distributer has been announced. The news was confirmed by President Herbert J. Yates.
>
> Yates expects Republic earnings to rise from sales of films to television, rental of studio space, and film laboratory services. But the company is shutting down its exchanges throughout the world and will make no more pictures.
>
> This isn't exactly news. As a film studio Republic has been slowly dying for years. Yates merely signed the death certificate. Could Republic have been saved? It's a lot easier to make a post mortem than cure grave illness. Nevertheless, observers point out how Republic failed to meet the demands of a changing industry. Republic was ideally suited to turn out T.V. films at a low price, especially westerns. But the studio backed off. Instead the lot was rented to M. C. A.'s Revue Productions and Republic collected only a rental.
>
> Well, it's over now. Hollywood has no time for lamenting. The main concern here is which studio will be next?[29]

The fate of Republic Pictures and its president was the topic of conversation among those in the motion picture industry. It was no secret that Yates' constant backing of features starring his wife was a source of trouble for the executive. No figures were made available on how much Vera Ralston movies drained from Republic resources, but it was estimated by some stockholders to be in the millions. Aside from that issue, it appeared to most familiar with the interworking of the studio the Republic operation was doomed. When Republic was first in business, it was geared to produce inexpensive pictures. The advent of television did away with the market for inexpensive pictures. People could see all the routine entertainment they wanted on the home screen, and there was no need to spend money at the theaters.[30]

Motion picture executives, stuntmen and stuntwomen, and actors and actresses who had a relationship with Republic over the course of its twenty-three years in business openly discussed the ways the studio could have remained viable. Some suggested Republic could have become a class production company. The opportunity was there since Republic had a long association with top draw John Wayne. The studio had made a gallant attempt to become a class production company when working with John Ford, but Yates retreated from the field. Others suggested Republic could have devoted itself entirely to producing shows for television.[31]

Herbert Yates wasn't officially removed as president of Republic Pictures until July 1959. Victor M. Carter, a Los Angeles businessman, was in charge of a group of individuals who acquired control of the studio from Yates, his family, and several others. Carter was elected president. It was reported that the Carter group purchased four hundred thousand shares of Republic stock at a cost of six dollars a share.[32]

Herbert Yates' departure from Republic Pictures was widely publicized, but it wasn't the only time Yates' name would be mentioned in the press in 1959. Both Roy Rogers and John Wayne would make reference to the one-time leader of the studio where the actors worked.

During an interview with trade publications about his career, Roy Rogers confessed his belief that he had been blacklisted by the film studio. He blamed Herbert Yates for the fact that he hadn't done a film in eight years. "Oh, we've had deals come up and we've talked to people at studios about them," Rogers explained to the *Hollywood Reporter*. "But as soon as the negotiations got to the top men in the studios, the deals were suddenly dropped. I believe the producers blackballed me. Why? Because I had the nerve to fight Yates for four and a half years."[33]

Yates controlled eighty-six of Rogers' feature pictures and aimed to sell them to television. Rogers sued to stop him, arguing that actors had a right to share in the profits.[34]

By 1958 Republic Pictures had shut down because it failed to meet the demands of a changing industry.
AUTHOR'S COLLECTION

"I won the case all right, but then the Supreme Court reversed the decision," Rogers elaborated. "It cost me $100,000 in lawyer's fees and I don't get any help from other actors. The Screen Actors' Guild wouldn't go to bat because it was worried about all the actors who were under contract to studios then. . . . Well, I lost, and old movies started flooding T. V., without a cent of payment to actors. A lot of them are pretty hungry now."[35]

John Wayne's comments about Yates centered on his refusal to give the actor the money to do *The Alamo*. Wayne was reflecting on his pet project the day he was to begin shooting the picture. Yates promised Wayne would be able to make the movie when he was at Republic Pictures, but it never happened. Instead, Yates made his own movie based on the famous stronghold entitled *The Last Stand*. Yates' version did not star Wayne. Wayne left the studio over the situation and eventually was producer, director, and star of *The Alamo* under the banner of his own company.[36]

Just as Herbert Yates was making his exit from Republic Pictures in 1959, it was announced that Four Star Films was to lease the studio. Four

Star Films was owned by Dick Powell, David Niven, and Charles Boyer. The firm had outgrown the Fox western lot where they were located. The Republic studios provided them ample space to produce the five television series they were committed to make.

Yates was nearly eighty years old when he made his departure from the company he helped build. Gossip columnist Sheilah Graham caught up with the ex-executive in New York in November 1959. He was lunching with his son. "I'm a retired filibuster," the senior Yates told Graham. When asked what he meant, Yates explained that he was in an "active" war with those who drove him out of Republic.[37]

Less than a year after Yates left Republic Pictures, a fire at the studio's lumberyard caused an estimated $250,000 in damages. The cause of the blaze was never determined.[39]

In May 1962, the CBS Television Network took over the Republic Pictures' lot and began production on a number of new series including *Rawhide* starring Clint Eastwood. Yates kept abreast of the happenings within the company with the hopes of one day seeing it return to its former glory.[40]

On February 3, 1966, Herbert Yates died at his home in Sherman Oaks. Vera, his wife, was by his side. He had been in declining health since suffering three cerebral strokes in late September 1965. He was eighty-five years old when he passed away. Close friend and actor Forrest Tucker remembered Yates as a "very tough, often rough guy who knew how to be fair." Gene Autry recalled Yates as a great studio head. "I had many arguments and fights with him," the singing cowboy admitted, "but I respected him very much."[41]

Funeral services were held at the Oakwood Cemetery on Long Island in New York where Herbert Yates was laid to rest.[42]

In February 1967, CBS purchased Republic Studios' lot for $9.5 million. The name Republic Pictures remained, and under the well-recognized majestic eagle banner executives continued to search for a way to revitalize the brand and utilize the stockpile of product.[43]

The popularity of the action adventure series *Batman* prompted leaders at Republic to resurrect some of the studio's best-known chapter plays and release them to television. Cliffhanger films such as *Raiders of the Lost Ark* sparked additional interest in Republic Pictures' archives and for a brief period of time it appeared the studio would have another chance at the big time. Ultimately it was not to be. Spelling Entertainment Group bought the company's productions and later sold them to Paramount Pictures.[44]

Republic Pictures is remembered as being one of the most prolific and efficient operations in Hollywood's early years. The studio created the pattern for fast-paced, thrill-a-minute, killer B serials and hard-riding, gun-smoke-shrouded horse operas.

APPENDIX:
LIST OF REPUBLIC PICTURES FILMS

1930s

Release date	Title	Notes
May 15, 1935	*The Headline Woman*	Produced by Mascot Pictures
July 10, 1935	*Born to Gamble*	Produced by Liberty Pictures
August 19, 1935	*Westward Ho*	
September 5, 1935	*Tumbling Tumbleweeds*	
September 12, 1935	*Two Sinners*	
September 24, 1935	*The Crime of Dr. Crespi*	
September 25, 1935	*Cappy Ricks Returns*	
October 5, 1935	*Forbidden Heaven; The New Frontier*	
October 9, 1935	*The Spanish Cape Mystery*	
October 21, 1935	*Melody Trail*	
October 22, 1935	*1,000 Dollars a Minute*	
November 4, 1935	*Lawless Range*	
November 19, 1935	*Racing Luck*	
December 2, 1935	*Forced Landing; The Sagebrush Troubadour*	
December 3, 1935	*Frisco Waterfront*	
December 16, 1935	*The Singing Vagabond*	
December 28, 1935	*Hitch Hike Lady*	
January 18, 1936	*The Oregon Trail*	
January 20, 1936	*Dancing Feet; The Leavenworth Case*	
February 15, 1936	*The Lawless Nineties*	
February 17, 1936	*The Leathernecks Have Landed*	
February 22, 1936	*The Return of Jimmy Valentine*	

March 2, 1936	*Red River Valley*		December 14, 1936	*Happy Go Lucky*
March 4, 1936	*Laughing Irish Eyes*		December 21, 1936	*Beware of Ladies; The Old Corral*
March 9, 1936	*King of the Pecos*		December 23, 1936	*The Mandarin Mystery*
March 27, 1936	*Doughnuts and Society*		December 28, 1936	*A Man Betrayed*
April 3, 1936	*The House of a Thousand Candles*		January 4, 1937	*Riders of the Whistling Skull*
April 13, 1936	*Comin' Round the Mountain*		January 11, 1937	*Larceny on the Air*
April 14, 1936	*Federal Agent*		January 25, 1937	*Join the Marines*
April 18, 1936	*The Harvester*		February 15, 1937	*The Gambling Terror; Two Wise Maids*
April 20, 1936	*The Girl from Mandalay*		February 22, 1937	*Paradise Express*
May 1, 1936	*Frankie and Johnny*		February 28, 1937	*Round-Up Time in Texas*
May 11, 1936	*The Singing Cowboy*		March 1, 1937	*Circus Girl*
May 22, 1936	*Burning Gold*		March 3, 1937	*Hit the Saddle*
May 25, 1936	*The Lonely Trail*		March 22, 1937	*Bill Cracks Down*
May 26, 1936	*Hearts in Bondage*		March 24, 1937	*Lightnin' Crandall*
May 30, 1936	*Down to the Sea*		March 27, 1937	*Git Along Little Dogies*
June 2, 1936	*Navy Born*		March 29, 1937	*Navy Blues; Trail of Vengeance*
June 16, 1936	*Go-Get-'Em, Haines*		April 5, 1937	*Jim Hanvey, Detective*
June 22, 1936	*Guns and Guitars*		April 6, 1937	*Lawless Land*
June 25, 1936	*Ticket to Paradise*		April 22, 1937	*Bar-Z Bad Men*
July 6, 1936	*Winds of the Wasteland*		April 26, 1937	*The Hit Parade*
August 11, 1936	*Follow Your Heart*		May 4, 1937	*The Trusted Outlaw*
August 15, 1936	*The Gentleman from Louisiana*		May 5, 1937	*Gunsmoke Ranch*
August 19, 1936	*Oh, Susanna!*		May 12, 1937	*Rootin' Tootin' Rhythm*
September 11, 1936	*Sitting on the Moon*		May 13, 1937	*Guns in the Dark*
September 13, 1936	*Bulldog Edition*		May 15, 1937	*Michael O'Halloran*
September 22, 1936	*The Three Mesquiteers*		May 18, 1937	*Gun Lords of Stirrup Basin*
September 24, 1936	*Undercover Man*		May 24, 1937	*Affairs of Cappy Ricks; Come on, Cowboys*
September 28, 1936	*The President's Mystery*		June 7, 1937	*Border Phantom; Dangerous Holiday*
September 30, 1936	*Ride Ranger Ride*		June 14, 1937	*Yodelin' Kid from Pine Ridge*
October 5, 1936	*Cavalry*		June 21, 1937	*A Lawman Is Born; Rhythm in the Clouds*
October 26, 1936	*Ghost-Town Gold*		June 28, 1937	*It Could Happen to You*
November 9, 1936	*Country Gentlemen*		June 30, 1937	*Range Defenders*
November 16, 1936	*The Big Show*		July 7, 1937	*Doomed at Sundown*
November 18, 1936	*The Gun Ranger*		July 12, 1937	*Meet the Boyfriend*
December 1, 1936	*The Bold Caballero*		July 19, 1937	*The Red Rope*
December 9, 1936	*Roarin' Lead*		July 31, 1937	*Bulldog Drummond at Bay*

August 2, 1937	Boothill Brigade		May 11, 1938	Romance on the Run
August 20, 1937	Sea Racketeers		May 23, 1938	Gangs of New York
August 23, 1937	Public Cowboy No. 1		June 6, 1938	Desert Patrol
September 1, 1937	Escape by Night		June 13, 1938	Ladies in Distress
September 1, 1937	Ridin' the Lone Trail		June 15, 1938	Riders of the Black Hills
September 6, 1937	Heart of the Rockies; The Sheik Steps Out		July 4, 1938	Gold Mine in the Sky
September 8, 1937	All Over Town		August 1, 1938	Heroes of the Hills
September 24, 1937	Arizona Gunfighter		August 6, 1938	A Desperate Adventure
October 4, 1937	Boots and Saddles		August 11, 1938	Army Girl
October 4, 1937	Youth on Parole		August 15, 1938	Man from Music Mountain
October 11, 1937	The Wrong Road		August 22, 1938	Tenth Avenue Kid
October 18, 1937	The Trigger Trio		August 22, 1938	Durango Valley Raiders
November 8, 1937	Portia on Trial		August 28, 1938	Pals of the Saddle
November 13, 1937	Springtime in the Rockies		August 29, 1938	The Higgins Family
November 26, 1937	Manhattan Merry-Go-Round		September 4, 1938	Billy the Kid Returns
November 29, 1937	The Duke Comes Back		September 20, 1938	Overland Stage Raiders
December 6, 1937	The Colorado Kid; Wild Horse Rodeo		October 1, 1938	The Night Hawk
December 15, 1937	Glamorous Night		October 7, 1938	Prairie Moon
December 20, 1937	Exiled to Shanghai		October 8, 1938	Down in "Arkansaw"
December 22, 1937	Lady Behave!; Mama Runs Wild		October 29, 1938	I Stand Accused
January 11, 1938	Paroled - To Die		November 5, 1938	Rhythm of the Saddle
January 24, 1938	The Purple Vigilantes		November 14, 1938	Storm Over Bengal
January 29, 1938	The Old Barn Dance		November 21, 1938	Come On, Rangers
February 7, 1938	Outside of Paradise		November 28, 1938	Santa Fe Stampede
February 16, 1938	Born to Be Wild		December 2, 1938	Western Jamboree
February 21, 1938	Hollywood Stadium Mystery		December 5, 1938	Orphans of the Street
March 1, 1938	Prison Nurse		December 22, 1938	Red River Range
March 7, 1938	Call the Mesquiteers		December 26, 1938	Federal Man-Hunt
March 7, 1938	Thunder in the Desert		December 30, 1938	Shine On, Harvest Moon
March 18, 1938	King of the Newsboys		January 6, 1939	Fighting Thoroughbreds
March 28, 1938	Arson Gang Busters		January 10, 1939	The Mysterious Miss X
April 4, 1938	Invisible Enemy		January 23, 1939	Pride of the Navy
April 14, 1938	Outlaws of Sonora		February 3, 1939	Home on the Prairie
April 15, 1938	The Feud Maker		February 6, 1939	Woman Doctor
April 18, 1938	Call of the Yukon		March 6, 1939	I Was a Convict
April 20, 1938	Under Western Stars		March 13, 1939	Rough Riders' Round-up

March 19, 1939	*Southward Ho*
March 27, 1939	*Mexicali Rose*
April 12, 1939	*Frontier Pony Express; The Night Riders*
April 24, 1939	*Forged Passport*
April 25, 1939	*Street of Missing Men*
May 4, 1939	*Blue Montana Skies*
May 12, 1939	*Three Texas Steers*
May 15, 1939	*Man of Conquest*
May 20, 1939	*My Wife's Relatives*
May 26, 1939	*The Zero Hour*
June 2, 1939	*S.O.S. Tidal Wave*
June 9, 1939	*Mountain Rhythm*
June 19, 1939	*In Old Caliente*
June 27, 1939	*Wyoming Outlaw*
July 3, 1939	*Mickey the Kid*
July 12, 1939	*She Married a Cop*
July 26, 1939	*Should Husbands Work?*
July 31, 1939	*Colorado Sunset*
August 6, 1939	*Wall Street Cowboy*
August 10, 1939	*New Frontier*
August 14, 1939	*In Old Monterey*
August 21, 1939	*Smuggled Cargo*
August 28, 1939	*Flight at Midnight*
September 20, 1939	*Calling All Marines*
September 29, 1939	*The Arizona Kid*
October 6, 1939	*The Kansas Terrors*
October 13, 1939	*Sabotage*
October 27, 1939	*Jeepers Creepers*
November 3, 1939	*Main Street Lawyer*
November 10, 1939	*The Covered Trailer*
November 16, 1939	*Rovin' Tumbleweeds*
November 17, 1939	*Saga of Death Valley*
November 29, 1939	*Cowboys from Texas*
December 15, 1939	*South of the Border*
December 20, 1939	*Days of Jesse James*
December 31, 1939	*Money to Burn*

1940s

Release date	Title	Notes
January 12, 1940	*Heroes of the Saddle*	
January 23, 1940	*Wolf of New York*	
January 30, 1940	*Village Barn Dance*	
March 12, 1940	*Pioneers of the West*	
March 15, 1940	*Forgotten Girls*	
March 22, 1940	*Rancho Grande*	
March 26, 1940	*Ghost Valley Raiders*	
April 12, 1940	*Young Buffalo Bill*	
April 14, 1940	*Grandpa Goes to Town*	
April 15, 1940	*Dark Command*	
April 17, 1940	*In Old Missouri*	
April 22, 1940	*Covered Wagon Days*	
May 10, 1940	*Gaucho Serenade*	
May 10, 1940	*The Crooked Road*	
May 19, 1940	*Gangs of Chicago*	
May 24, 1940	*Rocky Mountain Rangers*	
June 6, 1940	*Women in War*	
June 19, 1940	*Wagons Westward*	
June 25, 1940	*Grand Ole Opry*	
June 29, 1940	*One Man's Law*	
July 1, 1940	*The Carson City Kid*	Distribution only
July 3, 1940	*Three Faces West*	
July 15, 1940	*Carolina Moon*	
July 20, 1940	*Scatterbrain*	
July 30, 1940	*The Ranger and the Lady*	
July 30, 1940	*Girl from God's Country*	
August 10, 1940	*Sing, Dance, Plenty Hot*	
August 16, 1940	*The Tulsa Kid*	
August 29, 1940	*Oklahoma Renegades*	
August 31, 1940	*Earl of Puddlestone*	
September 6, 1940	*Ride, Tenderfoot, Ride*	
September 11, 1940	*Girl from Havana*	
September 15, 1940	*Colorado*	

September 30, 1940	*Under Texas Skies*	
October 6, 1940	*Barnyard Follies*	
October 10, 1940	*Frontier Vengeance*	
October 11, 1940	*Melody and Moonlight*	
October 15, 1940	*Hit Parade of 1941*	
October 21, 1940	*Young Bill Hickok*	
November 1, 1940	*Who Killed Aunt Maggie?*	
November 11, 1940	*The Trail Blazers*	
November 15, 1940	*Melody Ranch*	
November 17, 1940	*Friendly Neighbors*	
November 22, 1940	*Texas Terrors*	
November 29, 1940	*Meet the Missus*	
December 5, 1940	*The Border Legion*	
December 20, 1940	*Behind the News*	
December 23, 1940	*Lone Star Raiders*	
December 27, 1940	*Bowery Boy*	
January 6, 1941	*Wyoming Wildcat*	
January 14, 1941	*Robin Hood of the Pecos*	
January 24, 1941	*Ridin' on a Rainbow*	
January 28, 1941	*Arkansas Judge*	
January 31, 1941	*Petticoat Politics*	
February 14, 1941	*The Phantom Cowboy*	
February 16, 1941	*Prairie Pioneers*	
February 28, 1941	*The Great Train Robbery*	
March 7, 1941	*A Man Betrayed*	
March 14, 1941	*Back in the Saddle*	
March 27, 1941	*Mr. District Attorney*	
April 4, 1941	*In Old Cheyenne*	
April 8, 1941	*Pals of the Pecos*	
April 10, 1941	*Two Gun Sheriff*	
April 12, 1941	*Sis Hopkins*	
April 17, 1941	*Rookies on Parade*	
April 22, 1941	*Lady from Louisiana*	
April 26, 1941	*The Singing Hill*	
May 5, 1941	*Country Fair*	
May 7, 1941	*Sheriff of Tombstone*	
May 12, 1941	*The Gay Vagabond*	
May 16, 1941	*Saddlemates*	
May 24, 1941	*Desert Bandit*	
May 27, 1941	*Angels with Broken Wings*	
June 20, 1941	*Nevada City*	Distribution only
June 24, 1941	*Kansas Cyclone*	
June 25, 1941	*Puddin' Head*	
July 10, 1941	*Gangs of Sonora*	
July 12, 1941	*Mountain Moonlight*	
July 15, 1941	*Sunset in Wyoming*	
July 20, 1941	*Hurricane Smith*	
July 24, 1941	*Citadel of Crime*	
July 31, 1941	*Rags to Riches*	
August 20, 1941	*Ice-Capades*	
August 25, 1941	*Under Fiesta Stars*	
August 29, 1941	*The Pittsburgh Kid*	
September 5, 1941	*Bad Man of Deadwood*	
September 10, 1941	*Outlaws of Cherokee Trail*	
September 12, 1941	*The Apache Kid*	
September 22, 1941	*Doctors Don't Tell*	
September 26, 1941	*Death Valley Outlaws*	
September 30, 1941	*Sailors on Leave*	
October 10, 1941	*Mercy Island*	
October 15, 1941	*Down Mexico Way*	
October 17, 1941	*Jesse James at Bay*	
October 24, 1941	*Gauchos of El Dorado*	
October 30, 1941	*Public Enemies*	
November 10, 1941	*The Devil Pays Off*	
November 12, 1941	*Sierra Sue*	
November 25, 1941	*Tuxedo Junction*	
November 25, 1941	*A Missouri Outlaw*	
December 12, 1941	*Red River Valley*	
December 15, 1941	*West of Cimarron*	
December 18, 1941	*Mr. District Attorney in the Carter Case*	
January 5, 1942	*Lady for a Night*	
January 13, 1942	*Arizona Terrors*	

January 16, 1942	Man from Cheyenne	November 4, 1942	X Marks the Spot
January 26, 1942	Pardon My Stripes	November 13, 1942	Valley of Hunted Men
January 30, 1942	Code of the Outlaw; Cowboy Serenade	November 16, 1942	Heart of the Golden West
February 2, 1942	A Tragedy at Midnight	December 16, 1942	The Traitor Within
February 17, 1942	South of Santa Fe	December 18, 1942	Secrets of the Underground
March 5, 1942	Sleepytime Gal	December 24, 1942	Ice-Capades Revue
March 6, 1942	Stagecoach Express	December 28, 1942	The Sundown Kid
March 11, 1942	Heart of the Rio Grande	December 30, 1942	Ridin' Down the Canyon
March 13, 1942	Yokel Boy	December 31, 1942	Johnny Doughboy
March 18, 1942	Raiders of the Range	January 8, 1943	Mountain Rhythm
March 25, 1942	Jesse James, Jr.	January 15, 1943	London Blackout Murders
March 26, 1942	Shepherd of the Ozarks	January 25, 1943	Thundering Trails
March 27, 1942	The Affairs of Jimmy Valentine	February 12, 1943	Dead Man's Gulch
April 1, 1942	Sunset on the Desert	March 3, 1943	Carson City Cyclone
April 16, 1942	The Girl from Alaska	March 10, 1943	Idaho
April 24, 1942	Westward Ho	March 12, 1943	The Blocked Trail
April 29, 1942	Home in Wyomin'	March 12, 1943	The Purple V
May 18, 1942	Romance on the Range	March 26, 1943	Hit Parade of 1943
May 18, 1942	Remember Pearl Harbor	April 6, 1943	Tahiti Honey
May 25, 1942	Stardust on the Sage	April 9, 1943	King of the Cowboys
May 31, 1942	In Old California	April 13, 1943	The Mantrap
May 31, 1942	The Cyclone Kid	April 16, 1943	Santa Fe Scouts
June 10, 1942	Moonlight Masquerade	April 20, 1943	Shantytown
June 16, 1942	The Phantom Plainsmen	April 27, 1943	Chatterbox
July 2, 1942	Sons of the Pioneers	April 30, 1943	Calling Wild Bill Elliott
July 15, 1942	Joan of Ozark	May 1, 1943	Daredevils of the West
July 27, 1942	Hi, Neighbor	May 10, 1943	A Gentle Gangster
July 31, 1942	The Sombrero Kid	May 15, 1943	Days of Old Cheyenne
August 17, 1942	Call of the Canyon	May 20, 1943	Swing Your Partner
August 17, 1942	The Old Homestead	May 21, 1943	Riders of the Rio Grande
August 24, 1942	Shadows on the Sage	May 28, 1943	False Faces
September 14, 1942	Sunset Serenade	June 11, 1943	The Man from Thunder River
September 15, 1942	Bells of Capistrano	June 14, 1943	Song of Texas
October 8, 1942	Flying Tigers	July 1, 1943	Fugitive from Sonora
October 24, 1942	Youth on Parade	July 5, 1943	Thumbs Up
October 27, 1942	Outlaws of Pine Ridge	July 8, 1943	Bordertown Gun Fighters

July 29, 1943	*The Saint Meets the Tiger*	April 9, 1944	*Rosie the Riveter*
August 12, 1943	*Silver Spurs*	April 17, 1944	*The Lady and the Monster*
August 15, 1943	*Black Hills Express*	April 24, 1944	*Trocadero*
August 18, 1943	*Beyond the Last Frontier*	May 5, 1944	*Jamboree*
August 19, 1943	*Wagon Tracks West*	May 13, 1944	*Cowboy and the Senorita*
August 21, 1943	*Someone to Remember*	May 14, 1944	*Tucson Raiders*
August 23, 1943	*The West Side Kid*	May 27, 1944	*The Tiger Woman*
August 26, 1943	*Headin' for God's Country*	June 9, 1944	*Silent Partner*
August 27, 1943	*Nobody's Darling*	June 15, 1944	*Man from Frisco*
September 5, 1943	*Sleepy Lagoon*	June 17, 1944	*Goodnight, Sweetheart*
September 13, 1943	*Hoosier Holiday*	June 24, 1944	*The Yellow Rose of Texas*
October 15, 1943	*A Scream in the Dark*	July 2, 1944	*Marshal of Reno*
October 18, 1943	*The Man from the Rio Grande*	July 14, 1944	*Call of the Rockies*
October 30, 1943	*The Man from Music Mountain*	July 20, 1944	*Silver City Kid*
November 13, 1943	*Here Comes Elmer*	July 26, 1944	*Secrets of Scotland Yard*
November 20, 1943	*Overland Mail Robbery*	July 31, 1944	*Three Little Sisters*
November 22, 1943	*The Deerslayer*	August 5, 1944	*Song of Nevada*
November 23, 1943	*Mystery Broadcast*	August 5, 1944	*The Girl Who Dared*
November 24, 1943	*Death Valley Manhunt*	August 11, 1944	*Bordertown Trail*
December 6, 1943	*In Old Oklahoma* Distribution only	August 12, 1944	*Sing, Neighbor, Sing*
December 15, 1943	*Pistol Packin' Mama*	August 13, 1944	*The Port of 40 Thieves*
December 29, 1943	*California Joe*	August 16, 1944	*The San Antonio Kid* Distribution only
December 30, 1943	*Whispering Footsteps*	September 12, 1944	*Strangers in the Night*
December 30, 1943	*Raiders of Sunset Pass*	September 14, 1944	*That's My Baby!*
December 31, 1943	*O, My Darling Clementine*	September 15, 1944	*San Fernando Valley; Stagecoach to Monterey; Atlantic City*
January 5, 1944	*Hands Across the Border*	September 30, 1944	*Cheyenne Wildcat*
January 5, 1944	*Pride of the Plains*	October 6, 1944	*Code of the Prairie*
January 27, 1944	*The Fighting Seabees*	October 12, 1944	*My Buddy*
February 19, 1944	*Casanova in Burlesque*	October 16, 1944	*Storm Over Lisbon*
March 3, 1944	*Beneath Western Skies*	November 6, 1944	*Lights of Old Santa Fe*
March 19, 1944	*Mojave Firebrand*	November 10, 1944	*End of the Road*
March 28, 1944	*My Best Gal*	November 7, 1944	*Sheriff of Sundown*
April 2, 1944	*Hidden Valley Outlaws*	November 15, 1944	*Vigilantes of Dodge City*
April 3, 1944	*The Laramie Trail*	November 30, 1944	*Faces in the Fog*
April 4, 1944	*Outlaws of Santa Fe*	November 30, 1944	*Brazil*
April 7, 1944	*Call of the South Seas*	December 1, 1944	*Firebrands of Arizona*

December 23, 1944	*Thoroughbreds*		
December 23, 1944	*Lake Placid Serenade*		
December 30, 1944	*The Big Bonanza*		
December 31, 1944	*Sheriff of Las Vegas*		
January 16, 1945	*Grissly's Millions*		
January 22, 1945	*The Big Show-Off*		
January 26, 1945	*The Topeka Terror*		
February 15, 1945	*Great Stagecoach Robbery*		
February 19, 1945	*A Song for Miss Julie*		
February 28, 1945	*Sheriff of Cimarron*		
March 21, 1945	*Utah*		
March 30, 1945	*The Great Flamarion*	Distribution only	
April 2, 1945	*Identity Unknown*		
April 5, 1945	*Earl Carroll Vanities*		
April 20, 1945	*Corpus Christi Bandits*		
May 10, 1945	*The Phantom Speaks*		
May 20, 1945	*Lone Texas Ranger*		
May 21, 1945	*The Vampire's Ghost*		
May 23, 1945	*Three's a Crowd*		
May 28, 1945	*Flame of Barbary Coast*		
June 2, 1945	*Santa Fe Saddlemates*		
June 4, 1945	*A Sporting Chance*		
June 19, 1945	*Bells of Rosarita*		
June 29, 1945	*The Chicago Kid*		
July 1, 1945	*The Man from Oklahoma*		
July 3, 1945	*Gangs of the Waterfront*		
July 9, 1945	*Steppin' in Society*		
July 10, 1945	*Road to Alcatraz*		
July 11, 1945	*Trail of Kit Carson*		
July 14, 1945	*Oregon Trail*		
July 14, 1945	*The Cheaters*		
July 16, 1945	*Hitchhike to Happiness*		
July 23, 1945	*Jealousy*		
August 16, 1945	*Tell It to a Star*		
September 1, 1945	*Swingin' on a Rainbow*		
September 7, 1945	*Phantom of the Plains*		
September 10, 1945	*Behind City Lights*		
September 14, 1945	*Bandits of the Badlands*		
September 15, 1945	*Along the Navajo Trail*		
September 15, 1945	*The Fatal Witness*		
September 15, 1945	*Love, Honor and Goodbye*		
September 20, 1945	*Scotland Yard Investigator*		
September 29, 1945	*Sunset in El Dorado*		
October 7, 1945	*Marshal of Laredo*		
October 20, 1945	*Don't Fence Me In*		
November 1, 1945	*Rough Riders of Cheyenne*		
November 2, 1945	*Girls of the Big House*		
November 14, 1945	*Colorado Pioneers*		
November 15, 1945	*Mexicana*		
November 16, 1945	*The Tiger Woman*		
November 17, 1945	*Captain Tugboat Annie*		
November 27, 1945	*An Angel Comes to Brooklyn*		
December 13, 1945	*The Cherokee Flash*		
December 13, 1945	*The Woman Who Came Back*		
December 21, 1945	*Wagon Wheels Westward*		
December 25, 1945	*Dakota*		
December 28, 1945	*Song of Mexico*		
January 25, 1946	*Gay Blades*		
January 27, 1946	*A Guy Could Change*		
February 2, 1946	*Days of Buffalo Bill*		
February 4, 1946	*California Gold Rush*		
February 16, 1946	*The Madonna's Secret*		
February 28, 1946	*Crime of the Century*		
March 9, 1946	*Song of Arizona*		
March 16, 1946	*Strange Impersonation*		
March 29, 1946	*Sheriff of Redwood Valley*		
April 10, 1946	*Murder in the Music Hall*		
April 11, 1946	*The Undercover Woman*		
April 17, 1946	*Alias Billy the Kid*		
April 18, 1946	*Home on the Range*		
April 20, 1946	*The Catman of Paris*		
April 27, 1946	*The Glass Alibi*		

May 9, 1946	Rainbow Over Texas		
May 10, 1946	Sun Valley Cyclone		
May 11, 1946	Passkey to Danger		
May 12, 1946	Winter Wonderland		
May 18, 1946	The French Key		
May 22, 1946	The El Paso Kid		
May 24, 1946	Valley of the Zombies		
May 31, 1946	In Old Sacramento		
June 8, 1946	One Exciting Week		
June 15, 1946	Man from Rainbow Valley		
June 28, 1946	Traffic in Crime		
July 5, 1946	Specter of the Rose		
July 10, 1946	My Pal Trigger	Distribution only	
July 12, 1946	Night Train to Memphis		
July 22, 1946	Rendezvous with Annie		
July 23, 1946	Red River Renegades		
July 29, 1946	Conquest of Cheyenne		
August 7, 1946	The Inner Circle		
August 9, 1946	The Last Crooked Mile		
August 12, 1946	G.I. War Brides		
August 19, 1946	The Invisible Informer		
August 22, 1946	Earl Carroll Sketchbook		
August 26, 1946	Under Nevada Skies		
September 3, 1946	The Mysterious Mr. Valentine		
September 9, 1946	Rio Grande Raiders		
September 12, 1946	Roll on Texas Moon		
October 18, 1946	Home in Oklahoma		
November 7, 1946	The Magnificent Rogue		
November 11, 1946	Plainsman and the Lady		
November 15, 1946	Santa Fe Uprising		
November 18, 1946	Affairs of Geraldine		
November 21, 1946	Sioux City Sue		
December 2, 1946	I've Always Loved You		
December 5, 1946	Out California Way		
December 15, 1946	Heldorado	Distribution only	
December 15, 1946	The Fabulous Suzanne		
December 23, 1946	Stagecoach to Denver		
December 23, 1946	That Brennan Girl	Distribution only	
January 22, 1947	The Pilgrim Lady		
January 25, 1947	Trail to San Antone		
January 31, 1947	Calendar Girl		
February 1, 1947	Last Frontier Uprising		
February 15, 1947	Angel and the Badman	Distribution only	
	Apache Rose; Vigilantes of Boomtown		
March 8, 1947	The Ghost Goes Wild		
March 22, 1947	Hit Parade of 1947		
April 1, 1947	Homesteaders of Paradise Valley;		
	Twilight on the Rio Grande; Yankee Fakir		
April 15, 1947	Bells of San Angelo		
April 24, 1947	Spoilers of the North		
May 5, 1947	Oregon Trail Scouts		
May 15, 1947	That's My Gal		
June 1, 1947	That's My Man		
June 6, 1947	Saddle Pals		
June 10, 1947	Web of Danger		
June 25, 1947	Northwest Outpost		
July 1, 1947	Rustlers of Devil's Canyon		
July 3, 1947	The Trespasser		
July 15, 1947	Robin Hood of Texas		
July 15, 1947	Springtime in the Sierras	Distribution only	
July 24, 1947	Blackmail		
July 28, 1947	Wyoming		
August 11, 1947	The Pretender	Distribution only	
August 15, 1947	Marshal of Cripple Creek		
August 30, 1947	Along the Oregon Trail		
September 8, 1947	Exposed		
September 15, 1947	Driftwood		
October 1, 1947	The Wild Frontier		
October 15, 1947	On the Old Spanish Trail		
November 9, 1947	The Fabulous Texan		
November 24, 1947	The Flame		
December 15, 1947	Bandits of Dark Canyon; Under Colorado Skies		

January 1, 1948	The Main Street Kid	January 5, 1949	Rose of the Yukon
January 10, 1948	The Gay Ranchero	January 22, 1949	Sheriff of Wichita
January 15, 1948	Slippy McGee	February 8, 1949	Daughter of the Jungle
February 1, 1948	Campus Honeymoon	February 25, 1949	The Last Bandit
February 22, 1948	Oklahoma Badlands	March 1, 1949	Wake of the Red Witch
February 23, 1948	Madonna of the Desert	March 8, 1949	Hideout
March 14, 1948	The Inside Story	March 15, 1949	Duke of Chicago
March 25, 1948	Lightnin' in the Forest	March 28, 1949	The Red Pony
March 28, 1948	Bill and Coo	March 29, 1949	Death Valley Gunfighter
April 1, 1948	California Firebrand	April 8, 1949	Prince of the Plains
April 15, 1948	The Bold Frontiersman	April 15, 1949	Streets of San Francisco
April 25, 1948	Old Los Angeles	April 29, 1949	Susanna Pass
April 25, 1948	Heart of Virginia	May 2, 1949	Frontier Investigator
April 26, 1948	King of the Gamblers	May 23, 1949	Law of the Golden West
April 30, 1948	Under California Stars Distribution only	May 29, 1949	Hellfire
May 13, 1948	Carson City Raiders	June 8, 1949	Outcasts of the Trail
May 24, 1948	The Gallant Legion	July 15, 1949	The Wyoming Bandit
May 25, 1948	I, Jane Doe	July 27, 1949	South of Rio
May 31, 1948	Secret Service Investigator	July 28, 1949	Flaming Fury
June 15, 1948	The Timber Trail	August 1, 1949	The Red Menace
July 15, 1948	Eyes of Texas; Marshal of Amarillo	August 15, 1949	Brimstone
July 26, 1948	Daredevils of the Clouds	August 29, 1949	Bandit King of Texas
September 1, 1948	Sons of Adventure	September 1, 1949	Post Office Investigator
September 3, 1948	Angel in Exile	September 5, 1949	The Kid from Cleveland
September 5, 1948	Night Time in Nevada	September 9, 1949	Down Dakota Way
September 11, 1948	Out of the Storm	September 15, 1949	The Fighting Kentuckian
September 15, 1948	Desperadoes of Dodge City; Son of God's Country	September 22, 1949	Flame of Youth
October 1, 1948	The Denver Kid	October 7, 1949	San Antone Ambush
	Moonrise Distribution only	October 15, 1949	Navajo Trail Raiders
October 7, 1948	Macbeth	October 15, 1949	Alias the Champ
October 31, 1948	The Plunderers	November 4, 1949	Ranger of Cherokee Strip
November 1, 1948	Angel on the Amazon	November 15, 1949	The Golden Stallion
November 5, 1948	Grand Canyon Trail; Sundown in Santa Fe	November 24, 1949	Pioneer Marshal
November 24, 1948	Renegades of Sonora	November 25, 1949	Powder River Rustlers
December 8, 1948	Homicide for Three	December 14, 1949	Sands of Iwo Jima
December 29, 1948	The Far Frontier		

1950s

Release date	Title	Notes
January 8, 1950	Bells of Coronado	
January 11, 1950	The Blonde Bandit	
January 30, 1950	Unmasked	
February 6, 1950	Gunmen of Abilene	
February 28, 1950	Tarnished	
February 28, 1950	Singing Guns	
March 1, 1950	Belle of Old Mexico	
March 12, 1950	Federal Agent at Large	
March 25, 1950	House by the River	
March 25, 1950	Code of the Silver Sage	Distribution only
March 26, 1950	Harbor of Missing Men	
March 31, 1950	The Vanishing Westerner	
April 1, 1950	The Arizona Cowboy	
May 1, 1950	Women from Headquarters	
	Salt Lake Raiders	Distribution only
May 10, 1950	The Invisible Monster	
May 18, 1950	Rock Island Trail	
May 22, 1950	The Savage Horde	
June 1, 1950	Hills of Oklahoma; Destination Big House; Twilight in the Sierras	
June 26, 1950	The Avengers	
June 30, 1950	Covered Wagon Raid; Trigger, Jr.	
July 8, 1950	Trial Without Jury	
July 20, 1950	The Old Frontier	
July 28, 1950	Jungle Stampede	
August 6, 1950	Vigilante Hideout	
August 15, 1950	The Showdown	
August 29, 1950	Lonely Heart Bandits	
September 6, 1950	Frisco Tornado	
September 15, 1950	Surrender	
September 18, 1950	Redwood Forest Trail	
September 18, 1950	Prisoners in Petticoats	
September 25, 1950	Sunset in the West	
October 15, 1950	Hit Parade of 1951	
October 23, 1950	Rustlers on Horseback	
November 15, 1950	North of the Great Divide; Rio Grande	
November 20, 1950	Under Mexicali Stars	
November 25, 1950	The Missourians	
December 15, 1950	Trail of Robin Hood; California Passage	
January 20, 1951	Pride of Maryland	
January 27, 1951	Belle Le Grand	
January 30, 1951	Rough Riders of Durango	
February 2, 1951	Spoilers of the Plains	
February 23, 1951	Missing Women	
February 28, 1951	Night Riders of Montana	
March 1, 1951	Silver City Bonanza	
March 3, 1951	Oh! Susanna	
March 5, 1951	Cuban Fireball	
March 23, 1951	Insurance Investigator	
March 30, 1951	Heart of the Rockies	
April 8, 1951	Thunder in God's Country	
April 26, 1951	Bullfighter and the Lady	
May 1, 1951	Buckaroo Sheriff of Texas	
May 15, 1951	In Old Amarillo; Wells Fargo Gunmaster	
May 30, 1951	Million Dollar Pursuit	
June 1, 1951	Fighting Coast Guard	
June 20, 1951	Secrets of Monte Carlo	
July 1, 1951	The Dakota Kid	
July 15, 1951	Rodeo King and the Senorita	
July 25, 1951	Lost Planet Airmen	Feature version of their 1949 film serial King of the Rocket Men
August 24, 1951	Fort Dodge Stampede	
September 15, 1951	Havana Rose	
September 15, 1951	Arizona Manhunt	
October 6, 1951	Adventures of Captain Fabian	
October 15, 1951	South of Caliente; Utah Wagon Train	
October 20, 1951	Honeychile	
November 6, 1951	The Sea Hornet	
November 15, 1951	Pals of the Golden West	
November 15, 1951	Street Bandits	

November 19, 1951	Desert of Lost Men	
December 5, 1951	The Wild Blue Yonder	
January 21, 1952	Captive of Billy the Kid	
January 26, 1952	Lady Possessed	
February 8, 1952	Colorado Sundown	
March 1, 1952	The Last Musketeer	
March 22, 1952	Leadville Gunslinger	
March 24, 1952	Oklahoma Annie	
April 1, 1952	The Fabulous Senorita	
April 15, 1952	Border Saddlemates; Hoodlum Empire; Wild Horse Ambush	
May 1, 1952	Gobs and Gals	
May 20, 1952	Black Hills Ambush	
June 1, 1952	Bal Tabarin	
June 15, 1952	I Dream of Jeanie	
June 20, 1952	Thundering Caravans	
July 25, 1952	Old Oklahoma Plains	
September 5, 1952	Woman of the North Country	
September 14, 1952	The Quiet Man	
October 1, 1952	Tropical Heat Wave	
October 8, 1952	Desperadoes' Outpost	
October 10, 1952	The WAC from Walla Walla	
October 10, 1952	Toughest Man in Arizona	
October 20, 1952	South Pacific Trail	
November 15, 1952	Woman in the Dark	
November 20, 1952	Thunderbirds	
November 25, 1952	Ride the Man Down	
February 1, 1953	Marshal of Cedar Rock	
February 15, 1953	San Antone	
February 25, 1953	Old Overland Trail	
March 20, 1953	Woman They Almost Lynched	
March 30, 1953	The Lady Wants Mink	
April 5, 1953	A Perilous Journey	
April 28, 1953	Fair Wind to Java	
May 2, 1953	The Sun Shines Bright	
May 8, 1953	Iron Mountain Trail	
May 15, 1953	Savage Frontier	
June 12, 1953	City That Never Sleeps	
July 15, 1953	Sweethearts on Parade	
August 5, 1953	Down Laredo Way	
August 8, 1953	Bandits of the West	
August 15, 1953	Champ for a Day	
September 8, 1953	El Paso Stampede	
September 28, 1953	Shadows of Tombstone	
October 21, 1953	Sea of Lost Ships	
November 15, 1953	Flight Nurse	
November 15, 1953	Crazylegs	
December 16, 1953	Geraldine	
December 15, 1953	Red River Shore	
January 15, 1954	Jubilee Trail	
February 10, 1954	Phantom Stallion	
March 25, 1954	Make Haste to Live	
April 1, 1954	Untamed Heiress	
June 1, 1954	Hell's Half Acre	
July 1, 1954	Laughing Anne	
August 15, 1954	The Outcast	
August 23, 1954	Johnny Guitar	
August 25, 1954	Roogie's Bump	
September 1, 1954	The Shanghai Story	
September 1, 1954	Tobor the Great	
December 3, 1954	Trouble in the Glen	
December 8, 1954	The Atomic Kid	
December 15, 1954	Hell's Outpost	
January 5, 1955	African Manhunt	
January 28, 1955	Carolina Cannonball	
February 18, 1955	Timberjack	
March 22, 1955	Yellowneck	Distribution only
May 5, 1955	The Eternal Sea	
May 12, 1955	Santa Fe Passage	
May 19, 1955	I Cover the Underworld	
June 2, 1955	City of Shadows	
June 15, 1955	The Road to Denver	Distribution only
June 23, 1955	Double Jeopardy	

July 7, 1955	*Lay That Rifle Down*	
August 3, 1955	*The Last Command*	
September 15, 1955	*Headline Hunters*	
September 29, 1955	*Cross Channel*	
October 13, 1955	*The Twinkle in God's Eye*	
October 17, 1955	*A Man Alone*	
October 27, 1955	*No Man's Woman*	
November 10, 1955	*Secret Venture*	
November 17, 1955	*The Vanishing American*	
December 15, 1955	*The Fighting Chance*	
January 6, 1956	*Flame of the Islands*	
January 20, 1956	*Jaguar*	
January 27, 1956	*Track the Man Down*	
January 30, 1956	*Hidden Guns*	
March 9, 1956	*Come Next Spring*	
March 15, 1956	*When Gangland Strikes*	
March 29, 1956	*Magic Fire*	
April 6, 1956	*Stranger at My Door*	
April 27, 1956	*Terror at Midnight*	
May 3, 1956	*The Maverick Queen*	
July 23, 1956	*Dakota Incident*	
August 4, 1956	*Thunder Over Arizona*	
August 17, 1956	*Lisbon*	
August 24, 1956	*A Strange Adventure*	
October 5, 1956	*Daniel Boone, Trail Blazer*	Distribution only
October 12, 1956	*Scandal Incorporated*	
October 19, 1956	*The Man Is Armed*	
October 26, 1956	*Above Us the Waves*	Distribution only
November 16, 1956	*A Woman's Devotion*	
December 21, 1956	*Accused of Murder*	
January 25, 1957	*Duel at Apache Wells*	
February 15, 1957	*Affair in Reno*	
March 8, 1957	*Hell's Crossroads*	
April 5, 1957	*Spoilers of the Forest*	
May 17, 1957	*The Weapon*	
May 31, 1957	*The Lawless Eighties*	
June 21, 1957	*Journey to Freedom*	
June 28, 1957	*The Unearthly; Beginning of the End*	
July 15, 1957	*The Last Stagecoach West*	
September 7, 1957	*Pawnee*	
September 15, 1957	*Taming Sutton's Gal*	
September 22, 1957	*The Wayward Girl*	
October 6, 1967	*Hell Canyon Outlaws*	
October 18, 1957	*Panama Sal*	
November 1, 1957	*Raiders of Old California*	Distribution only
November 11, 1957	*The Crooked Circle*	
November 15, 1957	*Eighteen and Anxious*	
November 25, 1957	*Man from Tangier*	Distribution only
December 6, 1957	*Hell Ship Mutiny*	Distribution only
December 13, 1957	*Gunfire at Indian Gap*	
December 25, 1957	*West of Suez*	
January 10, 1958	*Outcasts of the City*	
February 7, 1958	*Scotland Yard Dragnet*	Distribution only
February 28, 1958	*The Notorious Mr. Monks*	
March 21, 1958	*Morning Call*	
April 24, 1958	*Juvenile Jungle*	
April 24, 1958	*Young and Wild*	
May 30, 1958	*Man or Gun*	
June 1, 1958	*Girl in the Woods*	
June 6, 1958	*The Man Who Died Twice*	
June 11, 1958	*Street of Darkness*	
October 3, 1958	*No Place to Land*	
December 2, 1958	*Invisible Avenger*	Distribution only
January 23, 1959	*Plunderers of Painted Flats*	
February 13, 1959	*OSS 117 Is Not Dead*	Distribution only
February 25, 1959	*Hidden Homicide*	

ENDNOTES

Chapter 1: Herbert Yates' Republic

1 *Independent*, February 5, 1966

2 Ibid.

3 *Chicago Daily Tribune*, June 14, 1935

4 Ibid.; *The Cincinnati Enquirer*, June 14, 1935

5 Ibid.; *The Cincinnati Enquirer*, June 8, 1935

6 *The Sandusky Register*, August 11, 1935

7 *Brooklyn Daily Eagle*, August 10, 1935

8 *Altoona Tribune*, August 24, 1935

9 *Santa Ana Register*, August 7, 1936

10 Ibid.

11 *Cumberland Evening Times*, September 6, 1935

12 *Los Angeles Times*, November 2, 1935

13 *Los Angeles Times*, December 18, 1935

14 *Pittsburgh Post-Gazette*, January 2, 1935

15 *The Des Moines Register*, August 24, 1936

16 *The Detroit Free Press*, October 23, 1936

17 *Arizona Republic*, February 12, 1937

18 *Harrisburg Telegraph*, May 28, 1937

19 Ibid.

20 *Nevada State Journal*, June 10, 1937

21 Ibid.

22 *Reno Gazette Journal*, February 20, 1937; *Democrat and Chronicle*, July 10, 1937; www.b-westerns.com/levine

23 *San Antonio Light*, July 10, 1937

24 *El Paso Herald Post*, October 13, 1937

25 *The Bristol Daily Courier*, June 2, 1938

26 *The Akron Beacon Journal*, February 5, 1939

27 *The St. Louis Star & Times*, January 20, 1939

28 *The Morning News*, March 11, 1939

29 *The San Bernardino Sun County*, March 16, 1939

30 *Santa Cruz Sentinel*, May 12, 1939

31 *St. Louis Star & Times*, May 16, 1939

32 Ibid.

33 *Rochester News-Sentinel*, May 18, 1939

34 *Detroit Free Press*, May 30, 1939

35 Ibid.; *The Morning Herald*, February 17, 1940; *Eugene Guard*, October 1, 1939

36 *New York Herald Telegraph*, September 9, 1939

37 Ibid.; *Detroit Free Press*, September 13, 1939; *The Desert Sun*, October 6, 1939

Chapter 2: The Making of a Cowboy

1 *Harrisburg Telegraph*, January 19, 1935

2 *The Courier Journal*, September 27, 1935

3 *The Daily Reporter*, December 24, 1935

4 *The Times*, October 16, 1960

5 *Gene Autry: His Life & Career*, p. 49

6 Ibid., p. 44

7 Ibid., p. 71

8 *Hollywood Reporter*, January 26, 1931

9 *Dallas Morning News*, April 12, 1938

10 Ibid.

11 *Detroit Free Press*, June 22, 1951; *The Philadelphia Inquirer*, October 19, 1951; *Variety*, June 20, 1951

12 *Variety*, October 19, 1951; *The Star Press*, June 28, 1951

13 *John Wayne: The Man & the Myth*, pp. 55–57

14 *The Young Duke: The Early Life of John Wayne*, pp. 55–56

15 Ibid., pp. 58–59

16 *John Wayne: The Life & Legend*, pp. 91–92

17 *John Wayne: American*, p. 175; *The Overlook Film Encyclopedia: Stunts*, p. 106

18 *Republic Studios: Between Poverty Row & the Majors*, pp. 15–17

19 Ibid., 19

20 *Shooting Star: A Biography of John Wayne*, pp. 252–54, www.glamourgirls ofthesilverscreen.com

21 *Hollywood Reporter*, November 13, 1952

22 Ibid.

23 Ibid.

24 *Republic Pictures: Between Poverty Row & the Majors*, pp. 22–29

Chapter 3: Ghouls, Freaks of Nature, and the Walking Dead

1 *The Great Movie Serials: Their Sound & Fury*, pp. 52–53

2 *Valley of the Cliffhangers*, pp. 112–14

3 *Pittsburgh Post-Gazette*, January 11, 1980

4 *Cliffhanger*, pp. 74–75

5 *The Edwardsville Intelligencer*, November 29, 1973

6 *Blood 'n' Thunder Cliffhanger Classics*, p. 171; *Classic Cliffhangers*, p. 202–3

7 *The Brooklyn Eagle*, December 12, 1943

8 *The Freeport Facts*, July 5, 1955

9 *The Film Encyclopedia*, p. 175

10 *Science Fiction Serials*, p. 42–43

11 *The Daily Plainsman*, October 6, 1946

12 Ibid.

13 *Pittsburgh Post-Gazette*, May 22, 1944

14 *Cumberland Evening Times*, September 2, 1944; *Republic Horror: The Serial Studio's Chillers*, p. 173

15 *Los Angeles Times*, February 15, 1946

16 *Mount Carmel Item*, November 8, 1946

17 Ibid.

18 Ibid.

19 Ibid.; *The Evening News*, August 9, 1946; *Pittsburgh Post-Gazette*, August 22, 1946

20 *Clarion Ledger*, July 27, 1991

21 *Science Fiction Serials*, pp. 179–81

22 *The Morning Call*, February 27, 1972

23 *The Guardian*, March 21, 2002; *Los Angeles Times*, March 18, 2002

24 *In a Door, Into a Fight, Out a Door, Into a Chase*, pp. 535–36

25 *Encyclopedia of American Film: Serials*, pp. 113–14

Chapter 4: The Biggest Little Studio

1 *Brooklyn Daily Eagle*, April 28, 1939

2 *Honolulu Star-Bulletin*, May 19, 1939

3 *The Ottawa Journal*, May 4, 1940

4 *The Morning Call*, April 28, 1940

5 *The Indianapolis Star*, May 11, 1940

6 Ibid.

7 *Pittsburgh Post-Gazette*, May 10, 1940

8 *Hollywood Reporter*, October 3, 1940

9 *Variety*, November 29, 1940

10 Ibid.

11 *The Bakersfield Californian*, February 11, 1954

12 *Waco Tribune Herald*, March 30, 1947

13 *Honolulu Star-Bulletin*, January 7, 1947

14 *The Times Herald*, October 28, 1945

15 *Motion Picture Herald*, June 22, 1946

16 *Pittsburgh Post-Gazette*, December 18, 1940

17 *Los Angeles Times*, February 4, 1849; *Beatrice Daily Sun*, March 27, 1849

18 *The Newark Advocate*, March 14, 1949

19 *John Wayne: American*, p. 313

20 *Hollywood Reporter*, June 29, 1948

21 *Joplin Globe*, June 30, 1948

22 *The Courier Journal*, October 29, 1950

23 *Chicago Tribune*, April 17, 1950

24 Ibid.

25 Ibid.; *Daily News*, September 18, 1950

26 *The Philadelphia Inquirer*, August 28, 1948; *Variety*, September 10, 1948

27 *Variety Movie Guide*, pp. 487–88

28 *The Western Films of John Ford*, pp. 146–48

29 *The Tennessean*, November 11, 1950

30 *The Hollywood Reporter*, October 30, 1950

31 Ibid.

32 *Albuquerque Journal*, November 18, 1959

33 *The Hollywood Reporter*, October 30, 1950

34 Ibid.

35 Ibid.

36 Ibid.

37 *Inside Oscar*, pp. 340–43

38 Ibid.

39 *John Wayne: American*, pp. 368–70

40 *The Hollywood Reporter*, November 13, 1952

41 Ibid.

Chapter 5: The Amazing Lydecker Brothers

1 *Encyclopedia of American Film Serials*, pp. 197–98

2 Memo between Herbert Yates and H. Lydecker, February 14, 1942

3 *Encyclopedia of American Film: Serials*, pp. 28–29

4 *The Overlook Film Encyclopedia*, pp. 53–54

5 http://filesofjerryblake.com

6 *Elizabethville Echo*, June 29, 1944

7 *The Legendary Lydecker Brothers*, pp. 126–27

8 *The Havre Daily News*, January 12, 1945

9 *The Legendary Lydecker Brothers*, pp. 143–44

10 *Democrat and Chronicle*, March 19, 1949

11 *The Filmgoers Guide to the Great Westerns: Stagecoach to Tombstone*, p. 52

12 *The Rushville Republican*, August 5, 1954

13 *The Filmgoers Guide to the Great Westerns: Stagecoach to Tombstone*, pp. 55–56

Chapter 6: Republic Goes to War

1 *The Akron Beacon Journal*, June 19, 1942; *Poughkeepsie Journal*, July 16, 1942

2 Ibid.; *Ogden Standard Examiner*, January 3, 1943

3 *Hutchinson News*, November 15, 1942

4 Ibid.; *The Jackson Sun*, August 29, 1943

5 *The Sydney Morning Herald*, February 14, 1944

6 Ibid.

7 http://www.imdb.com/title/tt0034742/

8 *Rushville Republican*, March 18, 1944; www.tcm.com Fighting Seabees

9 *Star Tribune*, March 26, 1944

10 *Variety*, April 27, 1944

11 *Altoona Tribune*, October 20, 1944

12 Ibid.

13 *Waco Tribune Herald*, October 6, 1946

14 *Variety Movie Guide*, pp. 523–25

15 *John Wayne: American*, pp. 318–20

16 *Brooklyn Daily Eagle*, December 31, 1949

17 *The Pittsburgh Press*, December 30, 1949

18 *Los Angeles Times*, August 12, 1949

19 *Republic Studios: Between Poverty Row & the Majors*, pp. 74–75; *Valley of the Cliffhangers*, p. 193; *Hartford Courant*, July 26, 1942

20 *The Edwardsville Intelligencer*, November 29, 1973

21 *The Havre Daily News*, November 13, 1942; *News Journal*, July 31, 1942

22 *The Daily Times Davenport*, October 7, 1942

23 Ibid.

24 *The Daily Journal*, October 10, 1942

25 *The Morning News*, February 18, 1943

26 *Miami Daily News Record*, April 5, 1943

27 *Lancaster Eagle-Gazette*, January 18, 1944

28 *The News Journal*, September 14, 1943

Chapter 7: The Stuntmen

1 *Democrat and Chronicle*, November 30, 1947

2 *The Fun of Living Dangerously*, pp. 6–7

3 Ibid., pp. 7–10

4 *The News Chronicle*, October 4, 1929

5 *Los Angeles Times*, April 17, 1960

6 Ibid.; *Lansing State Journal*, October 3, 1971

7 *Stuntman!*, pp. 42–43

8 *Encyclopedia of American Serials*, pp. 127–30

9 *The Palm Beach Post*, January 27, 1977

10 *The Frankenstein Archive*, pp. 52-53

11 *Santa Ana Register*, January 27, 1977

12 *Hollywood Stunt Performers*, pp. 282–83

13 *Great Movie Serials*, pp. 280–81

14 Ibid.

15 *Serials-ly Speaking*, pp. 91–92

16 *Hollywood Stunt Performers*, pp. 113–14

17 Ibid., pp. 178–79

18 Ibid., pp. 111–12; *Arizona Republic*, October 19, 1967

19 www.b-westerns.com/stunt10.htm

Chapter 8: The Second Hollywood

1 *Oakland Tribune*, August 15, 1954

2 Ibid.

3 *The Times Recorder*, September 6, 1935

4 *The Hollywood Reporter*, April 13, 1938

5 *Brooklyn Daily Eagle*, May 2, 1938

6 *Carroll Daily Herald*, August 23, 1938; *The Hollywood Reporter*, May 7, 1938

7 Ibid.

8 Ibid.; *The Republic*, December 15, 1938

9 *The Newark Advocate*, November 4, 1938

10 *The Independent Record*, November 12, 1938

11 Ibid.

12 *Encyclopedia of American Serials*, pp. 58–59

13 *New Deal Cowboy*, pp. 83, 111

14 *Public Cowboy No. 1*, pp. 117–18

15 *Reading Times*, December 16, 1939

16 *Lubbock Evening Journal*, August 5, 1947

17 *The Plain Speaker*, October 11, 1940

18 *Encyclopedia of American Serials*, pp. 63–68

19 *The Anniston Star*, August 2, 1942; *The News Leader*, August 21, 1943

Chapter 9: Republic's Leading Ladies

1 *John Wayne: American*, pp. 283–85

2 *The New York Times*, March 3, 1947

3 *Democrat and Chronicle*, December 18, 1948

4 *Beatrice Daily Sun*, March 27, 1949; *Oakland Tribune*, February 28, 1947

5 *The Brownsville Herald*, October 21, 1953

6 *Lubbock Evening Journal*, January 19, 1954; *Los Angeles Times*, November 26, 1953

7 *The Bakersfield Californian*, May 28, 1954; *Los Angeles Times*, October 7, 1954

8 *Los Angeles Times*, February 13, 1955

9 *Abilene Reporter*, March 27, 1956; *Orlando Evening Star*, September 21, 1955

10 *Independent*, July 5, 1957; *The Plain Speaker*, July 9, 1957

11 *Los Angeles Times*, October 5, 1957

12 *Arizona Republic*, October 11, 1958; *The Times*, March 27, 1960

13 *Philadelphia Daily News*, August 28, 1961

14 *The Argus*, January 27, 1972

15 *The Sunday Herald*, April 6, 1947

16 *The Hollywood Reporter*, August 7, 1943; *The News Leader*, August 7, 1943

17 *The Hollywood Reporter*, February 3, 1943

18 *The Jackson Sun*, April 26, 1943

19 *Big Spring Daily Herald*, September 19, 1943

20 *The Tampa Tribune*, February 24, 1985

21 *The Cowboy and the Senorita*, pp. 25–30

22 Ibid.

23 Ibid.

24 Ibid.

25 Ibid.

26 *Los Angeles Daily News*, August 4, 1970

27 *Movie Line Magazine*, April 1944

28 *The Newark Advocate*, February 15, 1945

29 *The Tampa Tribune*, February 8, 2001

30 *Los Angeles Times*, February 8, 2001

31 *The Guardian*, February 28, 2003

32 *The Havre Daily News*, September 6, 1941

33 *The Havre Daily News*, July 7, 1941

34 *Chicago Tribune*, February 17, 2003; *The Brooklyn Daily Eagle*, November 7, 1944

35 *John Wayne: American*, pp. 274–75

36 *Tallahassee Democrat*, January 20, 1946

37 *Variety*, November 12, 1945

38 *The Brooklyn Daily Eagle*, April 15, 1946

39 *The Overlook Film Encyclopedia*, pp. 154–55; *Photoplay Magazine*, June 4, 1947; *Argus Leader*, July 26, 1945

40 *Pittsburgh Post-Gazette*, October 20, 1949

41 *John Wayne: American*, pp. 217–21

42 *Los Angeles Times*, October 16, 1950

43 *Kansas City Times*, March 17, 1952

44 *Lansing State Journal*, March 15, 1953

45 http://www.imdb.com/title/tt0045743/

46 *Santa Cruz Sentinel*, June 15, 1962

47 *Chicago Tribune*, February 17, 2003

48 *Visalia Times-Delta*, February 15, 2003

Chapter 10: Fade to Black

1 *Los Angeles Times*, August 20, 1958

2 *The New York Times*, February 2, 1941

3 Ibid.

4 *Motion Picture Herald*, June 22, 1946

5 *Hollywood Reporter*, October 26, 1946

6 *Hollywood Reporter*, October 31, 1949; *John Wayne: American* pp. 274–75; *Democrat and Chronicle*, October 4, 1946

7 *Motion Picture Herald*, November 24, 1951

8 *Motion Picture Herald*, November 24, 1951

9 *The Daily Republic*, March 15, 1952

10 *Los Angeles Examiner*, April 3, 1952; *Variety*, April 3, 1952

11 *Variety*, April 3, 1953.

12 *Variety*, April 11, 1952

13 *Variety*, April 12, 1952

14 *Variety*, May 14, 1952

15 *Variety*, July 23, 1952

16 *Honolulu Star Bulletin*, November 5, 1952

17 *The Times*, November 13, 1952

18 *Los Angeles Times*, January 27, 1953; *Los Angeles Times*, March 4, 1953

19 *The New York Age*, July 11, 1953

20 *The Times*, November 3, 1953

21 *Variety*, July 21, 1954

22 *Variety*, April 6, 1955

23 *Albuquerque Journal*, February 11, 1954

24 *Albuquerque Journal*, November 23, 1954

25 *Hollywood Reporter*, November 23, 1957

26 *Los Angeles Times*, April 2, 1958

27 Ibid.

28 *Press Courier*, May 19, 1958

29 *Hollywood Reporter*, April 8, 1958

30 *Lansing State Journal*, April 8, 1958

31 *Green Bay Press-Gazette*, April 8, 1958

32 *The Des Moines Register*, September 3, 1959

33 *Hollywood Reporter*, July 12, 1959

34 Ibid.

35 Ibid.; *The Burlington Free Press*, December 15, 1959

36 *The La Crosse Tribune*, November 25, 1959

37 *The Miami News*, November 24, 1959

38 *The Pittsburgh Press*, December 4, 1956

39 *The Daily Times, News*, June 6, 1960

40 *The Monroe News-Star*, May 24, 1962

41 *Independent*, February 5, 1966

42 *Los Angeles Times*, February 4, 1966

43 *Variety*, September 14, 1993

44 Ibid.

BIBLIOGRAPHY

Books

Barbour, Alan G. *Cliffhanger: A Pictorial History of the Motion Picture Serial.* New York: A & W Publishers, Inc., 1977.

Cline, William C. *Serials-ly Speaking: Essays on Cliffhangers.* Jefferson, NC: McFarland Publishing, 1994.

Cusic, Don. *Gene Autry: His Life & Career.* Jefferson, NC: McFarland, 2010.

Davis, Hank. *Classic Cliffhangers: Volume 2 1941-1955.* Parkville, MD: Midnight Marquee Press, Inc., 2008.

Donev, Stef. *The Fun of Living Dangerously: The Life of Yakima Canutt.* New York: Macmillan McGraw-Hill, 2000.

Drake, Oliver, and Yakima Canutt. *Stunt Man: The Autobiography of Yakima Canutt.* Norman, OK: University of Oklahoma, 1997.

Duchemin, Michael. *New Deal Cowboy: Gene Autry & Public Diplomacy.* Norman: University of Oklahoma, 2016.

Elley, Derek, and Richard Attenborough. *Variety Movie Guide.* New York: Prentice Hall, 1992.

Enss, Chris, and Howard Kazanjian. *The Cowboy & the Senorita: A Biography of Roy Rogers & Dale Evans.* Guilford, CT: TwoDot Books, 2005.

Enss, Chris, and Howard Kazanjian. *The Young Duke: The Early Life of John Wayne.* Guilford, CT: Globe Pequot Press, 2007.

Etulain, Richard W., and Glenda Riley. *The Hollywood West: Lives of Film Legends Who Shaped It.* Golden, CO: Fulcrum Publishing, 2001.

Eyman, Scott. *John Wayne: The Life and Legend.* New York: Simon & Schuster, 2015.

Freese, Gene Scott. *Hollywood Stunt Performers, 1910s–1970s: A Biographical Dictionary.* Jefferson, NC: McFarland Publishing, 2004.

Glut, Donald. *The Frankenstein Archive: Essays on the Monster, the Myth, the Movies, and More.* Jefferson, NC: McFarland Publishing, 2002.

Hardy, Phil. *The Overlook Film Encyclopedia: The Western*. New York: Overlook Press, 1995.

Harman, Jim, and Donald Glut. *The Great Movie Serials: Their Sound and Fury*. New York: Doubleday, 1972.

Henderson, Jan Alan. *The Legendary Lydecker Brothers*. New York: Createspace Independent Publishing, 2010.

Hughes, Howard. *The Filmgoers Guide to the Great Westerns: Stagecoach to Tombstone*. London: I. B. Tauris, 2008.

Hulse, Ed, Rex Layton, Daniel Neyer, and Brian Taven. *Blood 'n' Thunder Cliffhanger Classics*. New York: CreateSpace Independent Publishing Platform, 2012.

Hurst, Richard M. *Republic Studios: Between Poverty Row and the Majors*. Metuchen, NJ: Scarecrow Press, 1979.

Katz, Ephraim. *The Film Encyclopedia*. Springfield, OH: Crowell Publishing, 1979.

Kinnard, Ray. *Science Fiction Serials: A Critical Filmography of the 31 Hard SF Cliffhangers*. Jefferson, NC: McFarland Publishing, 2008.

Langley, Christopher. *Images of America: Lone Pine*. Charleston, SC: Arcadia Publishing, 2007.

Loy, Phillip R. *Westerns & American Culture, 1930–1955*. Jefferson, NC: McFarland Publishing, 2001.

Mathis, Jack. *Valley of the Cliffhangers*. Barrington, IL: Jack Mathis Advertising, 1975.

Mathis, Jack. *Republic Confidential: The Players*. Barrington, IL: Jack Mathis Advertising, 1992.

Mayer, Geoff. *Encyclopedia of American Film: Serials*. Jefferson, NC: McFarland Publishing, 2017.

McFadden, Brian. *Republic Horrors: The Serial Studio's Chillers Kohner*, Madison & Danforth, 2013.

McFadden, Brian. *Republic Mysteries: The Serial Studio's WhoDunIts*. Kohner, Madison & Danforth, 2015.

Munn, Michael. *John Wayne: The Man and the Myth*. Berkeley, CA: Berkeley Press, 2005.

Needham, Hal. *Stuntman! My Car-Crashing, Plane-Jumping, Bone-Breaking, Death-Defying Hollywood Life*. Boston, MA: Little, Brown and Company, 2011.

Olson, James, and Randy Roberts. *John Wayne: American*. Lincoln, NE: Bison Books, 1997.

Place, J. A. *The Western Films of John Ford*. New York: Citadel Publishing, 1977.

Swann, Thomas Burnett. *The Heroine or the Horse: Leading Ladies in Republic Films*. New York: A. S. Barnes, 1977.

Warren, Holly George. *Public Cowboy No. 1: The Life and Times of Gene Autry*. Oxford: Oxford University Press, 2009.

Wiley, Mason, and Damien Bona. *Inside Oscar: The Unofficial History of the Academy Awards*. New York: Ballantine Books, 1986.

Witney, William, and Francis Nevins. *In a Door, Into a Fight, Out a Door, Into a Chase: Moviemaking Remembered by the Guy Next Door*. Jefferson, NC: McFarland Publishing, 2005.

Zolotow, Maurice. *Shooting Star: A Biography of John Wayne*. New York: Simon & Schuster, 1974.

Newspapers

Abilene Reporter, Abilene, Texas, March 27, 1956

The Akron Beacon Journal, Akron, Ohio, February 5, 1939

The Akron Beacon Journal, Akron, Ohio, June 19, 1942

The Akron Beacon Journal, Akron, Ohio, November 6, 1950

Albuquerque Journal, Albuquerque, New Mexico, November 18, 1950

Albuquerque Journal, Albuquerque, New Mexico, February 11, 1954

Albuquerque Journal, Albuquerque, New Mexico, November 23, 1954

Altoona Tribune, Blair County, Pennsylvania, August 24, 1935

Altoona Tribune, Blair County, Pennsylvania, October 20, 1944

The Amarillo Globe-Times, Amarillo, Texas, April 8, 1958

The Anniston Star, Anniston, Alabama, August 2, 1942

The Argus, Fremont, California, January 27, 1972

Argus-Leader, Sioux Falls, South Dakota, May 28, 1940

Argus-Leader, Sioux Falls, South Dakota, July 26, 1945

Arizona Republic, Phoenix, Arizona, February 12, 1937

Arizona Republic, Phoenix, Arizona, May 13, 1937

Arizona Republic, Phoenix, Arizona, October 11, 1958

Arizona Republic, Phoenix, Arizona, October 29, 1967

Asbury Park Press, Asbury Park, New Jersey, November 13, 1952

The Bakersfield Californian, Bakersfield, California, February 11, 1954

The Bakersfield Californian, Bakersfield, California, May 28, 1954

The Baltimore Sun, Baltimore, Maryland, November 17, 1971

Battle Creek Enquirer, Battle Creek, Michigan, November 9, 1950

Battle Creek Enquirer, Battle Creek, Michigan, April 29, 1953

Beatrice Daily Sun, Beatrice, Nebraska, March 27, 1949

Big Spring Daily Herald, Big Spring, Texas, February 3, 1943

Big Spring Daily Herald, Big Spring, Texas, September 19, 1943

The Bonham Daily Favorite, Bonham, Texas, November 5, 1950

The Bristol Daily Courier, Bristol, Pennsylvania, June 2, 1938

Brooklyn Daily Eagle, Brooklyn, New York, August 10, 1935

Brooklyn Daily Eagle, Brooklyn, New York, May 2, 1938

Brooklyn Daily Eagle, Brooklyn, New York, April 28, 1939

Brooklyn Daily Eagle, Brooklyn, New York, December 12, 1943

Brooklyn Daily Eagle, Brooklyn, New York, November 7, 1944

Brooklyn Daily Eagle, Brooklyn, New York, April 15, 1946

Brooklyn Daily Eagle, Brooklyn, New York, December 31, 1949

Brooklyn Daily Eagle, Brooklyn, New York, December 28, 1950

The Brownsville Herald, Brownsville, Texas, October 21, 1953

The Burlington Free Press, Burlington, Vermont, December 15, 1959

Carroll Daily Herald, Carroll, Iowa, September 23, 1938

Chicago Daily Tribune, Chicago, Illinois, June 14, 1935

Chicago Daily Tribune, Chicago, Illinois, May 11, 1947

Chicago Daily Tribune, Chicago, Illinois, November 17, 1950

Chicago Tribune, Chicago, Illinois, May 27, 1986

Chicago Tribune, Chicago, Illinois, February 17, 2003

The Cincinnati Enquirer, Cincinnati, Ohio, June 8, 1935

The Cincinnati Enquirer, Cincinnati, Ohio, June 14, 1935

The Cincinnati Enquirer, Cincinnati, Ohio, May 17, 1937

The Cincinnati Enquirer, Cincinnati, Ohio, August 30, 1961

The Cincinnati Enquirer, Cincinnati, Ohio, March 14, 1991

The Clarion-Ledger, Jackson, Mississippi, July 27, 1991

The Courier Journal, Louisville, Kentucky, September 27, 1935

The Courier Journal, Louisville, Kentucky, July 30, 1950

The Courier Journal, Louisville, Kentucky, October 29, 1950

The Courier Journal, Louisville, Kentucky, November 2, 1950

Cumberland Evening Times, Cumberland, Maryland, September 6, 1935

Cumberland Sunday Times, Cumberland, Maryland, May 21, 1944

The Daily News, Huntingdon, Pennsylvania, September 18, 1950

The Daily Plainsman, Huron, South Dakota, August 13, 1942

The Daily Plainsman, Huron, South Dakota, October 6, 1946

Daily Press, Newport News, Virginia, March 15, 1991

The Daily Reporter, Coldwater, Michigan, December 24, 1935

The Daily Republic, Fairfield, California, March 15, 1952

The Daily Times, Mitchell, South Dakota, October 7, 1942

The Daily Times, New Philadelphia, Ohio, August 9, 1950

The Daily Times, Wisconsin Rapids, Wisconsin, December 3, 1951

The Daily Times News, Burlington, Vermont, June 6, 1960

The Dallas Morning News, Dallas, Texas, April 12, 1938

Democrat and Chronicle, Rochester, New York, July 10, 1937

Democrat and Chronicle, Rochester, New York, October 4, 1946

Democrat and Chronicle, Rochester, New York, May 18, 1947

Democrat and Chronicle, Rochester, New York, November 30, 1947

Democrat and Chronicle, Rochester, New York, December 18, 1948

Democrat and Chronicle, Rochester, New York, March 19, 1949

The Des Moines Register, Des Moines, Iowa, August 24, 1936

The Des Moines Register, Des Moines, Iowa, August 20, 1944

The Des Moines Register, Des Moines, Iowa, September 3, 1959

The Desert Sun, Palm Springs, California, October 6, 1939

Detroit Free Press, Detroit, Michigan, October 23, 1936

Detroit Free Press, Detroit, Michigan, May 30, 1939

Detroit Free Press, Detroit, Michigan, September 13, 1939

Detroit Free Press, Detroit, Michigan, June 22, 1951

Dixon Evening Telegraph, Dixon, Illinois, April 6, 1967

The Edwardsville Intelligencer, Edwardsville, Illinois, November 29, 1973

El Paso Herald Post, El Paso, Texas, October 13, 1937

Elizabethville Echo, Elizabethville, Pennsylvania, June 29, 1944

Eugene Guard, Eugene, Oregon, October 1, 1939

The Evening News, Sault St. Marie, Michigan, August 9, 1946

The Freeport Facts, Freeport, Texas, July 5, 1955

The Guardian, London, United Kingdom, March 21, 2002

The Guardian, London, United Kingdom, February 28, 2003

Great Bend Tribune, Great Bend, Kansas, August 30, 1961

Green Bay Press Gazette, Green Bay, Wisconsin, April 8, 1958

Harrisburg Telegraph, Harrisburg, Pennsylvania, January 19, 1935

Harrisburg Telegraph, Harrisburg, Pennsylvania, May 28, 1937

Hartford Courant, Hartford, Connecticut, July 26, 1942

The Havre Daily News, Havre, Montana, September 6, 1941

The Havre Daily News, Havre, Montana, September 7, 1941

The Havre Daily News, Havre, Montana, November 13, 1942

The Havre Daily News, Havre, Montana, January 12, 1945

Honolulu Star-Bulletin, Honolulu, Hawaii, May 19, 1939

Honolulu Star-Bulletin, Honolulu, Hawaii, May 4, 1940

Honolulu Star-Bulletin, Honolulu, Hawaii, November 5, 1952

Hutchinson News, Hutchinson, Kansas, November 15, 1942

Independent, Long Beach, California, July 5, 1957

Independent, Long Beach, California, February 5, 1966

The Independent Record, Helena, Montana, November 12, 1938

The Indianapolis Star, Indianapolis, Indiana, July 11, 1937

The Indianapolis Star, Indianapolis, Indiana, May 11, 1940

The Indianapolis Star, Indianapolis, Indiana, November 23, 1957

The Indianapolis Star, Indianapolis, Indiana, November 25, 1960

The Jackson Sun, Jackson, Michigan, August 26, 1943

The Jackson Sun, Jackson, Michigan, August 29, 1943

Joplin Globe, Joplin, Missouri, June 30, 1948

Kansas City Times, Kansas City, Missouri, March 17, 1952

The La Crosse Tribune, La Crosse, Wisconsin, November 25, 1959

Lancaster Eagle-Gazette, Lancaster, Ohio, January 1, 1944

Lansing State Journal, Lansing, Michigan, March 15, 1953

Lansing State Journal, Lansing, Michigan, April 8, 1958

Lansing State Journal, Lansing, Michigan, October 3, 1971

Lincoln Journal Star, Lincoln, Nebraska, May 10, 1959

Los Angeles Daily News, Los Angeles, California, August 4, 1970

Los Angeles Examiner, Los Angeles, California, April 3, 1952

Los Angeles Times, Los Angeles, California, November 2, 1935

Los Angeles Times, Los Angeles, California, December 18, 1935

Los Angeles Times, Los Angeles, California, December 27, 1940

Los Angeles Times, Los Angeles, California, February 15, 1946

Los Angeles Times, Los Angeles, California, May 10, 1946

Los Angeles Times, Los Angeles, California, August 19, 1946

Los Angeles Times, Los Angeles, California, February 4, 1949

Los Angeles Times, Los Angeles, California, August 12, 1949

Los Angeles Times, Los Angeles, California, October 16, 1950

Los Angeles Times, Los Angeles, California, July 16, 1951

Los Angeles Times, Los Angeles, California, March 15, 1952

Los Angeles Times, Los Angeles, California, January 27, 1953

Los Angeles Times, Los Angeles, California, March 4, 1953

Los Angeles Times, Los Angeles, California, November 26, 1953

Los Angeles Times, Los Angeles, California, October 7, 1954

Los Angeles Times, Los Angeles, California, February 13, 1955

Los Angeles Times, Los Angeles, California, January 6, 1958

Los Angeles Times, Los Angeles, California, March 8, 1958

Los Angeles Times, Los Angeles, California, April 2, 1958

Los Angeles Times, Los Angeles, California, August 20, 1958

Los Angeles Times, Los Angeles, California, November 20, 1958

Los Angeles Times, Los Angeles, California, April 17, 1960

Los Angeles Times, Los Angeles, California, February 4, 1966

Los Angeles Times, Los Angeles, California, April 14, 1994

Los Angeles Times, Los Angeles, California, February 12, 1997

Los Angeles Times, Los Angeles, California, February 8, 2001

Los Angeles Times, Los Angeles, California, October 5, 2001

Los Angeles Times, Los Angeles, California, March 18, 2002

Lubbock Evening Journal, Lubbock, Texas, August 5, 1947

Lubbock Evening Journal, Lubbock, Texas, January 19, 1954

Miami Daily News Record, Miami, Florida, April 5, 1943

The Miami News, Miami, Florida, October 6, 1957

The Miami News, Miami, Florida, November 24, 1959

The Monroe News-Star, Monroe, Louisiana, May 24, 1962

The Morning Call, Allentown, Pennsylvania, August 18, 1938

The Morning Call, Allentown, Pennsylvania, April 28, 1940

The Morning Call, Allentown, Pennsylvania, August 31, 1942

The Morning Call, Allentown, Pennsylvania, February 27, 1972

The Morning Herald, Uniontown, Pennsylvania, February 17, 1940

The Morning News, Wilmington, Delaware, March 11, 1939

The Morning News, Wilmington, Delaware, February 18, 1943

Mount Carmel Item, Mount Carmel, Pennsylvania, November 8, 1946

Nevada State Journal, Reno, Nevada, June 10, 1937

The News-Chronicle, Shippensburg, Pennsylvania, October 4, 1929

The News Journal, Wilmington, Delaware, July 31, 1942

The News Journal, Wilmington, Delaware, September 14, 1943

The News Leader, Staunton, Virginia, August 7, 1943

The News Leader, Staunton, Virginia, August 21, 1943

The Newark Advocate, Newark, Ohio, November 4, 1938

The Newark Advocate, Newark, Ohio, February 15. 1945

The New York Age, New York, New York, July 11, 1953

New York Herald, New York, New York, September 9, 1939

New York Times, New York, New York, February 2, 1941

New York Times, New York, New York, March 3, 1947

New York Times, New York, New York, August 5, 1951

New York Times, New York, New York, December 24, 2016

The Newark Advocate, Newark, Ohio, March 14, 1949

Oakland Tribune, Oakland, California, February 28, 1947

Oakland Tribune, Oakland, California, October 16, 1952

Oakland Tribune, Oakland, California, August 15, 1954

The Ogden Standard-Examiner, Ogden, Utah, May 10, 1942

The Ogden Standard-Examiner, Ogden, Utah, January 3, 1943

Orlando Evening Star, Orlando, Florida, September 21, 1955

The Ottawa Journal, Ottawa, Ontario, Canada, May 4, 1940

The Palm Beach Post, Palm Beach, Florida, January 27, 1977

Philadelphia Daily News, Philadelphia, Pennsylvania, August 28, 1961

The Philadelphia Inquirer, Philadelphia, Pennsylvania, January 27, 1938

The Philadelphia Inquirer, Philadelphia, Pennsylvania, August 28, 1948

The Philadelphia Inquirer, Philadelphia, Pennsylvania, October 19, 1951

Pittsburgh Post-Gazette, Pittsburgh, Pennsylvania, January 2, 1935

The Pittsburgh Press, Pittsburgh, Pennsylvania, September 7, 1943

The Pittsburgh Press, Pittsburgh, Pennsylvania, December 4, 1956

Pittsburgh Post-Gazette, Pittsburgh, Pennsylvania, May 10, 1940

Pittsburgh Post-Gazette, Pittsburgh, Pennsylvania, May 22, 1944

Pittsburgh Post-Gazette, Pittsburgh, Pennsylvania, August 22, 1946

Pittsburgh Post-Gazette, Pittsburgh, Pennsylvania, December 18, 1948

Pittsburgh Post-Gazette, Pittsburgh, Pennsylvania, October 20, 1949

Pittsburgh Post-Gazette, Pittsburgh, Pennsylvania, August 28, 1961

Pittsburgh Post-Gazette, Pittsburgh, Pennsylvania, January 1, 1980

The Plain Speaker, Hazleton, Pennsylvania, October 11, 1940

The Plain Speaker, Hazleton, Pennsylvania, July 9, 1957

Poughkeepsie Journal, Poughkeepsie, New York, July 16, 1942

Press-Courier, Oxnard, California, May 19, 1958

Reading Times, Reading, Pennsylvania, December 16, 1939

Reno Gazette Journal, Reno, Nevada, February 20, 1937

The Republic, Columbus, Indiana, December 15, 1938

Rochester News-Sentinel, Rochester, New York, May 18, 1939

Rushville Republican, Rushville, Indiana, March 18, 1944

Rushville Republican, Rushville, Indiana, August 5, 1954

The St. Louis Star & Times, St. Louis, Missouri, January 20, 1939

The St. Louis Star & Times, St. Louis, Missouri, May 16, 1939

The Salt Lake Tribune, Salt Lake, Utah, December 28, 1948

The Salt Lake Tribune, Salt Lake, Utah, October 30, 1950

San Antonio Light, San Antonio, Texas, July 10, 1937

The San Bernardino County Sun, San Bernardino, California, March 16, 1939

The Sandusky Register, Sandusky, Ohio, August 11, 1935

Santa Ana Register, Santa Ana, California, August 7, 1936

Santa Ana Register, Santa Ana, California, January 27, 1977

Santa Cruz Sentinel, Santa Cruz, California, May 12, 1939

Santa Cruz Sentinel, Santa Cruz, California, June 15, 1962

Shamokin News-Dispatch, Shamokin, Pennsylvania, April 22, 1953

South Florida Sun Sentinel, Fort Lauderdale, Florida, September 5, 1994

The Springfield Leader, Springfield, Missouri, October 24, 1929

Star Gazette, Elmira, New York, August 21, 1957

The Star Press, Muncie, Indiana, June 28, 1951

Star Tribune, Minneapolis, Minnesota, March 26, 1944

Star Tribune, Minneapolis, Minnesota, July 7, 1957

The Sunday Herald, Provo, Utah, April 6, 1947

The Sydney Morning Herald, Sydney, New South Wales, Australia,
    February 14, 1944

Tallahassee Democrat, Tallahassee, Florida, January 20, 1946

The Tampa Tribune, Tampa, Florida, February 24, 1985

The Tampa Tribune, Tampa, Florida, March 14, 1991

The Tampa Tribune, Tampa, Florida, February 8, 2001

The Tennessean, Nashville, Tennessee, November 5, 1950

The Times Herald, Port Huron, Michigan, October 28, 1945

The Times Recorder, Zanesville, Ohio, September 6, 1935

The Times Recorder, Zanesville, Ohio, October 13, 1940

The Times, San Mateo, California, November 13, 1952

The Times, San Mateo, California, November 3, 1953

The Times, Shreveport, Louisiana, October 18, 1950

The Times, Shreveport, Louisiana, March 27, 1960

The Times, Shreveport, Louisiana, October 14, 1960

The Times, Shreveport, Louisiana, October 16, 1960

Visalia Times-Delta, Visalia, California, February 15, 2003

Waco Tribune Herald, Waco, Texas, October 6, 1946

Waco Tribune Herald, Waco, Texas, October 20, 1946

Waco Tribune Herald, Waco, Texas, March 30, 1947

The Wall Street Journal, New York, New York, May 25, 1964

Historical Quarterlies/Magazines/ Newsletters/Memos

Channels, Betting on Republic's Bonanza, January 1989

The Film Daily Cavalcade, Republic Pictures, 1939

The Golden Age of Republic Serials, Screen Facts No. 17, 1968

The Golden Age of Republic Serials, Part 2, Screen Facts No. 18, 1968

The Hollywood Reporter, April 13, 1938

The Hollywood Reporter, May 7, 1938

The Hollywood Reporter, October 3, 1940

The Hollywood Reporter, August 7, 1943

The Hollywood Reporter, May 1, 1944

The Hollywood Reporter, October 20, 1946

The Hollywood Reporter, October 26, 1946

The Hollywood Reporter, June 29, 1948

The Hollywood Reporter, November 29, 1948

The Hollywood Reporter, October 31, 1949

The Hollywood Reporter, April 6, 1955

The Hollywood Reporter, September 13, 1955

The Hollywood Reporter, November 23, 1957

The Hollywood Reporter, April 8, 1958

The Hollywood Reporter, July 12, 1959

The Hollywood Reporter, April 5, 1993

The Hollywood Reporter, July 9, 1996

The Independent, June 23, 1945

Memo between Herbert Yates and H. Lydecker, February 14, 1942

Memo on contracts of John Wayne, 1948, File 1919, Charles K. Feldman
    Papers, Republic Pictures File Folder

Motion Picture Herald, April 2, 1938

Motion Picture Herald, June 22, 1946

Motion Picture Herald, November 24, 1951

Movie Collectors World #609, August 4, 2000

Movie Line Magazine, April 1944

The New Captain George's Whizzbang, No. 16: Vol. 3, No. 4, 1968

Photoplay, June 4, 1947

Republic Pictures Press Release, July 10, 1996

Variety, October 3, 1940

Variety, November 29, 1940

Variety, April 4, 1943

Variety, April 27, 1944

Variety, May 1, 1944

Variety, July 28, 1944

Variety, October 16, 1944

Variety, November 12, 1945

Variety, August 20, 1947

Variety, September 10, 1948

Variety, June 20, 1951

Variety, October 10, 1951

Variety, October 19, 1951

Variety, April 3, 1952

Variety, April 12, 1952

Variety, May 14, 1952

Variety, July 23, 1952

Variety, July 21, 1954

Variety, April 6, 1955

Variety, September 14, 1993

Variety, November 7, 1996

Variety, September 9, 1998

Websites

http://filesofjerryblake.com

http://nzpetesmatteshot.blogspot.com/2010/09/big-boys-toys-howard-and-theodore.html

http://www.imdb.com/name/nm0946759/ Herbert J. Yates

http://www.imdb.com/title/tt0045743/ Fair Wind to Java

http://www.imdb.com/title/tt0034742/ Flying Tigers

www.b-westerns.com/levine.htm Nat Levine

www.b-westerns.com/canutt

www.b-westerns.com/stunt10.htm

www.glamourgirlsofthesilverscreen.com

www.vttbots.com/page20.html

www.tcm.com The Fighting Seabees

INDEX

ABOUT THE AUTHORS

Chris Enss is an award-winning screenwriter who has written for television, short subject films, live performances, and for the movies, and is the co-author *of Love Untamed: Romances of the Old West*, *Gilded Girls: Women Entertainers of the Old West*, and *She Wore A Yellow Ribbon: Women Patriots and Soldiers of the Old West* (with JoAnn Chartier); and *The Cowboy and the Senorita*, *Happy Trails*, *The Young Duke*, and *Thunder Over the Prairie*—soon to be a motion picture—with Howard Kazanjian. Other books include *Frontier Teachers: Stories of Heroic Women of the Old West* and *The Doctor Wore Petticoats*. She lives in Grass Valley, California.

Howard Kazanjian is an award-winning producer and entertainment executive who has been producing feature films and television programs for more than twenty-five years. While vice president of production for Lucasfilm Ltd., he produced two of the highest grossing films of all time: *Raiders of the Lost Ark* and *Star Wars: Return of the Jedi*. He also managed production of another top-ten box-office hit, *The Empire Strikes Back*. Some of his other notable credits include *The Rookies*, *Demolition Man*, and the two-hour pilot and first season of *J.A.G.* He lives in San Marino, California.